STELL

Stella Bowen was born in Adelaide, South Australia; her father died when she was three years old. She left school at the age of seventeen, briefly attending art classes in Adelaide. However, on her mother's death in 1914, Stella Bowen sailed for England. She enrolled at Westminster School of Art, where she was taught by Sickert, and shared a studio with a drama student friend. Together they met the avant-garde of London, gave large parties, and became friends with Ezra Pound, T.S. Eliot, Arthur Waley, May Sinclair, Violet Hunt, G.B. Stern, Wyndham Lewis, Yeats, Mary Butts – and Ford Madox Ford. Ford, at the time he and Stella met, was in the army, having been on active service in France. After the war Stella and he went to live in Sussex, in a cottage on the South Downs, and their daughter Julia was born in 1920. But after a few years the harsh winters in the country drove them from England. When Harold Monro offered them his villa at Cap Ferrat for the winter of 1922, they jumped at the chance. They lived in the South of France for a while, then moving to Paris where they remained for several years. This was the legendary Paris of the twenties. Living in a Montparnasse studio, Ford began the *transatlantic review* and he and Stella entertained their friends, including Cedric Morris, Hemingway, Pound, Joyce, Robert McAlmon, Gertrude Stein and Peggy Guggenheim.

On the collapse of the *review*, Stella and Ford went to Toulon, where their neighbours were Juan Gris and his wife. They returned to Paris, but by this time their relationship had begun to disintegrate. Ford had had an affair with a penniless young girl who 'possessed nothing but a cardboard suitcase and an astonishing manuscript' but went on to become the famous novelist Jean Rhys. Ford and Stella separated some years after this affair was over, and she began to earn her living by painting portraits, a living that became increasingly more precarious. By the mid-thirties it became apparent that she would have to move back to England. The years of the Second World War she spent mainly in London, and in 1943 she was appointed an Official Artist by the Australian War Memorial Board. Her last commission was of the Victory Parade in June 1946, completed shortly before her death at the age of fifty-two.

DRAWN
FROM LIFE

STELLA BOWEN

With a New Introduction by
JULIA LOEWE

Virago

Published by VIRAGO PRESS Limited 1984
41 William IV Street, London WC2N 4DB

First published by Collins Publishers Limited 1941

British Library Cataloguing in Publication Data

Bowen, Stella
 Drawn from Life.
 1. Bowen, Stella   2. Painters – Great Britain – Biography
 I. Title
 994.04'2'0924   ND497.B67

 ISBN 0-86068-655-8

Reproduced, printed and bound in Great Britain by
Hazell Watson & Viney Limited,
Member of the BPCC Group,
Aylesbury, Bucks

The cover shows a detail from "Tusnelda's
Interior" by Stella Bowen, reproduced
by kind permission of Julia Loewe

INTRODUCTION

My mother's life spanned the years between the close of the
nineteenth century and the late 1940s, a half century that
began with muslin dresses, tennis parties and cricket matches
in South Australia and ended with the Second World War and
its aftermath in England. Her personal journey and growth
showed at least as remarkable a change as that of the world
around her. Her own description of her journey in *Drawn
from Life* cannot be bettered; the only comment I can make is
that, though it reads as if it had just come fresh into her mind,
the fact is that she laboured over it a very great deal – as she
said, she had listened to enough talk by writers about writing
to know what it takes to turn out a professional job, and
writing was not her profession . . . hence her anguish. I know,
I was there!

I have among my possessions two photographs which
reveal, in a way, the changes she went through during the
period that I knew her – one from her middle thirties (around
1926) and another taken twenty years later. The first shows
her as a serious and reflective young woman, the second, from
a year or two before her death, shows her tolerant smile, her
wise, kind eyes, and the two together sum up this personal
journey perfectly.

She claims in the first chapter of her autobiography that she
was a shy, tongue-tied girl who did not shine in the decorous,
middle-class, suburban circle into which she had been born,
but I remember very well that when my husband and I spent a
few years in Australia in the early fifties, my uncle Tom,

Stella's brother, said to me in a rather bewildered way, "I don't know what she meant by all that stuff about being such a social failure. She may not have been a belle of the ball, but her friends were certainly all the more *interesting* people in Adelaide . . . "

Her love, her mind, were all bound up in painting — she had, of course, many other interests as well — and as a young woman, she pursued her aim in a single-minded, quiet way that seems surprising when one thinks of young women's position in those days, especially in the "Colonies". Of course, the fact that she had a small but sufficient independent income made a difference, but I believe that she would have found a way to learn her art no matter what her circumstances had been. She was basically apolitical, though her heart was in the right place. (Who can doubt, now, that it was right to be a pacifist in the First World War, and equally right to wish to fight the Nazis in the Second?) She supported the idea of suffrage (though she did not get directly involved in the cause), and she learned a great deal during the years of the First World War about social conditions, politics, and intellectual life that had never come her way in Adelaide.

Her mind was quick and receptive, her heart warm, and wherever she went, she made friends — from the famous and sophisticated, such as T. S. Eliot, James Joyce and Edith Sitwell, to the various village women and cleaning ladies who were always as fond of her as she was of them. Her sole criteria were that friends be neither cruel nor phony, nor yet (perhaps the worst crime) boring. The most remarkable thing about her was her unaggressive strength — everybody could, and did, rely on her, and she was always ready to help. Indeed, she more than once said to me plaintively that she sometimes wished she had a shoulder to lean on, instead of being the shoulder leant on!

Her single-minded determination to live her own life (except during the years with Ford Madox Ford, when his needs so overshadowed her own that she had perforce to help him live *his* life, but she also learnt a great deal during that period that she could not have learnt any other way) was remarkable for its total lack of activist "alarums and excursions". She just made her own choices and went ahead with them. Her favourite proverb was an old Spanish one that was also a favourite of Ford's: "Take what you want, said God, take it, and pay for it."

This is not to say that choices were always easy or casually decided. She would often worry over a decision for days or even weeks, weighing all the pros and cons, until one morning she would wake up with her mind clear, her decision made, and from that point she carried on – a feminist by example, but one without banners and slogans.

I first remember her when I was a small child in France soon after "we went to Paris, France, by way of Fittleworth" as she used to say, paraphrasing Hilaire Belloc. I suppose, considering our circumstances, that I did not see as much of her as I feel I did. Of course, the reason is clear to me now – I always felt enveloped in her love and care, and always had her total attention when we were together. I suppose, as the sociological jargon now puts it, it was "quality time" – but of a very high quality indeed! I was always treated as a person and not simply as a child.

Looking back, it was a different world. Anxiety about money, sometimes acute, did not, for instance, preclude taking my little nursemaid Lucy to France with the family, and indeed there was always a (varying) amount of domestic help on hand. Now, of course, "two-career families" are commonplace, and many machines have replaced the almost non-existent servants, and day-care centres have taken the place of nursemaids, even for affluent couples.

When she and I returned to England on our own, and I discovered a different mother speaking English – much more assured than she had been in her rather haphazard French –

we did go through a period of poverty: I wonder if really understanding books have been written about the very special comradeship of mother and daughter facing the world together . . .

During this period (with the cleaning woman who also came in to cook the Sunday joint, of course) we both made nearly all our own clothes. In fact, I still treasure her old hand-turned sewing machine on which we made them. I was glad that my training in dressmaking and costume design at the London Theatre Studio was of some assistance at this point. However little money she had to spend on clothes, she was always able to look like someone special, which indeed she was. All this, of course, came to an end with clothes rationing during the Second World War.

I was fortunate in that I never had to go through the common period of teenage revolt, because Stella was always an intelligent friend and mentor as well as a mother to me, with lots of common sense, so what need had I to revolt against her? With Ford, on the other hand, whom I saw only seldom at that time, I had many rows, but it is a comfort to me that by the time he died, when I was eighteen, I had made my peace with him.

*

For those who want to know "what happened then . . . " Stella's life after the completion of *Drawn from Life* did see her decision to return to London, where she found a small *pied-à-terre* in Paulton's Square, Chelsea, while retaining Green End, our cottage in Essex. The *pied-à-terre* was the lower half of a four-storey house with a pleasant garden at the rear end; at the front, a view of the neglected square shorn of its iron railings, which had been melted down for munitions. To make ends meet, she sublet the lower half of her flat to Francesca Fried, the widow of a refugee Austrian psychiatrist, who was then working as a psychiatric social worker. She was an energetic and capable woman of great spirit who ultimately returned to Vienna, where she helped create a school for war orphans.

After several frustrating attempts to find paid work that would help the war effort ("Yes, but can you type?" — she couldn't , and was considered too old to learn), she found part-time work for a correspondence course in painting, boring but paid, and later taught several live art classes. Painting portraits in London was next to impossible in the period during and following the Blitz, but she managed well enough for a while.

I, in the meantime (who *could* type and spoke perfect French), went into the Army, and worked in liaison with the Free French Forces. In 1943 I married a young documentary film scriptwriter then working on propaganda films for the Allies.

While financial matters continued to be a worry, Stella's affairs were at last taking a turn for the better. The correspondence courses and art classes continued, and she was gradually gaining recognition in her own country. She recorded a number of talks on the BBC's Pacific service, beamed at Australia — informal reports of life in England at that time, delivered in an easy, natural way which sounded effortless, but which nonetheless cost her considerable anguish, as the writing of *Drawn from Life* had done. These talks had two important results: her Talks Director, Theaden Hancock, and her husband Keith became the last of the many close friends that she made, and the broadcasts themselves were instrumental in her being appointed an Official War Artist for the Australian government.

Keith and Theaden (later Sir Keith and Lady) Hancock were an Australian couple somewhat younger than Stella whose friendship did much to warm and ease the few remaining years of her life. Keith was an historian working at the Cabinet Offices on the official civil history of the war, while Theaden was one of the few women in an administrative position at the

BBC at that time. They were kind, gentle and scholarly people who appreciated Stella's work as an artist, as well as the strength of her character and her personality. Her portrait of Theaden is one of the best examples of her later work. Sir Keith is now retired from the Australian National University at Canberra; Theaden died a few years after their return to Australia.

During this period I had managed to get myself billeted at Stella's in Paulton's Square while working in liaison with the Free French. This short period was the last time we would share a home. After I got married and moved away, Stella felt sure enough of herself to take on the lease of a whole house in Danvers Street, just off Paulton's Square. On 30 November 1943, she had received an exciting letter from Australia House in London which read:

Dear Madam,
We have been asked by the Australian War Memorial Board to invite you to accept a three month's engagement as Official Artist . . .

So began the final passage of Stella's life, in which she worked as an Official Artist (on ever-renewed contracts) until her health gave way in early 1947. She painted many pictures during those years, from portraits of Australian military bigwigs to loading up Australian aircraft and group portraits of their crews. Doubtless it was to some of these assignments, as well as to other occasions, that she used to refer to when she said, "I only smoke in moments of acute social embarrassment."

To her apprehensive amusement, in order to enable her to move freely in those very restricted areas, she was given the rank of captain and put into uniform. A more unlikely Aussie captain surely never existed.

To list all the pictures she painted for the War Memorial Board would be impossible, but she visited a number of airfields from which Australian squadrons were operating, and such pictures as "Bombing Up a Lancaster", "Halifax Crew, Driffield", and "A Sunderland Crew Comes Ashore at Pembroke Dock" were the results. The group portrait of one of these crews had to be finished from memory, as the plane was reported missing at the end of the raid . . .

It was on one of these airfields that she first heard of the V–1's (commonly known as doodle bugs), when Roland and I were working in London. With all her maternal instincts aroused, she went to the Commanding Officer for information and got lots of meaningless technical talk, until she finally asked him, "Just how many people can these bombs kill?" To which the C.O. harrumphed, "Oh, you mean the lethal capacity? I haven't the faintest idea . . . "

When German resistance collapsed, and the Prisoners of War started coming back, she painted several pictures at Gowrie House, Eastbourne, where returning Australian prisoners were welcomed back to England – "Reception Desk at Gowrie House" and "A Repatriated POW is Processed" being among the more successful.

When she was not painting "in the field" she was finishing her pictures or painting such portraits as "Admiral Colvin" and "Sir Charles Burnett" in her new home, a small delightful house where finally she again had a real studio with good light – the "proper working conditions" at last! It was in the warm comfortable basement kitchen there that my husband and I had many wonderful evenings with her. Roland still speaks with love and gratitude of the way in which, during the long blackout evenings, she "educated" the brash young Cambridge graduate and smoothed his corners, even as hers had been smoothed by the Chinese scholar Arthur Waley and Margaret Cole, among others, during the First World War. It was on the radio in Danvers Street that the three of us heard the exhilarating news of the liberation of Paris and went wild; also where we first heard of the agreement on the Veto in the Security Council of the United Nations made at Yalta. I still remember the look on Stella's face — "Well, so that's it". The UN was as powerless as the League of Nations had been.

She was a wonderful cook, and knew how to make the most of our meagre rations (helped considerably by food parcels from our Australian relatives and American friends!). During this period, also, there were many weekend trips to Green End, which we were all three allowed to visit, since it belonged to her, although the area was closed to visitors for a while because of the threat of invasion. These trips always included the transportation of what Roland and I called "little blue things" — various domestic objects of different sizes, and with varying degrees of difficulty on wartime trains from Danvers Street to Green End, or vice versa. (The first of these happened to be a pair of small blue cushions, hence the nickname.) She was always thinking of ways to improve one or the other house, to make them more pleasing to the eye, and she succeeded finally in having two charming domiciles.

All the close contacts she had with Australians during that period revived her desire to visit her native land and family and hold a series of exhibitions there, but this never got beyond the planning stage.

Her last commission and final picture was of Australian troops marching past the reviewing stand as part of the official Victory Parade in June, 1946.

She was barely able to finish this picture because her health began to break down. Stella's final illness began in the early part of 1947, and she spent the last few months of her life in her bed at home, growing steadily weaker. She did live long enough, however, to see her grandson, Julian David. She felt him all over, saw that he was perfect, and ceremoniously put one drop of champagne on his lips for good luck. She died peacefully on 30 October 1947, three weeks after his birth.

We have always regretted that she never lived to realize her hope that she would one day sit in the sunshine on the wooden bench against the front wall of Green End and play with her grandchild.

Among the many letters I received after her death, one of the most moving came from Sir Keith Hancock, who summed her up as well as anyone could: "Stella was the most courageous, vital and harmonious personality I have ever known . . . Her death is a waste, for she had so much to live for and such a genius for living. But since it had to come, I am glad it came as it did, without any suffering or any distortion of that, brave, ardent and rational spirit . . . "

*

It is now – as everybody keeps on pointing out – *1984*. Roland and I, Julian and his wife Maggy, all live in Southern California; Roland and I are retired, while Julian is a successful journalist and science writer, and the immensely proud father of enchanting, mischievous two-year-old, Erica. Many things have happened in the mere century since Stella's birth, and as her great-granddaughter starts on her own journey through life, I wonder what further developments, both good and bad, the future will hold for Erica and all other women – if, indeed, there is to be a future for anyone on this planet?

Julia Loewe, Los Angeles, 1984

CHAPTER ONE

Adelaide

THE LAND where I was born is a blue and yellow country, although when the sun pours out of a cloudless sky, there is very little colour to be seen. The blazing sky itself is almost empty of blue, and the yellow ochre of the dried grass is silvered by the glare. Even the shadows are less blue than painters like to pretend, and the air is so dry that the distance has the same quality as the foreground, and you can judge of space and perspective only by the diminishing scale in size. Local colour—flowers in the garden, or a little girl's dress—is sucked out and bleached by the sun, and the extreme visibility is tempered only by a shimmering heat-haze rising in the middle distance from the baked earth. The world is seen as a pattern of light and shade.

If you want to see a pattern of colour, to see the flower-beds as a rich mosaic and the child's frock a miracle of pink, you must come north where the sun is veiled in mist, and to your undazzled eyes, colour comes into its own. I never knew verdure until I came to England, and I have never forgotten my first surprised delight in the separate veils of blue which define each stage of the English distance.

On the first day of an Australian heat wave, you shut and darken all the doors and windows of your home. Underneath the corrugated iron roof lies a layer of insulating seaweed. The hours pass in a dim and listless obscurity, until eight o'clock—or perhaps nine—when it has become cool enough

9

outside to open up the windows. After dark, all the houses are empty, and from every garden comes the sound of quiet voices, relaxing into sociability.

Perhaps at midnight you carry your mattress on to the lawn, where a mass of pinky-white oleander flowers, sweeping to the ground beside you, reflect such brilliance from the moon that you must needs turn the other way. You wonder whether what your nurse said is true, and that the moon can change you into an idiot with a crooked face; but you are too tired to care much.

When the early dawn arrives, to chase you indoors with its dog-barkings and its cock-crowings and its glare, you are still unrefreshed and quite unready for to-morrow. The house is closed again before the sun gets up, and you go back to bed to sleep again till breakfast-time.

Your English cousin, seeing trees bending in the wind, says: " Doesn't it look fresher ? Couldn't we go out ? " But if she ventures her nose into that scorching oven-blast, straight from the desert—"I don't think it would be safe," she'll say.

Sand and grit are everywhere, and flies of course, and no water for the garden. And all the talk is of the bushfires to the north.

But the business of the town goes on as usual, the men don't even wear white suits, and the hours of work are the same as on the days when it is cool. When the change comes, which may be in five days, or in fifteen, the wind swings round quite suddenly, and a great freshness blows up from the sea. Doors bang and the trees bend the other way and the temperature may drop 20° in half an hour. Everyone collapses.

After that, comes a period of the kind of weather that good Australians refer to when they talk about their wonderful climate. The kind of weather in which you remember bathing all day long in the bluest sea in the world, and eating all the fruit you could stomach—figs warm from the trees, grapes (we were very fussy about the kinds we thought worth eating), oranges, of course—and once you really start eating oranges there is no reason why you should ever stop—passion-fruit, apricots, peaches and nectarines, all the fruits of the earth and no stint. It was considered inevitable, but unimportant, that we children should make ourselves a little ill sometimes in the fruit season.

And you remember the grey-green gum trees which give no shade, and the pine trees and the pepper trees which are not much better in this respect, and the great light spaces of the open landscape, in contrast with the luxuriant gardens, painfully maintained in times of drought, with their green lawns and deep shade, verandas screened by trellised vines and flowering creepers, plumbago, bougainvillea, hibiscus, mimosa (but we call it wattle) and dozens of flowers whose names I have forgotten.

And of course there were hammocks under the vines.

I wish I knew the truth about that strangely dim and distant life in Adelaide before the war. I have reconstructed it in my memory as a queer little backwater of intellectual timidity—a kind of hangover of Victorian provincialism, isolated by three immense oceans and a great desert, and stricken by recurrent waves of paralysing heat. It lies shimmering on a plain encircled by soft blue hills, prettyish, banal, and filled to the brim with an anguish of boredom.

I must be wrong. There must have been more in it than ever met my eye. My poor small eye was placed very close to the ground, and my view was doubtless a worm's-eye view. But it was the only view I had. . . .

I was born in the sort of house that must inevitably end its days as a boarding house. It was sizable, rather gloomy, at

a sufficiently good but not fashionable address, detached, with
two little lawns and a summer-house in front and a back
yard behind containing clothes lines, a stable and a coach
house, a see-saw and a swing. Being in Australia, it had a
front veranda with balcony above, and its roof was largely
smothered in Banksia roses, bougainvillaea and other greenery.
There was a trellis of vines covering the path from the front
to the back and figs, apricots, lemons and oranges grew
around the back yard.

There was a pampas-grass in the garden, and an aspidistra
in the drawing-room.

There were no modern conveniences. The nicest thing
about it was the view. Being placed high on the edge of the
town's oldest suburb, it looked down over low-lying park
lands where cattle grazed, over the distant slums surrounding
Port Adelaide, where factory chimneys trailed smoke wreaths,
and delicately drawn ship-masts reared themselves against the
most spectacular sunsets I have ever seen.

Trains going north ran across the middle of this view.
They ran for three days as far as the desert, and then came
back again. I hated the thought of that dead-end!

I never went more than a few hours north on that line
myself, when visiting those of my girl friend's whose parents
had sheep stations in the fertile belt near the coast. The life
on those stations was the most characteristically Australian
life I ever saw. It had its own style and its own flavour and
it could never have been the same anywhere else. In the
towns, except for the modifications imposed by the climate,
we were just pale imitations of something which was already
moribund in England. . . .

Going to England was called " going home," even by
people who had never been there and whose fathers had never
been. We all talked with varying degrees of Australian accent,

of which we were ashamed when we became aware of it. We
regarded a real English accent with positive reverence.

At Christmas, which came at midsummer with the temperature at—perhaps—100° in the shade, we sat down at midday to turkey and flaming plum pudding, having sent each
other cards depicting robins in the snow.

We were, in fact, a suburb of England. But it was different
in the country. If you were a hearty sort of person who
liked riding, and the great open spaces (and they certainly
were very great and very open), and if you did not mind
living in an ugly bungalow with a corrugated iron roof, and
liked rough-and-ready polo, and racing, and driving big
distances in derelict cars to visit your nearest neighbours; if
you liked jogging on horseback through the dusty sunlight
behind a herd of sheep and had no hankering after the Arts
or other sophistications, then you might well hold the view
that life on a station was the only life worth living.

But I was a town girl.

My mother was the daughter of a low-Church vicar from
Melbourne. Her favourite brother, who came to visit us sometimes, was a high-Church parson with the piercing eye and
the long, crooked upper lip of the actor or the preacher.
He was full of culture—the consciously-whimsical, English-
essayist kind of culture that flourishes in the Anglican Church
and never disturbs anybody's faith. He would have done very
well in a vicarage in Kent, with just that little bit of fifteenth-
century wrought-iron or fourteenth-century stone-work about
which he could have had man-to-man chats with his Bishop.
In Melbourne, he had to be content with his books. He was
the only male relative who counted in our lives, my father
having died when I was three, just before my brother's
birth. I think that to my Mother, Uncle Charlie represented the limit of what was permissible in the way of colour,

dash, and broadmindedness. I believe he was a very good preacher.

My mother was a gentle and loving saint whose life was lived in willing obedience to all those pious maxims which governed Victorian womanhood. When I knew her, she was above all a widow. An enlarged photograph of my father (who must have been a rather charming, cheerful little man, addicted to water-colour sketching and the making of wonderful maps) hung above the mantelpiece of every room in our house, and we always referred to him as Dear Father. My mother wore deep mourning for him until she died.

It is a privilege to be associated with anyone whose life is a simple and perfect demonstration of all that they believe, and it is an especially valuable privilege for a child. No compromise, and no lapse from her own high standard of conduct can ever have clouded my mother's conscience. But conscience was her sole criterion. Reason, or the discoveries of science, were irrelevancies which had to be trimmed to fit in with that arbitrary sense of right and wrong which, however artificially induced in the first place, ends by being all-too-naturally clung to by the simple-hearted. My mother's piety and selflessness were spontaneous and absolute, and the only failing that could possibly be attributed to her was a gentle and naïve snobbishness, which persisted in spite of straitened circumstances and social timidity. Her friends were the Bishop's wife, the Governor's wife, the wives of the University professors and the higher clergy. There being no aristocracy in Australia, the professional classes led the way, and my mother never quite hit it off with my father's relatives, whose outlook was not predominantly Church of England and whose forebears had been in the building trade. In these circumstances, she was not impressed by the fact that the husband of one of my aunts had been Lord Mayor of Adelaide, and the other, who owned the Conservative daily paper, had received a knighthood in England when attending a press conference. Nevertheless, the cousins in both these families, who were more modern, better educated, and tougher-minded than my mother's people, were a godsend to me as I grew up into the perplexities of adolescence.

When I fish into my memory between the ages of six and twelve, I land such small fry of trivial happenings that I am in two minds whether to dish them up or throw them back into the waters of oblivion.

I can remember many teas at Bishops' Court, an imitation Gothic building, which had a lovely musical-box with dancing sailors hidden in a dark corner under the staircase, where a spike in the carving had a potato stuck upon it, to protect our young heads. The Bishop's little girl was between the ages of my brother and myself, and we all played decorous games in the garden, which became less decorous only when shared by Harold Tennyson, the youngest of the Governor's three sons, who at six was given to such passions of rage when crossed, that he was the terror of us milder children. Lord Tennyson called these tempers "a rush of blood to the head" and prescribed its immersion in a pail of cold water. But in the absence of authority, no such reprisals were possible, and when I was invited to stay to tea with Harold after the Government House dancing class, and he sloshed my new white fur-trimmed coat with green slime out of the goldfish pond, I was much too frightened to complain to his nurse, who gave me a good scolding for getting so dirty.

My young brother Tom was also given to childish rages of a spectacular sort, but I did not then know, what I have since observed, that these small unmanageables generally turn into the most valuable adults.

I must have been about nine at the time of the dancing

classes. Eight little boys and eight little girls were instructed by Miss Young, Adelaide's most exclusive dancing teacher, whose father had, they said, been born in the very ballroom where our lessons took place. That ballroom was my idea of true elegance. Banquettes of crimson plush, white and gold walls with panels of crimson brocade, great mirrors from floor to ceiling, and immense crystal chandeliers. I imagined Society in England to be one vast extension of this kind of glory.

Watching us, the mammas would sit on pale blue tufted satin chairs with Lady Tennyson in the inner drawing-room. The other reception rooms were all flowery chintz and white paint, and the house, a vaguely Georgian affair planted squarely in a large garden in the centre of the town, had a portico for carriages in case people arrived in the rain. When it was sunny, there came from the lawn the perpetual click of bat on ball as Mr. Jose, the handsome and muscular tutor in holy orders, bowled endlessly to Lionel Tennyson, already destined to become a star cricketer.

Aubrey, the second boy, was a member of the dancing class and my first partner in the polka. To think that we learnt the polka and the lancers before learning the waltz!

I was a stodgy and law-abiding little girl. I had a straight fringe and long dark ringlets, artificially induced. I was always dressed in white or cream—delaine, I think, was the material. There was one hat I did not like. It was a gathered chiffon affair on a vast wire frame, such as you may see in photos of the Diamond Jubilee (we were behind the times in Adelaide) and I used to walk next to the wall on the way to church so as to be able to rub the edge and spoil it, but I think that was almost the limit of my naughtiness.

My really besetting sin was reading, and this got worse. I would read in bed, against orders, extinguishing my candle

when I heard my mother's footsteps in the passage, and re-
lighting after she had passed. I would persuade myself that I
could get to school in ten minutes and read till I had but
seven left in which to cover a quarter of an hour's walk, and
arrive late again, and breathless. My mother spoke to me very
gravely about this self-indulgence.

There was no lack of reading-matter in our home. We had
the complete works of Carlyle, very handsomely bound ; all
the Victorian poets and essayists; the History of the Reforma-
tion, the Decline and Fall, and criticisms and biographies of
many writers whose own works we did not possess. There were
also the complete novels of Dickens, Thackeray, George Eliot
and Charlotte Brontë, which I was allowed to read, with the
exception of *Adam Bede* and *Jane Eyre*. But my earliest reading
consisted of Rosa Nouchette Carey, Charlotte Yonge, and
Juliana Horatia Ewing. I swallowed them all with enthusiasm,
and was easily convinced that nothing mattered in life but
unselfishness and piety. At one time I announced that I would
like to go as a missionary to Melanesia! . . .

On Sundays we were not allowed to read secular literature,
but there was a long series called "Sunday Echoes in Week-day
Hours," which illustrated the Collect, Gospel, or Epistle for
the day in a fictional manner. I can remember that the gilding
on this pill was definitely insufficient. I can also remember
suffering much from the compulsory hymn-singing around
the piano on Sunday evenings, chiefly, I think, because we sang
very badly, and my mother was no pianist.

Many years later, when I had occasion to accompany a
small child to the Catechisme de Saint Sulpice in Paris, I discovered that the Catholic ear for music is not necessarily
superior to the Protestant. The person who there played the
harmonium produced an erroneous and ghastly wail reminis-
cent of all the tin chapels in the world, to which it was im-

possible for the children to sing correctly. And let no Christian propagandist imagine that this sort of thing does not matter!

It mattered very much to me, as a child, that I had no gift for music. Of course I had piano lessons, with two hours daily practising. But owing to a complete lack of musical facility, the whole thing was a dreadful bore, and I had enough ear to dislike the sounds I made. And then one of my cousins, who had been studying the violin in Leipzig, came home and gave a recital in the Town Hall. Nora was a handsome creature and a real musician. There was a Bach concerto on the programme which I thought divinely beautiful (I suppose it was the first real music I had ever heard) and Nora thereupon became my ideal person and Bach my favourite composer. He still is! But the piano lessons after that became more insupportable than ever. If Nora Kyffin Thomas had only been a painter, my artistic leanings might have escaped earlier in that direction; but at that time I had never seen a decent picture nor met a real artist. It is true that I was sent as a child to the School of Design on Saturday mornings because I was supposed to have a gift for drawing and my mother knew that one should not neglect one's gifts. There I learnt to draw cubes, cones, pots, scrolls, and plant-life, and later to paint (in *water-colour*, if you can believe it) still-life groups consisting of a fan, a slipper, and a string of beads, or a vase with a peacock's feather stuck in it and a satin bow tied round its neck. (The School of Design was the Municipal Art School, and ladies went there to buy original designs for their embroidery. They were always of water-lilies.) But these classes stopped when I began to work for school exams. Not so the music, however, since my mother felt that had a social value far beyond anything I could get from Art!

My adored Nora had a very strong-minded friend called

Ethel Cooper, an excellent pianist and composer, who also played the trombone for visiting orchestras and might often be seen, camouflaged by a black coat and man's tie, amongst the wind instruments at the Theatre Royal. It was she who suggested to me that the cornet was much easier than the piano, and that if I really wanted to enjoy music, I could join her own Woman's Orchestra as a cornet player. "Women must come to Wind," she said firmly. So I said, would she ask my mother if I might learn the cornet instead of the piano, which she did, but of course my mother wouldn't hear of anything so unnatural.

Behind out house was a Catholic convent, and by looking through the red or blue corners of the bathroom window-panes, I could see the nuns walking amongst their lemon trees. They kept a boarding school, and my mother was distressed to discover a little Protestant girl amongst the boarders. She obtained permission to take this child to our church, and when we knocked at the convent door to collect her on Sunday mornings I was always impressed by the nun's smiling composure in contrast to my mother's nervous embarrassment. Of course, I considered it was very deceitful of the nun to smile, when she must have been furious at the loss of her prey! All the same, I thought their chapel (I peeped in) was much prettier than our Parish church.

Our drawing-room was very dark because the bow-window was under the veranda. It contained a Bechstein semi-grand piano and a reproduction of a Raphael Holy Family standing on an easel, under a large palm. On the walls were my father's water-colours in gold frames, and over the door hung an oriental portière on a hinged brass rod, which squeaked.

I do not remember ever to have enjoyed myself in this room.

But I had a room of my own, which, provided that I spent no money on it and did everything myself, I was allowed to arrange and decorate as I liked. I am sorry to say that I stencilled it all over with dreadful peacocks! I adored this room, and the privacy which I there enjoyed was my most valued privilege.

My young brother was content with the use of the ink-stained school-room. He was a much more active, normal, outgiving person than I, and managed his life much better. He was hardy, good-looking, tempersome and cheerful. He was very popular. But I was too old for him. We shared a governess when we were quite young, but afterwards I was sent to a small and select private school run by a friend of my mother's—a charming and cultivated lady whose lessons in English literature were a delight, but who taught me little Latin, less mathematics, and no science. At fifteen I was sent to a large and quite unselect school for two years, in order to be put through the Senior Public Examination. This was a salutary and stimulating experience, for I was forced to keep pace with a large class, and quickly to make up my deficiencies in science, which I enjoyed. I acquired a respect for hard facts and straight thinking from a certain Miss Benham, who was the first teacher I had ever met who would not put up with a blur or a wobble in answer to a question, and who insisted on speed. She discovered in me a natural aptitude for geometry—where after all there is something visual to go by—but I was completely blind to algebra.

After passing the Senior Exam, I left school at seventeen and have remained to this day a disgracefully uneducated person in any academic sense. This book is about an education of another sort. . . .

I must still have been at school when Kathleen (Nora's youngest sister) began lending me books by Wells and Shaw.

They blew through my poor little home-made mind like a thrilling but alarming tornado. I felt it to be dangerous— but how desirable—to regard the human will as a precious life-force instead of merely something to be subdued and trimmed to fit a pious pattern. I hoped soon to become brave enough to face the cold and searching light of logic and reason. . . .

I was at this time extremely distressed by the realization that the Church of England was not in the least interested in æsthetic values. I was at the "Beauty is Truth, Truth Beauty" stage of adolescence. I also realized that the Church of England was not in the least interested in scientific thought, and I could not understand why, if God created man in His own image, He did not intend him to exercise the reasoning powers which He had given him. It is funny and pathetic now, to trace the long, slow path that the young of my day had to tread towards any intellectual freedom. To-day we try to confer this freedom ready-made upon our children—and they do not even thank us for it! They are asking for a law, obedience to which will keep them safe and cosy. Maybe this is not entirely reaction against the older generation, but a natural fear of the atrocious aspect of the world to-day. Wishful thinking has come back.

At a quite early age, I exercised my embryonic reasoning powers to elucidate some of the facts of life, about which no one had been willing to enlighten me. If hens laid eggs, then it was logical to suppose that puppies and even babies came from inside their mothers. And the idea that you had to be married in order to have children did not seem reasonable in face of the fact that dogs and cats evidently had no need of any ceremony. This was borne out by reading stories in which fallen women were mentioned, and their attempts to conceal their shameful maternity. It soon became obvious that the arrival of the offspring was not due to chance, but to some definite and conscious act of intimacy. Why such intimacy should ever occur, when the penalties were so frightful, puzzled me until I hit upon the explanation that it must in itself be highly pleasurable. This led straight to an understanding of what was meant by physical passion in contrast to spiritual love. Physical passion was of course extremely discreditable, but I suspected that, since it was part of the system on which the rest of creation worked, it was probably very difficult to confine it to the wedding-ring principle. Having arrived unaided at these conclusions, I considered that I had solved the entire sexual question, and at that time thought very little more about it. My one care was to spare my mother the embarrassment of enlightening me with her own construction of these unpalatable facts, and myself the embarrassment of admitting that I "knew." As a matter of fact, she attempted no enlightenment until I was eighteen, and was then easily persuaded that there was not anything I wanted to know. She was, however, a little hurt that I wouldn't talk about it, nor allow her to correct any undesirable impressions I might have received.

I was eager to leave school when the time came, for by then there had settled in Adelaide a red-headed little fire-brand of a woman who was not only an excellent painter, fresh from Paris, but a most inspiring teacher. She had opened a studio in the city, and I should think was the only person in South Australia to employ a nude model. She had about twenty pupils—mostly older women, and none from amongst my mother's circle of friends, but I was absolutely determined to study with her. The piano lessons had by now been abandoned, and my mother was persuaded that it would be right for me to cultivate my talent for art, provided it was in moderation. So, in spite of her dislike of the nude model (who after all was only a little girl of fourteen) I was allowed to go to Rose MacPherson's classes on two days a week.

Going up the stairs to that studio were the happiest moments of my life. All sorts of new æsthetic sensibilities began sprouting in my spirit like mushrooms.

I was taught to paint by tone-values, to study degrees of light and shade, and to make a direct attack upon the canvas. I found this method still in vogue in the first art school I subsequently attended in London. It is not the method which I now follow, and I could wish that I had had an architectural rather than a photographic sense developed in those early lessons. It would have saved a lot of time.

All the same, Rose MacPherson's knowledge, integrity, and dynamic enthusiasm did wonders in setting all my machinery in motion. And what else is a teacher for?

After my mother's death, I found a pathetic entry in her diary, deploring the undue influence of Miss MacPherson who was convinced that I would one day escape to Europe in order to study. "You know, Mrs. Bowen, you won't be able to keep her," she had said, and to my poor mother this must have sounded like the knell of doom. She lived entirely for us children. Even her activities as secretary to the Mother's Union were but an extension of her own parenthood. And she was a simple person whom it would have been easy to make happy if one had not become such a prickly young egotist. Brother Tom was still at school, and anyway he had the prerogatives of his sex. Boys did leave home. Girls didn't. So my mother and I got in trouble together and were both quite unhappy for some months, whilst I went chasing sententiously after alien gods which I probably called Beauty and Freedom!

But I am glad to remember that just before her last illness I had promised that I would never again ask to leave home. If she had lived, I think she would eventually have let me follow my own ideas, and would even have come with me wherever I wanted to go. . . .

Miss MacPherson's art classes were short-lived. She could not stand the *petit bourgeois* Adelaide atmosphere, and was bothered by the animosity of the School of Design. To my dismay, she suddenly packed up and went back to Paris, leaving me bereft of all contact with the world of painting. I tried to get up a club to share a model with the pupils who remained, but it died of inanition. I worked by myself, of course, but there was no one to criticize my efforts. It was at this moment that I began to beg—unsuccessfully—to go to Melbourne to study.

There was, however, another side to life. Naturally. There was sport and there was dancing.

In Adelaide your social popularity depended pretty exactly upon your proficiency at tennis. Not to play at all was unthinkable—it debarred you from almost all the day-time entertainment that there was. If you were a bad player, you nevertheless tried to run hard and to seem keen, and if you were cheerful, humble, and energetic, you were tolerated. It was necessary to be tolerated, because otherwise what would you do on Wednesdays and Saturdays ? Everyone else would be at the Oval where the Adelaide lawn tennis club had sixteen lovely grass courts, and everything was properly done. My father used at one time to be honorary secretary of this club and my mother still came down sometimes to tea. . . .

It took courage to cross those immense lawns alone, hoping that you had on enough petticoats (it was a crime to reveal that you were a bi-ped above the hem-line, a difficult thing to conceal in the slanting Australian sunshine), hoping that you would be able to find a four, and that it wouldn't be quite the worst four, as it was last week, and that you would still find employment after six o'clock when the male population began to turn up for mixed doubles.

There were no men of leisure in Adelaide—everyone was in business who was not studying for a profession. The Australian brother was usually much less civilized than the Australian sister, who had utilized her leisure to cultivate her person and her manners, and even her mind. Brother would often be a pimply young simpleton, either too shy to speak, or boisterously hearty. The few who weren't—the good dancers and the good talkers who were interested enough in femininity to be interesting themselves—behaved like the lords of the earth and had everything their own way.

The Adelaide Oval was very prettily situated. There were trees all round and you could see the distant hills from the tennis courts, while the grandstand faced the whole range of Mount Lofty. And what with the Test Matches, and inter-state and intercollegiate football and cricket, as well as the international tennis, the Oval was a great centre of social life.

It was there that I acquired that hatred of all sport and especially cricket, which has lasted all through the years. I can neither explain this nor excuse it, but even to-day, there is something about a band playing, flags flying in the sunshine, green grass, and the scramble in the tea-tent, that fills me with a huge, irrational, agonizing depression. . . .

Next to sport, almost the only activity open to an Adelaide girl was dancing. I was a pretty good dancer, but alas! the conversational ease, and above all the brightness of manner considered essential to a good time, were never acquired by me. Of course I had "come out," in white net over white satin, trimmed with my mother's honiton lace which she had heroically had bleached for the occasion, and with a bouquet of white flowers. And I had another dress of peach-coloured satin trimmed with diamanté, and a third of yellow chiffon trimmed with brown velvet. But in spite of these aids to success, I didn't catch on at all. It was not that I expected to find anyone to talk to about Art, but I think that in my solemn way I must have been looking for someone who would talk to me about Life, and this made me so heavy in hand that I became the hostesses' despair. There was no subterfuge I did not practise to conceal my partnerless condition, from lurking darkly in the garden to hiding in the cloakroom. I found that a parked car was no use as a hidie-hole as it was bound to be occupied. . . .

The supper extras were the real trouble because if you didn't have a partner you didn't get any supper, and if your hostess discovered this she would begin to fuss, and send you in with some old gentleman who had already supped, and your shame would become public.

It is true that there was some improvement in this state of things when my friend Margaret came home from England where she had been sent to be "finished." She was the daughter of a rich and adoring widower, and had plenty of aunts to entertain for her. She was a wise and easy-going young woman whom I had known well as a child at Victor Harbour during our long summer holidays. We used to do each other's hair and teach each other new stitches in needlework. In those days she and I were known locally as the Two Fishes because of our aquatic proclivities. We bathed in a piece of deep sea fenced in against sharks, stingarees and octopuses, but unfortunately the tides on those parts are unpredictable and unaccountable, and sometimes the sea would rise in the night and pour over the piles and deposit a large shark. This would be waiting to welcome the first bather, who fortunately was always a man, because the women's bathing hours were later in the day!

Well, Margaret with her fine blonde looks and a wardrobe from London (*three* white evening-dresses for her coming out!) and lots of polish, was quite a glamorous person, and ready to take me in hand and instruct me in the better conduct of my life. Her simple theory was that the first essential was to make everybody very fond of you, and afterwards you would be allowed to do as you pleased.

Margaret's friendship led an even more dazzling person called Hilda, to take me up as well. Hilda had been to Europe three times, played excellent tennis and really important golf, and was blessed with the quickest tongue and the most effervescent vitality I had ever met. But the chief thing about Hilda was her remarkable mother. Mrs. Fisher was every bit as slender, elegant, and spirited as her daughters. She had a pretty wit and used to say things which my mother would certainly have stigmatised as "not quite kind," and I thought her marvellously brilliant.

It was from this family that I first learnt to respect the hard-headedness that goes into the making of anything first-rate—even if it is only a party! The Fishers entertained enormously and their parties were the best in town. But the principle on which they picked their guests was not that which would have prevailed in my home. Instead of "I think Angela ought to be asked, dear, she gets out so little," it was "I'm not going to have Angela, mother, the boys can't bear her and anyway I've got enough girls." I also remember my shock when Hilda went to play in a golf tournament on the day that her mother was going under an anæsthetic for some trivial operation. That could never have happened in my home; but then, my mother's daughter could never have become a golf champion—or even, it seemed, a painter!

We were pretty well chaperoned in those days. The enter-taining was all done for the unmarried girls, who found a sad falling off in partners as soon as they acquired a husband. Even the Belle of the Town, after quite a popular marriage, had difficulty in filling her programme. "Brightness" was the quality most prized in a débutante; but the worst thing that could happen to her was to be considered fast. A dashing young lady who came visiting in Adelaide from Perth scandalised everyone by lunching alone with a man in a restaurant. Another girl, down from the country for the occasion, had two glasses of unaccustomed champagne at a Government House ball, which turned a shy rustic into a flushed chatter-box, and I can still remember the shocked comments that were whispered between the long curtains that swayed between the ballroom and the garden.

We also had one example of real vice—an erstwhile dis-tinguished barrister who lived in open sin with a woman he could not marry. Of course we never met them. They were merely pointed out, with bated breath, at concerts and so on. They were quite old, and had been together for years.

Once my mother saw a young man lay his hand for an instant on my arm to emphasize a remark. She told me after-wards that I ought never to let people touch me. Needless to say, I was never kissed!

All the same, it is probably reasonable to suppose that I should have ended by marrying some serious young man and settling down for ever in Adelaide, if it had not been for my mother's death. Since the brief period of Miss MacPherson's art classes my appetite for painting had had nothing to feed on, whilst the ministrations of Margaret and Hilda had helped to diminish my sense of social inferiority. I can well remember the intoxication of having my conversation listened to, for the first time, by five people at once! Also, I had by

then given up all hope of going to Melbourne, where I had a
cousin who was a painter and another who was a pianist and
where there was a big Art School, for my mother's health
was failing and it was not possible to suggest leaving her.

Her last illness was my first experience of tragedy. When
they told me she could not recover, I was terror-struck. The
freedom that I had longed for was coming towards me, but
I did not want it. Not just then. But even in the most poignant
moment of loss, I knew that some day I should want it again,
and that I should know what to do with it when it came.

My mother died superbly, in a gentle radiance of religious
faith. She had no doubts whatever that she was going straight
to join my father, so she was not in the least afraid, and not
in the least sorry for herself. She displayed incredible courage,
first in concealing from us all the seriousness of her disease,
and afterwards in facing its horror with composure. It was
a great performance. In the desolation at her loss that smote
upon Tom and myself, we told each other that we must stay
very closely together and everything must always be as she
would have wished. . . .

What actually happened, however, was that Uncle Charlie,
as our guardian, sent Tom to a boarding school and decreed
the sale of our home, and I seized the opportunity to persuade
him and the Trustees to let me go to England for a year, until
Tom should have left school. They bought me a return ticket,
allowed me £20 a month, placed me in charge of the Fishers
(travelling as far as Marseilles) and arranged for me to stay
as a paying guest with the secretary of the Mothers' Union
in Pimlico. . . .

That was in April, 1914, and I have never gone back.

CHAPTER TWO

England in War Time

THE GREAT THING about a sea voyage is that you miss the changing landscape between one country and another. There is no clue in sea and sky to foretell what the next picture will be like.

Even train journeys, if they are to strange and distant places, have for me an element of the miraculous. I find it impossible really to believe in my bones, what I know well enough in my brain, that by this time to-morrow my own precious bodily person will be sitting, eating, and walking at that strange destination—that when I unpack this suitcase, which I am now closing, it will be to put these same familiar articles into—let us say—an Italian chest of drawers which is already waiting, destined to receive them—that I shall have seen with these eyes and spoken with this tongue to my long lost friend in person—that she will be actually and casually there, available for gossip, just like anybody else.

The present is the only reality—but to be able to carry the present through space—that is really a dazzling experience!

It was pretty dazzling to come to Europe in the spring of 1914. The ship became a kind of buffer state between two worlds—a state where the stiff and timorous fledgling was able to try her conversational wings amongst strangers who had never been told that Stella Bowen was quite a dull girl!

I had my first glimpse of cosmopolitan life at the Galle

Face Hotel, in Colombo, which was full of passengers from a liner from the Far East and where there was a ball, with coloured lights in the palm trees and moonlight on the sea. I loved the romantic background, although I was by no means enterprising enough for the appropriate romantic episode. I had £20 a month, I was free, and I was beholden to nobody, but these precious gifts were but coins to be fingered lovingly and not as yet to be spent. It was nice, however, to be treated like other girls with the small change of gallantry, "how well you dance," and a basket of fruit to your cabin.

The temperature in Colombo was actually lower than it had been in Adelaide when we left home. But being officially " the tropics," no one exerted themselves at all. There was limitless service, punkahs swaying, lots of ice, white linen suits, and complete inertia through the middle of the day. I saw a rich, fat Cingalese gentleman stuck all over with heavy gold ornaments which went oddly with his European clothes, lolling in a rickshaw and looking more objectionable than anyone I had ever imagined. I went in a rickshaw myself and felt miserably apologtic to the slim brown creature who padded along between the shafts. I saw the unimaginable squalor of the native quarter, the crawling heaps of brown limbs, the begging babies, the sickness. I admired the skill, industry and soft-voiced charm of the Hindu tailor who offered to copy your favourite suit in twenty-four hours for a pittance. All this is the Empire, I told myself, and no criticism of it entered into my mind. Not then.

Back on the boat, we found that we had shipped many more passengers, and this time they were not Australians. People from China, and the Straits, and from India itself. There was one lovely tall girl with sublime clothes and a wonderful leopardskin coat, who was married to a most unappetising little monkey of a husband, three times her age.

They told me it was for his money and I thought the girl an utter fool. If you have £240 a year of your own, that sort of thing doesn't make sense! But it gave me something to think about with regard to women's economic position. I had been told that I should find the Suffrage movement raging in England, but I did not expect that it would interest me very much. It was so unromantic!

I found London grimmer, dirtier, more cramped and less spectacular than I had expected. Bond Street was a bitter disappointment and Park Lane not splendid at all. I stayed as a paying guest in St. George's Square, Pimlico, with an unexceptionable family where there were two daughters and two sons. The younger son was on vacation from Oxford and he was detailed to show me the sights. His rather furry top-hat and greenish morning coat (they were in reduced circumstances) struck me as being a silly and unbecoming way to dress, and although I think he was quite a nice boy he was then at the pasty and pimply stage and I could not feel that he was much of an asset as an escort. He probably thought the same about me. I was completely dumb and my clothes were all wrong. Knowing that I should arrive just before the summer, I had provided myself with a selection of embroidered white muslin dresses and white shoes, and not much else! The two girls in this family, with their mother, were sunk deep in church work. They were marvellously good. And they were nice looking and well bred and their clothes were well cut. But they never got asked to any parties. Once in the season they were lent a box at the Opera, and once at the Albert Hall. But they were real home girls, which would have seemed quite natural to me but for the glaring contrast of their elder brother's life. He was a pretty enough Naval Lieutenant with a job at the Admiralty, and his dressing table mirror was stuck all round with invitations to the grandest balls in town. He would go out night after night in shining raiment, the while we sat down to our mutton chops and steamed pudding. But it was only after staying with my Bishop, and observing how the daughters of retired colonels in Kent were treated in comparison with their brothers, that I learnt to accept this state of things as normal in England. In Australia it was the girls rather than the boys, who represented their families in the social field. And the girls certainly had as much spent on their education as the boys, and were probably given a bigger allowance afterwards, since they were not expected to earn their own living. Another thing that I found curious in England was a meek acceptance of a fifth-rate social status which went hand in hand with a fulsome loyalty to the system that assigned to you that mediocre grade. In Australia we didn't look up to anybody, and if certain people sometimes looked down, they knew better than to expect to meet an admiring gaze from below!

The Bishop and his wife, who lived in a large Georgian house surrounded by lawns, rhododendrons and greenhouses, were extraordinarily kind to me. They had not seen me since, as a tearful little girl beside my equally tearful mamma, I had waved goodbye as they stood in the middle of a tug filled with clergymen on a choppy sea, on their way to the liner which was to carry them back to England.

The Bishop was smooth and round and genial, but rather shy. His wife was pink-faced and white-haired, short and plumb and gracious, very well connected and with a great resemblance to Queen Mary. She was bustling and unselfconscious and had real distinction. Unfortunately her young daughter was quite unable to unfold in this atmosphere, and remained a tightly-closed and rather unhappy little oyster, in spite of the united efforts of Marty (the housekeeper with sixty years of service with the family) and Nannie (thirty years) and Mummie and Grannie and Auntie B, who all smothered her with love and sought to prise open her mind and her heart. She was dowdy and shy, and she knew it, and when—as sometimes happened—her social duties included talking to a young man, it didn't help to have the whole family lined up, lovingly watching to see how she got on. Yet if she had got on *too* well, there would have been the dickens to pay!

I, too, felt constrained in her mother's kindly presence, for I had come to Europe in the hope of becoming an adult, and Bishop's Court put me right back under the old cotton-wool lid of fixed ideas, and sweetness-and-light, under which the chilly blast on independent thought can never penetrate. So I must have seemed like another unsatisfactory young oyster to my hostess (who would come to my bedside with, "How I *wish* you could have been here *last* week, dear. I wanted you to meet a girl we had here who is the *greatest* fun, I *know* you'd love her for she's as *gay* and as *modern* and as *full* of high spirits as anyone could wish—and so *intensely* interested in church work"—and what does one answer? I didn't know), yet without her warm-hearted hospitality and constant kindness I'd have been lonely and forlorn indeed during those first months in England.

It was on my second visit to Bishop's Court that I was gratified to discover that I was considered to have a certain nuisance-value as a young female. There were thirteen ordination candidates staying in the house and wherever you went, black coat-tails could be seen vanishing around the corner ahead. It was decided that the eyes of the deacons must not rest upon the daughter of the house nor yet upon myself before they were safely ordained. In consequence, we two were banished to Marty's room for all our meals until after the ceremony, when we were allowed to take tea in the hall, hemmed in behind a long table, and guarded at each end by the Bishop and his wife, where we had the felicity of viewing the massed curates across the buns and scones.

Later, when I had started going to an art school, the Bishop's wife said how nice it was for me to have such an interest, but of course, she did not see why it was necessary to study from the nude. However, someone had told her that it was all " very nicely done. The model is first draped, and then posed, and then the drapery is just—er—lifted off!" I did not undeceive her.

I first saw the amazing grandeur of the English spring from the front seat of the Bishop's limousine. He sped about his diocese confirming people, and provided that I came inside the car when it approached its destination, I was allowed to go and sit with the chauffeur after we had got well away again.

I can never forget my first sight of the infinitely repeated layers of young green beech leaves, spraying down from the huge, delicately-drawn trees. I had never imagined such a prodigality of verdure nor such radiantly blue distances. I had never known the air with such a lift and sparkle.

But the atmosphere inside the house was still very much like Adelaide, except for the greater ceremoniousness, which I hope improved my manners.

Presently, however, I had to leave my Pimlico family, owing to the return of a son from India whose room I had been occupying, and then chance pitched me into a milieu so unbelievably different from anything I had known or imagined, that I nearly exploded in the effort not to seem nonplussed. It came about because the Bishop's wife had a widowed sister who was just a tiny bit flightier than herself, and the sister had a daughter who was quite a good deal flightier than her mother. This daughter had a friend who was an artist in Chelsea, and the Bishop's sister-in-law arranged for me to go there for a visit as a paying guest—because she thought I needed young society. The Bishop didn't like it, but the letter had already been written.

The artist was Peggy Sutton, a good-humoured and lively lady with a baby daughter and a lazy, intelligent husband with a civil service job—I think in the education office. They had a studio flat in the King's Road and they said they would take me to the Café Royal and to the Crabtree Club. They did. At the Café Royal (which in those days still wore a cosy, old-fashioned aspect, with red plush and gilt curlicues) I saw all manner of queer, noisy and exotic folk. One glance sufficed to convince me that they were not actuated by any of the principles which guided the lives of those with whom I had hitherto come in contact. This, I said to myself, is a sink of iniquity, and how awful it would be if anyone were to see me here! The idea that nobody would care tuppence whether I was there or not, never entered my head, which was still filled with the naïve self-importance of the small-town dweller.

The Crabtree night club was even worse than the Café Royal. Beer marks on plain deal tables, wooden benches, and a small platform on which a moon-faced youth made music for a bevy of gyratory couples. Models in trousers, page-boy hair bobs, mascara'd eyes, unmanly youths and unfeminine girls, and *nobody* in evening dress! To me, it was the acme of low life. I believe that there were a number of distinguished and amusing artists there, but I wouldn't know, though I do remember hearing Marinetti reciting his zoom-bang poetry in Italian. . . .

With Peggy and her husband I visited my first English bar-parlour. It was in that nice pub on the Chelsea embankment

at the foot of Oakley Street, but even there I suffered from a
feeling that it wasn't lady-like. I do blush for myself at this
period. I have no idea whether the Suttons were aware of my
amazement at all I saw and heard at their flat, or whether I
succeeded in camouflaging my derangement. It was the sort
of place where one would get up in the morning and discover
that the bathroom was occupied by a Sleeping Beauty who had
climbed in through the window at three a.m., having failed
to get home to her suburb after a party. This was considered
quite reasonable and proper. One would be taken to call on
a certain Phillip at 10 p.m. to help him get straight in a new
domicile, and find a young woman alone with him, quite
unchaperoned, helping him sort out his books. Another
young woman would go up the river on a midsummer
night with a man friend and discuss, without embarrassment,
the prospects of getting back to London before sunrise.
I had imagined that if you broke the really sacred conventions by going alone to a man's rooms, or staying out all
night, you were necessarily bad. It dawned upon me soon,
however, that the young women in Chelsea who broke
these rules all the time, were quite nice girls, and just like
anybody else, except that they were rather better educated,
and appeared somehow to have disposed of their families.

The dishevelled host at a studio party, sitting on a rickety
bed in an open shirt with a beer bottle between his feet and
a girl in each arm, would arise quite unselfconsciously to greet
you with the most polished Oxford manner—the sort of
manner which would have fluttered the dovecots of Adelaide
into getting out the best silver and ordering a chicken. I
could not understand its connection with squalor, and I could
not guess that most of these people would also end their days
in prosperous bourgeois respectability, getting out the best
silver themselves, and ordering many chickens!

I was in the country when war broke out, staying on a farm with my old school teacher who had lately arrived from Adelaide. I was completely unaware of the European situation, or even of its precise geography. I had been brought up on Imperialist-Jingo history but had very little feeling of patriotism, having arrived too recently in England. I had no sense whatever of my place in the British Empire nor of the British Empire's place in history. I had no personal connection with the fighting forces.

Then Hilda and Mrs. Fisher arrived in London, and being much more aware of what was happening, declared that we ought to take up work of National Importance. In consequence, I joined Hilda for a period of work on a Children's Care Committee in the East End, where early war conditions were creating chaos.

By this time I was boarding with a doctor's family in Harley Street. I was extremely lonely, and the depression created by the war, but more particularly by my introduction to the slums, kept me in a haze of unhappiness. The slums were a revelation of awfulness. I had to write reports on the homes I visited and my reports were so uniformly black that they were of no value. I had to learn to distinguish between black, near-black and grey. . . .

I had to take a child with ringworm to the Out-Patients Department of the Hackney Hospital . . . and on Skin-Disease Day. I was kept waiting interminably, in crowds, on benches, in draughts. The doctor was intensely disagreeable and sent us to wait on another bench for X-ray treatment. After two hours, without having received treatment, we were told to come back in four weeks' time. The whole excursion had taken four hours, a half-day's work. It was easy to see why the poor didn't avail themselves of the medical services unless they were bullied into it.

Homerton was a nightmare. I wish I could say that my social conscience was born from that moment, but it wasn't. I wanted to run away from it all, and start painting. I did, however, begin to realise a few facts and to talk about social questions with a new friend I made at the Children's Care Committee. This was Mary Butts, who was working in the East End to get practical experience of social conditions as a sequel to her studies at the London School of Economics. She was a flaming object in that dreary office, with her scarlet hair and white skin and sudden, deep-set eyes. She looked what she was—a girl who came from a lovely old home in Dorset and a family which had given her good manners and an expensive education, but had entirely failed to inspire her with the current ideas of her class. In particular, she was at loggerheads with her mother, who was always opening bazaars and never (she alleged) gave straight answers to awkward question. I am sure Mary made the questions as awkward as possible! Unlike me, still timidly trying to extricate myself from a background of prejudice and humbug and muddled thinking, and tentative about setting up views of my own (I had to stop, and look, and listen first), Mary had fought her own more formidable background tooth and nail from the start, and had a vast set of very definite views of her own, about which she was extremely vocal.

She loved a good fight, and spread considerable desolation in her home by wrestling with her mother for the possession of her young brother Tony, then at Eton. As part of Tony's education, Mary decided one fourth of June to take a party to visit him composed of people calculated to explode the stuffy, upper-class conventions under which the boy was supposed to be languishing. The party consisted of a Hindu student called Chanda, a young Jewish poet and pacifist called John Rodker, a Greek male ballet-dancer of great beauty called Jean Varda, a lovely friend of mine called Phyllis, and myself. I was wearing a pair of exquisite spike-heeled shoes which some-one had given me and which pinched horribly, so we all went on to the greensward beside the river so that I could take them off, and we danced on the grass, for the edification of the decorous groups who were strolling about with their top-hatted offsprings. Then our poet took us all to call on Aldous Huxley, who at that time was a housemaster, and he simply hated us. But since we liked him, we stayed quite a long time. After tea in Tony's rooms, we felt that we had had a very successful day, and Mary was convinced that we had done Eton all the good in the world. I must say that young Tony bore it all very well.

When I first met Mary at Hackney Wick, she delighted to endoctrinate me concerning the potential splendour of the Working Man and the inept futility of our Royal Family. I thought this was just plain treason, but I listened.

When I got to know her better, I found Mary to be an aristocratic anarchist rather than the socialist she then im-agined herself. She was always full of turgid, high-pressure mthusiasms and indignations, and it was essential to her to devise suitable objects for the exercise of these faculties. She would use her fine brains to build up a brilliant, if crazy theory which then became a fruitful nesting-place for all the bats she had in the belfry. The fact that the original evidence on which this structure was founded had never been seriously examined and was often a plain piece of silliness did not matter. It did not disturb her theory-building activities, and the consequent intellectual and emotional fireworks. In a word, Mary was an artist, and the fireworks were often ex-tremely beautiful.

I can very well remember Ford Madox Ford's enthusiasm when I first showed him a manuscript of Mary's. It was

Ashe of Rings I think, which was not published until long afterwards. She was a born writer of great sensitiveness and distinction, with a capacity for rich and sensuous imagery that was just a gift from Heaven. But she never offered me a coin of wisdom that did not ring false, and wisdom, alas! was what I then sought. I was bothered by her fiction-writer's capacity (new to me then, familiar now) to take some fact, and fabricate from it a dramatic grotesquerie in which she appeared firmly to believe and about which she would weave a whole tissue of dark and magical meaning, rife with spells and portents upon which she was quite prepared to act. I was still at the stage of being interested in the size and shape of the fact as I had known it, and wanting to have a clearer light thrown on it. I was like the child who wants to be assured that the fairy-tale is really true.

If I had been as wise then as I am now, I should have known that the way to enjoy any artist is to attend to his work, and not allow one's self to be confused by that lesser thing, his character. I should never have wasted a moment in worrying about Mary's misconceptions, nor in trying to find order and reasonableness in her life. I should have regarded her purely as a rather beautiful person who must be encouraged to go on producing beautiful prose, cost what it might in human wreckage. And I should have taken care not to be let in for any tidying-up jobs!

As it was, Mary, in those early days, took on for me the aspect of an exotic and foolhardy bird of whom I was rather frightened, but for whose offer of friendship I was immensely grateful at a period when I was seldom at my ease with anybody. I had no friend of my own sort with whom I could feel really sisterly and I was waiting—quite consciously and miserably—to find one. Hilda was getting engaged, and soon followed her fiancé to India to be married, I was hideously lonely, and Mary's presence did a great deal to brighten those barren days, even if it could not do much to warm them.

I have always thought, however, that if one were ill, destitute, a refugee, or in any really spectacular mess, Mary's doorstep would be the right doorstep on which to be found in a fainting condition. She would receive you and your woes with open arms, without question and without caution. No nonsense about deciding whether you were a deserving case! Mary would thrive on the drama of the situation and you would thrive on her championship.

I wish she were not dead. . . .

During all this time, I considered myself as merely a visitor in England, with a return ticket which should take me back to Adelaide to keep house for my brother. Then suddenly Tom cabled to say that he was leaving school prematurely to enlist, and added " your return optional."

With that, I sold my return ticket and enrolled immediately at an art school as a full-time pupil. Hearing of a students' hostel in De Vere Gardens, and armed with a reference from the Bishop, I introduced myself into this extremely select establishment. It was a good move, because it brought me at last into contact with my own kind. It was here that I met Phyllis Reid.

Phyllis was a lovely girl from Birmingham who was studying voice production and dramatic art at Miss Fogarty's school at the Albert Hall. She had immense light green eyes with black rims, set wide apart. Her slender figure was most excellently modelled through the middle, and her massive light-brown hair had curly yellow edges. The eyebrows were a jetty black, the eyelashes extravagant, and the jaw-line admirable. But although I appreciated all these assets (none better, for I've always been profoundly influenced by good looks) what really drew me first to Phyllis was the similarity between her origins and my own. She had been lectured in her youth in the same words, and been inculcated with the same principles. Her home had, of course, been closer to London than mine, so that there had been certain modifications. For instance, it was agreed that, in exceptional circumstances, girls might leave home and earn their own living, and there was, indeed, more insistence on the dignity of labour than there had been in my home. And on the political side there was a positive emancipation. Phyllis's people were all ardent Liberals and Suffragists and Phyllis herself had walked in a suffrage pilgrimage. But on the moral side we had been brought up on identical slogans. When the green eyes had attracted some attentions from a married man, and their young possessor had very properly questioned her mother about the possibility of married men being in love with people other than their wives, Mrs. Reid had replied that there *might* be such people, but that fortunately Phyllis was never likely to meet any of them. Well, obviously that did not wash.

So Phyllis, like me, was doing some independent research, and we had a vast amount to talk about. She was able to enlighten me about the Suffrage movement, and I her about such phenomena as Peggy Sutton's Chelsea folk, and Mary Butts. We had many cocoa parties and midnight confidences; student stuff, comforting and necessary.

The hostel was a very high-class establishment. Prayers were held each morning in a drawing-room with a vast polished floor and handsome antique furniture. You might go out twice a week until 12 p.m. if you gave due notice of where you were going. If you wished to receive a male caller, you must commandeer the drawing-room, which then had a notice pinned on the door, " Reserved for Miss Blank." So there was nothing casual about such visits, and if your caller stayed after 10 p.m. the Principal would come in and turn him out. With a charming smile, of course, for she was a most prepossessing and well-bred young woman with a porcelain skin and beautifully fixed, prematurely-grey hair. It was only when you lived in the house that you began to chafe under her regime. I think she disliked us all.

Phyllis chafed more than I did, that being her nature. I have always found it relatively easy to submit to outward control, so long as I am allowed to keep my thoughts to myself, but Phyllis had never willingly submitted to anything in her life, and is always ready to give her reasons to all whom it may concern.

The result was a migration from the hostel to a furnished studio where we two set up house together. This emancipation was won only after a hard tussle with the Reid family, whose consent to Phyllis's studying in London had been conditional upon her remaining under suitable control at the hostel. However, I was taken to Birmingham for inspection, and must have inspired a certain confidence, since we finally got permission to move into Pembroke Studios.

Here our adult life may be said to have begun. For three years we shared a studio which belonged to a painter who had gone to the front, and we gradually began to collect friends and add up experiences from amongst all the odd folk who were left out of the war. Many of these were socialist-pacifists, several were conscientious objectors, and it was fine to discover so many intelligent people ready to support the opinion that no good could come out of war. Finding myself a natural pacifist, I continued to do a certain amount of infant welfare work rather than war work, and gave up rolling bandages at a Red

Cross depot because I could not bear the blood-thirsty conversation of the old ladies of Kensington. But most of my time was spent at the art school. This school was one of which I had heard formerly in Australia, not knowing that its best days were long since past. Here I soon felt that I was in a blind alley. After drawing innumerable large and heavily-modelled nudes in charcoal, I decided to migrate either to the Westminster School of Art or the Slade. I went first for an interview to the Slade, but was completely crushed by the aspect of the professor who received me. I don't know whether it was the famous Tonks or the famous Brown, but he was eight feet tall and conceived it as his duty to put the fear of God into me. I knew well enough that I could never draw under his eye of wrath, so when he asked me what day I was coming to start work, I stammered that I was not sure that I was coming at all—and took a bus to the Westminster. Here they told me that they didn't believe in grief and tears, that they had never had any suicides amongst their students, and that if I was tired of drawing nudes in charcoal it would probably be extremely bad for me to continue to do so, and that they would help me to discover what I *did* want to do!

With this kind of encouragement I opened my mind wide to the theories of painting put forth by that great painter and great personality, Walter Sickert. He came but once a fortnight, and spent perhaps four minutes with each student. But those four minutes provided more inspiration than four months' criticism elsewhere.

Sometimes he would sport an exuberant and virile beard, and sometimes his aspect would be that of a clean-shaven ascetic. Sometimes he would be Richard and sometimes Walter. But these metamorphoses changed nothing in his constant search for a fresh, naïve and honest eye amongst his pupils. He made short work of the old methods of painting by realistic tone-values. If, for instance, he were to see an onion on a window-sill, instead of talking about it as a spherical object carrying a certain weight of shadow with a crescent of light upon its upper edge, he would be more apt to discuss its root-formation, the stripes in its skin, and the movement of the leaves shooting out at the top. If there were anything cock-eyed or unique about his onion, so much the better. He didn't want it to symbolize all onions, but to be a special, individual and possibly faulty one. And he would be furious if you brought to its contemplation any preconceived ideas as to what an onion should be like. No generalizations!

In short, he taught one to trust ones faithful eyes, and to open them wide. I had never before been required to look at things so minutely, and having looked, to record them with so little fuss. He hated it if you touched the canvas twice in the same place. The first touch had a virtue all its own, he would say, and any correction you added only substituted a doubtful virtue for a positive one. In the same way, you were never permitted to erase a line. If it were wrong, you just made a heavier one in the right place. Then your drawing had the added interest of showing your first thoughts as well as your second. . . .

All this was extremely good discipline for me, though very revolutionary. It did not permit of the building-up of architectural patterns—but I had not yet discovered that the building-up of patterns composed, if possible, of living tissues, and seen in a kind of no-man's-land of diffused light, was the thing which was going to interest me most in painting. I had not yet been to Italy.

In the meantime, Sickert opened my eyes to the beauties of the accidental and the spontaneous, and got me right out of the dismal academic rut into which I had been sinking. He taught me the difference between something dead (on canvas) and something living. When, later, I got to know a very different painter—Pavel Tchelitcheff—I recognised this quality again. If either of these men lifts his hand to make a stroke on paper or canvas, the stroke has so much life in it that you expect it to crawl off!

I suppose that this gift of creating life at a touch is the most enviable gift that a painter can have. Perhaps it is even a necessary one—like "getting across" on the stage, or a prose style with the kind of vitality that gets itself read even by people who have no interest in what the author is trying to say.

Whilst I was at the Westminster, struggling to make my painting fresher and yet more controlled, Phyllis was studying dramatic art at the Albert Hall. She was one of Miss Fogarty's best pupils and certainly had the gift of "getting across." But strangely enough, she had no ambition to adopt a stage career. All she wanted, was to live in London and never go back to Birmingham. Consequently, when she was offered an engagement at the Birmingham Repertory Theatre by John Drinkwater, she foolishly turned it down.

I saw something of Miss Fogarty's school, and even painted some scenery for it, because Phyllis insisted that I should go with her to the elocution class. She said it would improve my speech and make me less self-conscious. I daresay it did both, but it was agony to me! I kept on at it, however, for the pleasure of watching Miss Fogarty rehearsing the class which followed. She was a short, stout, middle-aged lady in a smooth purple coat and skirt with a lace jabot and a tricorne hat with a veil, yet when she sprang to her feet to show some gawky girl how to play Ariel, there was nothing incongruous about it. The illusion was produced, and the means employed to produce it were then discussed. I was fascinated.

Altogether, we got a pretty good introduction to all the arts during that black and dreary war-time, when the men were mostly fighting, and the raiders kept coming over with their bombs at the full of the moon. I suppose that the people who were left behind, and who were interested in the arts of peace, tended to get into a huddle together, for company. Anyway we made friends.

It began when Peggy, my former Chelsea hostess, turned up to ask if we would lend our studio for a party. We were naturally delighted with the prospect of seeing our big room at last filled with people. The party was to say good-bye to some artist going to the front, and to it came Ezra Pound.

Ezra, who lived near by, decided that two personable young women who lived in a large studio, danced to a gramophone, and longed to be sociable, were fit and proper persons to be cultivated, especially as one of them (Phyllis) had an insatiable appetite for poetry. To me, he was at first an alarming phenomenon. His movements, though not uncontrolled, were sudden and angular, and his droning American voice, breaking into bomb-shells of emphasis, was rather incomprehensible as he enlightened us on the Way, the Truth, and the Light, in Art. He desired us to teach him to dance, and quickly evolved a highly personal and very violent style, which involved a great deal of springing up and down, as well as swaying from side to side, which caused him the greatest satisfaction although I am bound to say that it reflected little credit on his teachers!

He was not unbeautiful. His face, shaped like the ace of spades with a tuft on the chin, was topped by a big bank of light-coloured crinkly hair which went straight on up, continuing the line of the sloping forehead and the long, straight nose. Under the nose was an equally long, straight mouth with flexible corners. All the features would gather together in the kindliest twinkling movement whenever he was amused, which was often. He would then make a rhythmic, hooting noise which represented laughter.

Ezra was a dear, as we soon discovered. But when he first came to call after the party, with the proposal that we should join his weekly dinner club at Bellotti's in Soho, I was still too alarmed by his wild man's aspect to accept. I decreed that Margaret Postgate should go with Phyllis in my place, and if their report were favourable, I would go next time!

When I consider how benighted, forlorn, and unattached I had felt since coming to England, how lacking friends and how longing for the company of my betters, it is very shaming to remember that the inhibitions of Adelaide were still working to prevent my acceptance of that first Bellotti dinner!

Because of course from that point we met a whole heap of people; T. S. Eliot and Arthur Waley and Wadsworth and May Sinclair and Violet Hunt and G. B. Stern, and P. Wyndham Lewis and the poet Yeats. Also Ezra's beautiful wife Dorothy, who never attempted to keep up with her husband's exuberant pace and remained at home in a somewhat lofty seclusion. It was a great compliment when she brought her cool detachment and charming presence to some of our studio dances, and I felt very proud when I heard that she had pronounced that "the little Australian was quite charming!"

It was much easier for Phyllis to get herself into circulation. Not only had she her really remarkable looks, her superb dancing and an exceptional out-giving animation, but she loved poetry and read it beautifully. All this was part of her speech-training and it stood her in good stead with the poets and writers whom we then met. What stood her in less good stead were her tantrums which would often create crises which I had to try to tidy up. For this, although she was my senior by several months, I was called "Auntie Stella," and she, "Little P!"

It worked very well. Of course, she soon began to have affairs of the heart, which I did not share, but everybody who came to the studio was extremely nice to me and I never felt left out in the cold. I did not have any beaus to speak of, but I enjoyed the confidence of Phyllis's young men, who contributed quite a bit, indirectly, to my education.

And Ezra took the trouble to occupy himself with our joint education. I expect it was fun for him to harangue two girls who took him so very seriously, and it was certainly fine for us. But it was all rather difficult for there were so many things we were forbidden to admire, and so few exponents of the arts that he recommended. These were the days of the American "Little Review" and the reverberations of "Blast" were still shaking the air. The public was an imbecile, and the artist was to make no compromise with popular taste. "Getting across" was the last thing he should consider.

In theory it was all very precious and exclusive and rather puritanical. But there were lovely things for us to admire—Eliot's "Prufrock," Ezra's "Lustra"—Gaudier Bjeska's stone carvings and drawings of animals, and Wyndham Lewis's drawings. I liked the latter for their built-up architectural quality even though I did not, as yet, see much point in abstract art—a guilty secret which I concealed as best I could from Ezra! There was also James Joyce's "Portrait of the Artist." Joyce and Lewis were Ezra's twin gods, before whom we were bidden to bend the knee most deeply. I did not meet Joyce, until years later, in Paris, when I found him to be far less alarming than Wyndham Lewis, whose conversation held so many traps for the unwary that it was just a question of choosing which one you would fall into.

"That is a very lovely girl you've got with you, Miss Bowen."

"Yes, isn't she?"

"And that is a most successful frock she is wearing."

"Ah! That was a very hasty concoction. I made it for her this afternoon."

"Hasty concoctions are always best, don't you think?"

(No. Yes. How does this fit in with the architectural? He does not draw like that.)

Or, "Do you like soldiers, Miss Bowen?"

(Yes. No. This is a mean question. I'm not quick-tongued enough to say that I don't like uniforms but I sometimes like some of the people who have to wear them.)

Arthur Waley, though apparently a shy and diffident little man, was another teaser with a redoubtable tongue. At that period he had a post at the British Museum and was already an authority on Chinese and Japanese art, but he had not yet published those exquisite poems from the Chinese for which he afterwards became famous. He had a high and breathless little voice and an almost feminine love of gossip. He was rather beautiful, but you did not notice this at first, because his face was always averted. If he came to call, he entered without a word, scuttled to a chair and never knew what to do with his bowler hat and stick. He would be wearing a mackintosh, and it would take quite a long time to get him going, conversationally. When you *did* get him going, his talk was highly amusing, penetrating, and slightly malicious. He was as sensitive as he was unsentimental — a combination which I learnt to appreciate more as I grew older, and discovered that the thick-skinned sentimentalist is the worst kind of person in the world.

When he got bored, Waley would rush from the room in the middle of a sentence with a "Well I must be going now," before you had time to open the door for him; but this lack of social aplomb did not mean that he could not be formidable on occasion. I can remember sitting on the floor in a room full of strange people and Waley suddenly saying with malice, "Of course, Miss Bowen is waiting to find a great man. She has often talked to me about it!" A complete invention which covered me with such confusion that I was quite unable to defend myself!

It was trivialities like these that gave one the feeling of being a fly upon a pin, held up for inspection, by the highbrows. That the said highbrows should ever have bothered with us at all, remains a matter for suprise and gratitude. In my case, I can only suppose that they found my complete lack of education something of a novelty! The clean slate.

Before we got to know Ezra and Co., almost the only friend we had in London besides Mary Butts, was Margaret Postgate, who had been at Roedean with Phyllis. Postgate's Latin Grammar had been my most hated textbook at school, and Margaret's father had written it. He was an eminent professor and a thorough-going domestic tyrant of the Victorian sort. His outlook was so reactionary and his discipline so rigid that his two eldest children, Margaret and Raymond, were already in a state of violent rebellion when I met them. Margaret had just taken a brilliant classical degree at Girton and had been appointed junior classical mistress at St. Paul's Girls School at the stupendous salary of £120 a year, which freed her from the tyranny of the parental purse strings. But Raymond, a lanky and shock-headed young intellectual still at Oxford with scholarships insufficient to support him, was at his father's mercy when he declared himself a conscientious objector. The old man stopped supplies and turned Ray into a rabid revolutionary on the spot. Margaret's Waterloo came later, when she renounced her safe school-teaching job for a precarious secretaryship with the Fabian Research Department. Her father could not stop her, but his gorge rose and overflowed when, later, she married the Socialist writer G. D. H. Cole, and Raymond married George Lansbury's daughter, Daisy. He subsequently cut them both out of his life and out of his will, and refused even to see his grandchildren.

When I first saw Margaret, I thought her the most uncivilised girl I had ever met, as well as the cleverest. She was shy, untidy, and wild, with a little square face under an immense mop of dark hair, small shoulders hunched, long arms held in at the elbows, and narrow hands with long gesticulating fingers. A high forehead, a wide, humorous mouth, and a very short chin. And however much she might edge away from strangers, and despise the small change of mannerly greetings, no bushel capable of hiding her light has ever been discovered! She is still one of my dearest friends.

Until Ray and Margaret appeared upon the scene, I had never met anyone who wanted to reform society politically. The rather amateurish enthusiasm of Mary Butts for the "potential splendour of the working man" was by no means the same thing as their absorbtion in routine political work. I was troubled when I discovered that they considered a socialist revolution to be an absolute necessity. One is not born with a consciousness of the rights and wrongs of the social system, and I acquired mine late in life because my natural orientation was towards the particular and the individual. I was enormously interested in my own life, and passionately curious about that most individual of all activities—artistic creation.

I was just learning to find my way about in the curious jungle into which fate had pitched me and ready to resist the idea that this landscape needed ploughing-up and re-planting, with all the old landmarks destroyed. That would mean learning my way about all over again! And the idea that the new landscape, although freed from the disgrace of puny and strangled vegetation, would represent nothing more inspiring than a tidy market-garden with rows of equal cabbages was not very inspiring. I wanted a few orchids, and it had not dawned on me that these feelings were conditional upon my continuing to receive £250 a year.

There were certainly no orchids in Tothill Street, but the comrades were a very good lot of cheerful, selfless, and quite serious minded youngsters. Some of them had been to prison as conscientious objectors. When they were all gathered together, they would sit on the floor and sing songs—mostly ribald skits upon the powers in Whitehall. Bound by a common faith, they could relax easily into a happy intimacy which contained more spontaneous and warm gaiety than any gathering of those little separate egos who usually make up a party. But their play was of a somewhat rudimentary kind, since dedication to a cause seems to make personal relationships unimportant, and when personal relationships are unimportant they are not cultivated with skill. And dedication to a cause appears also to make æsthetic considerations seem unimportant (though why I do not know) so they are not cultivated with skill either. On the whole, the comrades seemed quite impervious to ugliness. Francis Meynell was the only one whom I can remember as having any leaning towards the decorative side of life, or any desire to give pleasure by the conscious exercise of good manners. I stuck up for the idea that these things were not frivolous, but had to do with style and form in living, like technique in painting, and I could not see that they had any particular connection with capitalism, nor realise that the system which made it easier for a woman to marry £1000 a year than to earn it, gave an artificial commercial value to feminine beauty and personality and produced a huge class of female parasites whose chief activities were self-adornment and the maintenance of a web of personal relationships; I have always adored carefully tended good looks, and I do not care how artificial they are. An appearance of this sort is a work of art, entailing skill, patience, and self-discipline, and it must be carried off by the appropriate manner. It is not worth undertaking by people who are not gifted for it, and if it requires money, this might just as well be raised by passing round the hat as by any other means! So although I was ready to be convinced by socialist principles I was bothered by the comrade's contempt for "grooming" and "glamour" as capitalist vices, and also by the very unsatisfactory position they seemed prepared to assign to the artist in their brave new world. I still thought you could have everything at once.

I began to get some idea, however, of the sinister, predatory power of this grooming-and-glamour business through the friends of a girl violinist who lived next door to us. Our studio was one of twelve built round a courtyard which was planted with lilac and syringa bushes, and waited on, rather sketchily, by the porter's wife. It had a gallery containing our two beds in which we were invisible from below when lying down, but could look over the balustrade if we sat up. Beyond the studio there was nothing but the entrance, and the bathroom which was between ourselves and No. 3, from whence there issued perpetually the sounds of the loveliest music. One night the music was so heavenly that we stayed in the bath until 3 a.m. listening to it. Next day there was a knock on the door and a very chic and diminutive young woman with a curly smile came to inquire if we had been disturbed. She had had complaints from the neighbours and was anxious to be conciliatory about the all-night music, but "Ysaye had been too wonderful," she said. Very impressed, we said, "So *that* was who it was," and told her with what pleasure we had listened in. After that, we became constant visitors next door.

I think musicians have a very hard time in comparison with painters and writers in having to win their public by personal contact. Sylvia Sparrow earned a precarious living as a violinist and a society pet, and if any girl ever sang hard for her supper, she did! She was a fairy-like young person whose fragile appearance concealed a vast amount of grit, and she lived in a desperate treadmill of effort to keep her end up amongst the people who hired her to play in their houses and who came to her for lessons. These people provided us with a glimpse into what might be called Society. To them, we were "those two rather nice girls who live next door to darling Sylvia," and from them, I got a fair idea of the grim egotism that goes to the maintenance of a successful social façade. An artist was someone to be patronised if he could confer some distinction on oneself as patroness. Or someone who could create for one a really clever background or get-up. "Something that is really *me*!" or whose music would make a party more successful. "I love to surround myself with artists," as though they were something to be worn in the hair! One of these hostesses invited me with Sylvia for a week-end to her country estate, and there, except for being worried by the inadequacy of my clothes and my sang-froid, I found the atmosphere an easy let-down after the intellectual exactions of Ezra and the political theorising of the Postgates. Conversation circulated cheerfully around the coarser and simpler aspects of life. Being in need of a pill, I asked my hostess at bedtime if she could oblige me with one. "Dear me, no," she said, "haven't got such a thing. Bill," she shouted, "have you got any cascara for Miss Bowen?" Bill's door opened 'way down the passage. "No," he bellowed, "tell the girl to eat an apple!" Being unaccustomed to the fifth-form humour prevalent in English country houses I found this highly embarrassing. Years later, however, when I was painting the portrait of an aged M.F.H. in the Midlands, and had lost my Adelaide prudishness, I was able to remain equanimous when the old man, at the head of his dinner-table, explained to his inquiring grandson why the ladies left the table first. "Ask yourself, my boy. Ask yourself. Of course they have all this plumbing nowadays and I understand that in some houses you have to go to the bathroom. But why do you suppose that screen is in the corner? And why do you think your grandfather had the lower left-hand pane taken out of the window? . . . But it was your great-uncle Archibald who killed the virginia creeper . . . etc., etc."

To return to Sylvia. All sorts of prominent musicians would come and make music with her, just out of friendship. And with the help of a 'cellist colleague, she held a weekly class for ensemble playing to which her pupils would bring their friends, and it would be "darling Sylvia, we love coming here and mayn't we stay for a bite of food—just anything will do." And afterwards Sylvia would mutter, "Don't they know that I'm tired—tired—*tired*, that I was up till three last night and that I was teaching at nine-thirty this morning and that I had to darn my stockings and wash my blouse and that sausage and beer and bread and butter and cheese and fruit for ten people costs *money*, and that I have to go out to fetch it, and that they leave me with everything to clear up after leading two quartets of amateurs reading at sight for two hours?" Of course she never said such a thing aloud, or she would have brought her whole house of cards down about her ears. And it was quite a nice little card house, with lots of parties (that she could not afford to miss) and fees to be picked up as long as darling Sylvia's studio remained such an amusing place.

With new vistas opening around us, with our chosen studies, with Ezra to hold forth about literature, the Postgates to prod up our social consciences and Sylvia to provide glimpses of musical society, our education proceeded by leaps and bounds during those last years of the war. On the question of the war itself, we remained in a state of rather confused pacifism. The idea that the governments of Europe should have the right to conscript our whole generation, relegating everything creative to an ignominious position under the label of "civilian life," was horrible. War's purpose was destruction, which appeared to be the opposite of our function as would-be artists, or as women. We were thankful that we were allowed to keep out of it, though this attitude let us in for a fair deal of criticism. We did not come across many actual Colonel Blimps, but we had friends who blamed us for our unwillingness to "share the common experience," who considered that we were flabby-minded egotists, intent in irrelevancies and incapable of grasping the fact that we were living in the middle of an Epic.

Well, the Epic in question looks like a pretty tragic muddle in retrospect, and the heroes who died for it, the most deluded of victims. It solved nothing, and I'm glad that in those days we hated it and that we went on devoting ourselves to the arts of peace and trying to learn the things we wanted to know. Afterwards, when it became plain that the world had *not* been made safe for democracy, nor fit for heroes to live in, our pacifist ideals appeared to have been justified. But at the time, we suffered the usual torments and uncertainties of young people who don't go with the crowd. we were oppressed by the effort of nursing our own small spark of life under the shadow of the guns. Merely in material ways the gloom was heavy. Dark streets, horrid food, the manifold restrictions of D.O.R.A., queueing up for everything you wanted and being frightened by air raids. Then of course there was the perpetual weight on the imagination of the constant killing and wounding, and the profound depression at the plight of all soldiers, even in places of safety. Incidentally there was also a realization that the enthusiasm which soldiers on leave were apt to pursue feminine society was merely the outcome of their plight, and had nothing to do with any personality one might happen to possess!

My brother Tom came through the war without a scratch. He enlisted as a private but soon got recommended for a commission and came over from France to be trained. During his leaves he slept on our studio divan and gave us expensive meals in the West End. When he first turned up I had not seen him for over three years, and found him changed from a pink-cheeked schoolboy into a large, grown man, with a deep voice and a more solidly developed nose than in boyhood. He thought all our friends were freaks and said so, but got on with them beautifully. He was a dear, and a handsome fellow into the bargain. He fell in love with Phyllis, of course, but they both got over it in a fortnight.

When the war was over, he went back to Adelaide and married the girl to whom he had been writing ever since he left home. He is still married to her and they are raising a fine family in the house he bought in 1920.

On November 11th, 1918, we knew that there was going

to be an armistice at eleven o'clock, but we imagined that we should remain quite calm about it, so Phyllis went to keep a hairdressing appointment and I stayed at home. But of course, when the maroons sounded it was quite impossible to remain calm at all, and intolerable to remain alone. I ran into all the hairdressers shops in Kensington High Street looking for Phyllis, and when I could not find her, I went to Ezra's flat in Church Street and dragged him out. The streets were filling fast and we got on top of a bus going towards the city. In those days the tops of buses were not enclosed and we stood up in the front of ours, Ezra with his hair on end, smacking the bus-front with his stick and shouting to the other people packed on the tops of other buses jammed alongside ours, which were nosing a cautious route through the surging streets. Trafalgar Square was crammed to capacity and no vehicle could penetrate the living mass.

I can't remember how we got home.

Two days later I dined at the House of Commons with Frances Meynell, who had a ticket for a Labour Party dinner at which Lansbury and Ramsay MacDonald and Philip Snowden were the speakers. Everyone was very emotional. It was a good dinner, and I found myself seated between a Hindu who was a vegetarian and an Able-Bodied Seaman who was a teetotaller, and so was able to consume the oysters of the one and the champagne of the other. I imagined that Hindus and A.-B.'s were natural guests for the Labour Party to invite, and was having a cosy time with them in ignorance of the fact that one was a Belted Earl (Lord de la Warr—a conscientious objector on leave from a mine-sweeper in the North Sea) and the other was the brother of the New Christ (Mrs. Besant's Krishnamurti). After dinner we thought it would be appropriate to go and sing the Red Flag on the steps of the House of Lords, which we proceeded to do. Then we went to

Trafalgar Square, where the street lights were shining on the façades of the buildings for the first time in 4½ years and the bonfires were illuminating the seething, crazy masses of excited people. I can remember dancing round the Nelson Column hand in hand in a mile-long chain, falling on the steps and barking my shin, and being dragged up and on again. I can remember the perfectly sober Earl acting divinely drunk to an embarrassed policeman who was quite unable to control the crowd, "You dear ole bobby you," he burbled, clutching at the unwilling policeman for support, " ish all you fellars keepin' order like you do, as won ush the war."

I can remember seeing everyone looking happy, for the first time. And perhaps the last.

It must have been about nine months before the Armistice that we were introduced to Ford Madox Ford. We knew him very well by reputation because he was one of the writers whom Ezra allowed us to admire. *Ladies Whose Bright Eyes* and *The Good Soldier* were two of the best-thumbed books on our shelves, and Ford's war poems, *Footsloggers* and *Old Houses in Flanders*, were being discussed and admired at Harold Monro's Poetry Bookshop, whose weekly poetry readings we frequented. Indeed, Phyllis herself used sometimes to give readings there; I can remember her rendering of *Mr. Prufrock*, and our flattered pleasure when T. S. Eliot turned up, with his gentle and benevolent smile and a black satin chest-protector, at some of our beer-and-gramophone parties.

Ford was an innovation in our circle because not only was he in khaki, but he actually liked it. He was the only intellectual I had met to whom army discipline provided a conscious release from the torments and indecisions of a super-sensitive brain. To obey orders was, for him, a positive holiday, and the pleasure he took in recounting rather bucolic anecdotes of the army was the measure of his need for escape from the intrigues and sophistications of Literary London.

Ford was considerably older than the rest of our friends, and much more impressive. He was very large, with a pink face, yellow hair, and drooping, bright blue eyes. His movements were gentle and deliberate and his quiet and mellow voice spoke, to an Australian ear, with ineffable authority.

He had known everyone, and was full of stories, not only of Wells and Conrad and Henry James, but even of Liszt, Turgeniev, Swinburne and Rossetti whom he had known in childhood at the home of his grandfather, Ford Madox Brown.

I reacted violently against him at first on the grounds that he was a militarist. But I soon found that if he was a militarist, he was at the same time the exact opposite. When I got to know him better, I found that every known human quality could be found flourishing in Ford's make-up, except a respect for logic. His attitude to science was very simple. He just did not believe a word of it! But he could show you two sides simultaneously of any human affair, and the double picture made the subject come alive, and stand out in a third-dimensional way that was very exciting. What he did not know about the depths and weaknesses of human nature was not worth knowing. The hidden places of the heart were his especial domain, and when he chose he could put the screw upon your sense of pity or of fear with devastating sureness.

The stiff, rather alarming exterior, and the conventional, omniscient manner, concealed a highly complicated emotional machinery. It produced an effect of tragic vulnerability; tragic because the scope of his understanding and the breadth of his imagination had produced a great edifice which was plainly in need of more support than was inherent in the structure itself. A walking temptation to any woman, had I but known it!

To me he was quite simply the most enthralling person I had ever met. Worth all of Phyllis's young men put together, and he never even looked at her!

He began to tell me about himself, filling me with pride by confiding all his troubles and weaknesses. The most monumental of authors—the fountain, apparently of all wisdom, who appeared already to have lived a dozen lives now—amazingly—announced that he wished to place his person, his fortune, his future in my hands. Revealed himself as a lonely and very tired person who wanted to dig potatoes and raise pigs and never write another book. Wanted to start a new home. Wanted a child.

I said yes, of course. I accepted him as the wise man whom I had come across the world to find. I was ready, I felt stalwart and prepared for anything.

It did not appear to me as queer that an experienced, and highly-cultivated writer should desire to bury himself for ever in a country cottage with no one to talk to but a half-baked young colonial. I did not realise to what extent he would be putting his clock back, whilst I put mine forward. I still believed happiness to be a kind of present that one person could bestow upon another, and I thought it would be quite easy to bestow it upon Ford, and was passionately eager to try.

Ford, of course, knew a great deal more about human relationships than I, but though his mind was sceptical enough, the honest sentimentality of his heart had adopted the idea of love-in-a-cottage with complete sincerity. It was what he wanted, and when Ford wanted anything, he filled the sky with an immense ache that had the awful simplicity of a child's grief, and appeared to hold the same possibilities of assuagement. And in spite of discrepancies, or perhaps because of them, I think our union was an excellent bargain on both sides. Ford got his cottage, and he got the domestic peace he needed, and eventually he got his baby daughter. He was very happy, and so was I. What I got out of it, was a remarkable and liberal education, administered in ideal circumstances. I got an emotional education too, of course, but that was easier. One might get that from almost anyone! But to have the run of a mind of that calibre, with all its inconsistencies, its generosity, its blind spots, its spaciousness, and vision, and its great sense of form and style, was a privilege for which I am still trying to say "thank you."

CHAPTER THREE

Sussex

THE FIRST SPRING after the Armistice was like no other spring in our time. Nature's exuberance no longer seemed a mockery, and hundreds of thousands war-stiffened men and women began tremblingly to embark upon that new and longed-for life whose very naturalness made it seem unreal after the recent horrors.

Ford and I made our first home in a tumble-down cottage near the South Downs. We knew we were going to be very poor, because Ford had no money beyond what he earned and he had not written a novel since before the war. So when we heard of a farmer who had an empty cottage at five shillings a week, and found it to be very old, very charmingly situated, and named Red Ford, we took it immediately.

The fact that it had a big hole in the roof, and that water had to be carried in a pail from a "dip-hole" down the garden, did not disturb us unduly in the month of May. Nor did the long and muddy lane which was its only connection with the high road, nor the damp that soaked into the back wall and on to the wavy old brick floor. It *looked* all right, and that was the main thing. It looked like home.

It was built of old red brick and old red tiles, all greened over with mossy stains, and it was tucked under a little red sandstone cliff, and faced over a lush meadow which sloped downwards to a little stream, and upwards to a wood on the opposite side. The garden was bounded by a hedge thrown like a loop into the meadow, within which it stood, a proudly cultivated peninsula, above a sea of waving grass. In the hedge were some trees, big enough to support a hammock in which you might swing out over the field below.

Ford distempered the living-room and whitewashed the kitchen until the whitewash ran down into his armpit, and I painted all the doors and windows. We scraped together an assortment of second-hand junk as furniture, eked out by oddments given us by our friends. Ford bought a job-lot of old oak boards of which he was inordinately proud. "We'll have nothing but oak here," he said, and proceeded to build a cock-eyed lean-to outside the kitchen door to accommodate the oil stove on which we cooked, and which had a habit of belching smuts all over the tiny kitchen which was also the pantry and the scullery. When Ford's oak cook-house was finished, there was just one spot where you could stand upright as you tended your stew pots. When it rained, the floor became a puddle bridged by an oak plank. There was also a curtain of sacking hanging in the doorway, rather bothering to a person brushing through with both hands full of dishes.

In a slip of a room between the kitchen and the living-room, Ford used some more of his oak boards to construct a rough dining-table fastened for support to the side of the tiny staircase which led to the floor above. With two brass candlesticks and a pot of flowers, this table was also a great source of pride, and soon got so loaded with beeswax that its roughness became quite soft and gentle to the touch.

The rest of the oak boards were made laboriously into a sort of pigsty. The pig, however, died of a chill.

But if Ford was inexpert in the use of tools, he was extraordinarily skilful with his hands when it was a question of making things grow, or concocting some of his famous dishes. Then his movements were easy and sure, and everything he touched succeeded and came right. The garden, which had been neglected for years, soon began to blossom under his hands, and to supply our needs at table. And if the cook-house was a primitive hovel and the oil-stove a little horror, if the kitchen shelves were wobbly, the table a packing-case and the sink non-existent, it was nevertheless in these surroundings that I received my first—and how valuable!—instructions on the importance of food, for Ford was one of the great cooks. Of course he was utterly reckless with the butter and reduced the kitchen to the completest chaos. When he cooked, one kitchen-maid was hardly sufficient to wait upon him. But he did not mind how much trouble he took, and he never wasted scraps. Every shred of fat was rendered down, and every cabbage stalk went into the stock-pot which stood eternally on the living-room fire.

It was some time before I became skilful enough to deputise for him in the kitchen, but this became necessary when at last I persuaded him to start another book. Then he would retire upstairs to write, and leave me to wrestle with the dinner. At eight I would say, "are you ready to eat?" and he would reply, "in a minute." At eight-thirty I would say, "It is eight-thirty, darling," and he would reply, "Oh, give me another twenty minutes," and I would return to the kitchen and concoct something extra—another vegetable, or a savoury. At nine I'd say, "what about it?" and he'd tell me to put the meal on the table. At nine-thirty I would suggest putting it back on the fire, to re-heat. "What!" he'd cry, "dinner on the table all this time? Why ever didn't you tell me?" Well, we'd eat perhaps at ten, with enormous appetite, and discuss the progress of his book and of my cooking. We enjoyed ourselves.

But our visitors enjoyed it less, when they found the dinner-hour an ever-retreating mirage and their hunger an increasing passion. We tried to make it up to them by devising better and bigger meals, but even a greedy girl like Margaret Cole said she would have preferred a snack at seven-thirty to a banquet at—she alleged—eleven o'clock. There was no way, however, to alter the rhythm of Ford's habits, whatever form they took, and in all my life with him, I was never so foolish as to try. The habits varied at different times and in different places, but they always took precedence over everything else. At Red Ford we would spend the morning doing gardening and domestic chores; and after lunch we would go for such a big walk that tea was always late, and then Ford would go to his desk and I to the kitchen. We often had visitors for the week-end. Herbert Read and his wife came, and Francis Meynell, and Ray and Daisy Postgate, and Phyllis, of course, and Mary Butts, now married to the young poet, John Rodker. I suppose they thought it all incredibly primitive and I know that any self-respecting working woman would have refused to live in such a hovel. But I never saw it like that, and I'll swear that Ford never saw it like that either. His geese were always swans, and a tumble-down labourer's cottage, once he had made it his home and polished its woodwork and painted its walls, assumed in his eyes the dignity of a gentleman's country residence.

The simplicity of heart which made small things seem important, like the earliest salad, or the purchase of an old bit of brass or an effective arrangement of our meagre possessions, made Ford a delightful companion. He was never bored. It was not the first time that he had lived in a country cottage, and he liked instructing my ignorance in country lore. As for me, I was completely absorbed by it all. I have always liked doing things with my hands and up to a point, it was fun to overcome such setbacks as draughts, floods, smoke, and damp firewood. We were always expecting

our chickens to begin laying more eggs, our goat to give more
milk and our pig to put on more fat. It was important that
they should, for we were spending more money than we had
got, which was no way to prepare for the realization of our
dream, which was to buy a cottage of our own.

Then Ford had a windfall. He sold some film rights, and
the money he received, plus some capital I withdrew from
Australia, enabled us to buy "the" cottage, at Bedham.

Bedham was an extravagantly beautiful and quite in-
accessible spot on a great wooded hill about ten miles from
Red Ford. There was an immense view, and lovely paths
winding through beech woods all over the hillside. Our
cottage, white plaster and oak beams with a steep tiled roof,
was about three hundred years old and had settled well down
into its hillside. There was an orchard full of wild daffodils
running up to the hard road at the top of the hill, a small
wood full of bluebells lower down behind the cottage, and
below that, a big rough field. Ten acres in all, sloping
towards the view.

There is something inexpressibly touching and reassuring
about a very old cottage set in a gentle English landscape,
that has been inhabited for many generatons by ordinary
country folk. Something which seems to say; If you come
inside here, you can live your own true life in peace and
security and privacy. It will be safe to relax, safe to be honest,
and safe to bring your secret wishes into the light of day;
you will be protected from the world and if you are but
humble and modest enough, you will find sufficient delight
in the practical things which you must do in order to live
here, to fill your life. The cottage has seen many generations
out of their cradles and into their coffins and it will shelter
you as it has sheltered them.

But you must accept the life your cottage offers, just as

it is. You must not spend too much money on it, or you will chase away its healing, true-home spirit. And you must not try to be waited on to any great extent. The cottage does not like the idea of master and servant, nor the idea of money being locked up in its aged walls in the shape of gadgets, reinforcements and extensions.

I have seen cottages completely gutted, and their beautiful shells filled with brand new insides, where the original oak, salvaged at great expense reappears self-consciously between new plaster, above new floors, and beneath new ceilings. And the crimes that are committed upon fireplaces must be seen to be believed!

No. You must of course re-hang roofs when they leak badly and mend up holes when they appear, and do what is necessary against the damp and cold. And generally you crave for more light and may put another window in. But the minute you begin really pouring money into your cottage (and given a chance it will soak it up like a sponge), you take all the heart out of the place. Because what the cottage offers you is an escape from money and the monied life—that is its message and its value—and by making a capital investment of it, you destroy its *raison d'être*.

Across our common at Bedham there lived a Mr. Hunt and his lad who did all sorts of building and carpentering jobs. This was lucky for us, since they worked very simply, following the local fashion. They took away one of the inside partitions and removed the copper in the scullery, so as to give us a larger living-room. They also made a dormer window in the sloping roof upstairs, to lighten my dark bedroom. We took the old tiles off the pigsty for this, and also for a little porch to shelter the front door, and thatched the pigsty. But we made a mistake with the window, because Mr. Hunt was modern enough to use a plumb-line and a spirit-level, and made the window straight by the earth's centre instead of just using his eye and making it straight by the lines of the cottage. It was not that I had imagined the cottage to be on the level. I knew there was a slight list to starboard on my bedroom floor and that none of the perpendiculars were parallel. That was all right and the room looked perfectly at harmony with itself, until that wretched new window revealed the whole thing as practically a sinking ship, and you became absolutely sea-sick when you observed the angle at which the four-poster cut across the window-frame!

Well, it is quite easy to get used to living in a cock-eyed house and to manœuvring your furniture on the bumps and hollows of a brick floor. Ford always said that the Greeks built cock-eyed on purpose, because it was more alive, more interesting and restful to the eye, than mechanical precision. I believe he was right.

We moved over from Red Ford one summer day in 1920 and camped at Bedham whilst Mr. Hunt was still at work in the house. By this time we owned a high, ill-sprung dog-cart and a big, lively old mare whom I had learnt to drive. Ford went over early in the day with the farm wagon which was removing us, and I was left to load the dog-cart and drive over with the remainder of our goods and chattels. How I got them all aboard, and what kind of a spectacle I presented with pails, ladders, tools and bedding tied on all round, I do not know. I only know that since by now I was an expectant mother, this day impressed me as one of peculiar difficulty. Indeed, my dealings with the old mare became steadily more and more of a problem, because she was hard of hearing and hard of mouth and would have her own way, which was very terrifying on the bumpy roads around Bedham which switch-backed up and down, with a steep bank on one side and a sheer drop on the other. If the mare thought she would overtake another vehicle on a desperate corner, it was no use for the driver to have any ideas to the contrary. Similarly, she would stop at the foot of a hill, and refuse to budge until you had got out of the cart, to lead her up, when she would run you to the top at a spanking pace, and refuse to stop and let you get up again! On the other hand, if a rare motor car got into difficulties upon our steepest hill, the mare would put her best foot foremost and go sprinting up past it, as on the occasion when we had the pleasure of passing, without a flicker of recognition, a whole car-load of uninvited London busy-bodies coming to peep at Ford in his new retreat, gently rolling backwards down the hill!

One day in August when I was bringing home a load of timber and some sacks of meal, and expecting my baby in November, the mare so nearly pitched me out, bumping the wrong way down over the common, that I announced to Ford and to the old man who was then working in the garden for us, that I couldn't do any more errands on the roads. I thenceforth confined my activities to the house.

I stripped thirteen layers of paper off the living-room walls. Thirteen. And I took my little axe and chopped away all the worm-eaten bits from the old oak beams. I did not dig in the garden, but I did slip on the steep muddy orchard path and sprain an ankle badly enough to be kept relatively immobile during the last six weeks before the November event, which perhaps was just as well.

Ford's great idea of me was that I was immensely healthy and inexhaustibly energetic. I was healthy enough, but my energy never really came up to his ideal although I tried hard to make it. This, in spite of his theory—or one of his theories—that a man always liked his woman to be slightly ailing, so that she might be the more dependent upon his protection. Apparently this did not apply to me!

I have often had occasion to envy women with a fragile and helpless appearance, and the support that it invariably evokes! But never in all my life have I met anyone who has shown the slightest disposition to allow me to be helpless, though I can imagine no greater luxury. Perhaps I shall achieve it when I am really old.

Julie had a troublesome birth in a London nursing home on November 29th. There seems to be a conspiracy of silence about the horrors of childbearing and a pretty legend that the mother forgets all about it as soon as it is over. The hell she does! Nor does she forget the feeling of quivering helplessness both before and afterwards, and the indignity of having been reduced, even for a day, to the status of a squealing and abject animal.

I felt better about Nature's scheme after I had seen our goat give birth to twins on the lawn, without interrupting her dinner. I realised with relief that the rest of creation managed things a great deal better than we did!

Phyllis, now Mrs. Harry Birnstingl, and Margaret Cole were both expecting their first babies when I had mine, so I could not relieve my feelings by telling them what an awful experience it was, for fear of frightening them.

Julia was lovely. Even on the day she was born she was very pretty, and she soon became as smooth and pink-and-white and glowing as the heart of woman could desire. She developed a philosophical temper and an excellent digestion and she almost never cried. In my view she represented a definite improvement on Mop's and Phyllis's babies—girls also—who when they finally arrived were smaller and more fretful and ever so much uglier.

They are all three lovely girls now.

Mary Butts also had a baby almost on the same day as myself, and hers was simply colossal and very difficult to manage. Mary was quite unable to deal with her and left her to John to look after. John, being a Jew, had the paternal sentiment very well developed. Mary, on the other hand, was away in some sort of cloud-cuckoo land of her own and could not come to terms with anything so stupendously natural and immediate as a large and necessitous infant.

I came to terms with Julie pretty quickly, but not without difficulty, since I had never before had anything to do with an infant. I was terrified by her smallness and fragility, and when I had first to bath and handle her myself, I used to shake in every limb and perspire from every pore. Ford's mother was with me a good deal, but she was a very old lady and it was a long time since she had herself handled a new-born babe. I was gradually reassured, however, by Julie's natural equanimity, and soon learnt my job well enough.

Ford adored her. He simply doted. His large, slow person and quiet voice were just what young things liked, and his infant gave him a big new stake in the post-war world where he still felt pretty lost.

I don't think Julie was ever punished or ever scolded—certainly no one ever raised their voice at her—during the whole of her childhood. This might have spoilt her, except that she was naturally of a law-abiding disposition. Ford always called her "ma petite princesse," and spun the most enchanting fairy stories for her as soon as she grew old enough to enjoy them.

When we returned to Bedham with our brand-new off-spring at the New Year, we felt that life was really going to begin at last. The cottage and the child were both achieved, and both were lovely. The stage was set.

But we were hopelessly impoverished. Wages to Mr. Hunt and his lad, wages to old Standing who worked out-doors and to a young woman called Lucy who now worked in the house, the hundred and one purchases necessary for the equipment of a small holding, and finally the crashing expense of the nursing home, had more than emptied the exchequer. Ford imagined that the possession of ten acres was a guarantee of monetary profit and talked grandly and reassuringly about our becoming self-supporting. Of course we became nothing of the sort. The rough field was too rough to be cultivated, unless a large sum were spent on clearing it; Ford therefore decided to use it for breeding large black pigs on the open air system, and spent a good deal of money on two pedigree sows. Then the hedging and ditching of the field proved inadequate to restrain them, and money had to be spent on pig-proof fencing. Also, the mare cost as much to feed as a man, and we certainly never produced enough garden produce, eggs, firewood, etc., to justify old Standing's wages, and I soon began to suspect that our pig-breeding and vegetable gardening and chicken-rearing was uneconomical and amateurish. What we should have done, in the interests of solvency, would have been to cultivate only as much of the garden as we could manage without help, and cut down on the animals. Two litters of pigs, thirty hens, twenty ducks, three goats and the old mare, not to mention a cat and a dog, were more than we could have dealt with alone, and it was the necessity for outside help which destroyed the whole thing as a business proposition, and Ford was not the man to pay less than the highest current wages.

It could never have been a business proposition with Ford writing at his desk for several hours a day and myself heavily occupied with Julie. We had neither the time nor the farming experience to work our holding as it should have been worked, nor had we sufficient sense to limit our outdoor activities to the proportions of a manageable hobby. There was no good reason why a man of letters should also be expected to be a successful farmer, nor why, on the other hand, he should not bury himself frugally in the country if he wished, with a vegetable garden and a chicken-run to help out. But those pigs!

Their meals were cooked in an immense cauldron which hung, steaming perpetually, in a great hook above the living-room fire. This cauldron was very heavy to carry, very hot, and very black. The field where the pigs ran was very steep, and their sty some distance from it. They were always finding new gaps in the hedges and escaping on to the road and into the property of some irate neighbour. One morning one of them got out while I was pushing Julie in her pram along the road. This time it was dreadfully serious because there was a fine of £50 for allowing any animal on the road, on account of an epidemic of foot and mouth disease. And we had not got anything like £50. And Ford and Standing were too far off to be much use, so they shouted to me to go after the sow.

I expect it looked funny enough for a woman to be chasing a pig with a baby in a pram, but it did not seem funny to me. The sow was on the way to Fittleworth where the boar lived and that was three miles off. And since with the pram I could not get ahead of her to turn her back, I left Julie inside a cottage gate and seizing a big stick, managed by running along the embankment above the road to get in front of the amorous old beast and turn her round. I then collected the pram and by zig-zagging across the road, succeeded in driving the sow before me until we got home. All that Lucy said, when I collapsed scarlet and panting into a chair, was, "You done too much, mum," which rather deflated my pride in my achievement.

When a pig had to be killed, I took the pram further afield, out of earshot. Afterwards I made brawn from the head (you have to cut it up still hot in front of the fire, and mix it with all sorts of herbs and spices before packing it into the moulds), and sewed up the hams and sides in muslin, after they were salted, and hung them up to smoke in the great open chimney. Otherwise I had not much to do with the pigs. It was the goats that fell to my especial care.

We had an immense and turbulent billy-goat and a nanny called Penny, because of her resemblance to Ezra Pound, and two others. Penny would insist on sitting down on the pail whenever I tried to milk her, but the other two preferred to stand quiet until I had nearly finished and then plant a muddy, well-timed hoof into the milk. But these tricks were nothing to the fun they had when I came to change their pasture, twice a day. They were tied by long cords to the trees in the little wood, to eat the brambles, which they loved. (Ford said we kept the goats to destroy the brambles, rather than for their milk, although I weaned Julie on it), and when I came to untie them they would stand quietly until I had finished, and then plunge headlong down the hill, dragging me through the brambles till my poor arms were scored from wrist to elbow. They loved that. And I loved them! I even loved the pigs. I loved everything I did, inexpert and unaccustomed as I was at first, because it was all real, immediate and useful, and had to do with living things. And I loved being with someone with the same tastes and who lived through his eyes in the same way that I did. We took such perpetual and unanimous pleasure in the *look* of everything, the sky and the weather and the view and the garden and the arrangement of our cottage. "Come here a moment and

look at this." "Come see if those poppies are out since yester-
day." Come and look at the moon. . . . Come and look at
the sunset. . . . Come outside and see how the whitewash
glows in the dusk, and how lovely the room looks by fire-
light through the window.

You can almost live upon a view. Almost. Ford and I
subsequently lived in all sorts of places and with all sorts
of drawbacks, but they all had beauty of one sort or another.
It was more necessary to us than comfort and convenience,
and generally, as a commodity, cost less.

But if we managed to achieve beauty in our surroundings
at Bedham, and in our subsequent wanderings, there was
another commodity which was much less easily attained, the
provision of which, both there and afterwards, became one
of my chiefest difficulties. This was called "working conditions," and it meant seeing that Ford had somewhere to
write, and unmolested quiet whilst he was doing it. It meant,
of course, putting off meals until all hours, and acting as a
shock-absorber when problems and interruptions occurred
during working hours, and not only during working hours.
Ford would put it to me that he could not finish his book if
his mind was upset, and that I must manage to keep all worries
from him, which was difficult. It meant that I must not let
him know how overdrawn we were at the bank, nor how big
the bill from the corn mills had become, nor how badly we
needed a paraffin tank. His whole system rejected any knowledge of money matters, and if forced to contemplate them
at a bad moment, he would collapse into such a misery of
despair that our entire lives became paralysed. On the other
hand, the smallest unexpected cheque would inspire a mood
of ebullient optimism which led to an immediate orgy of
spending at the Petworth ironmongers, and a new bill to arrive
at the next awkward moment.

So I had to intercept bills and callers, and perform prodigies of domestic organisation to keep things quiet for him when we had people staying with us. In winter, when we were alone, he could write in peace in the landing-room upstairs, but this, the only spot in the cottage where his desk could stand, was also a thoroughfare to the little spare room and became untenable in summer, when we were never long without guests. So we built him a hut at the top of the orchard with the remainder of the famous oak boards which we had brought over from Red Ford. Of course, this hut received rain through the roof and wind through the sides, and I think Ford was very uncomfortable there, but at least his isolation was perfect.

I always resented his not having a proper study more than any of our other hardships. It was much more serious than the kitchen having a wet floor and the privvy being out of doors.

Poor Ford. If ever a man needed a fairy godmother, he did. A human spouse was quite insufficient, especially one who was less stalwart than she might have been, and whose monetary assets were of the slenderest. Ford was completely unmercenary, and also completely unable to plan or manage what money he had. I still thought of him almost as God the Father and it took me a long time—until it was too late in fact—to realise that the only sensible thing for me to have done would have been to assume entire control of all the spending, to turn a deaf ear to any alluring suggestions of pleasurable extravagance. But that would have required more strength of character than I possessed, and it would have humiliated Ford. He was all too ready, anyhow, to feel discouraged when things went wrong, and he found so many reasons for feeling frightened. If there was one thing for which I could ever reproach him, it would be for teaching me to dread fears and humiliations of which I had no previous knowledge.

Poor Ford! There was something about the sight of his large patient fingers tapping at the keys, that I always found infinitely touching. He was a writer—a complete writer— and nothing but a writer. And he never even felt sure of his gift!

He needed more reassurance than anyone I have ever met. That was one reason why it was so necessary for him to surround himself with disciples. He gave them much of himself; patient perusal and brilliant criticism of their efforts, and even when their work was mediocre, he always managed to put heart into them and make them proud of their calling and determined to screw the last ounce out of their talent. He had no professional secrets and would take any aspiring writer behind the scenes and explain exactly how he got his effects; the long, slow-moving passage heightening the effect of the subsequent quick crisis; the need for minute precision in a visual description; the different tension to be used in the short, long-short, or long story, the opening sentence which set the key for the whole work. In exchange for the help that he gave Ford received something very valuable—something that was good for him and without which he could scarcely live. He received the assurance that he was a great master of his art.

At Bedham, young writers began to turn up for weekends and I soon learnt how to promote the kind of talk they wanted. Who was it who said that conversation is the best indoor sport? It is certainly the best sport for Sussex winter evenings, those barbarous stretches of blackness which begin at four o'clock, with the weather raging outdoors and seeking every crack and cranny in the old house. It is then that the big log fire, the soft lamplight, and the fragrant, simmering stew-pot have an allurement that no amount of central heat, electric light, and well-served dinners in London can touch, and they exercise an irresistible invitation to the opening of conversational bosoms. The people round the fire have come from a long way off, and being isolated in space together, they soon begin to feel the urge to tell all! If there is some beer as well, that helps. . . .

Unfortunately, our decadent and benighted London friends much preferred to visit us in the summer! This was to their disadvantage, since in summertime there is something that needs doing out-of-doors every minute of the long daylight, and we had much less time to spare for our guests. I remember Ford setting Professor Laurence Marsden Price, an admirer from the University of Berkeley, California, to haymaking on a very hot July afternoon, which astonished as much as it amused the professor, and revealed to me for the first time that Americans don't wear braces! I remember, too, sending Margaret up a tree to pick greengages; and another American, who considered 8 a.m. to be practically the middle of the night, but swore he could knock together a log cabin in no time, being put to hew down some saplings, until old Standing in pity took his axe away, for fear lest he should cut off his toes.

Still, even in summer-time there were long talks about style, technique, and the tricks of the trade. There would be supper, late as usual, under the apple trees, Chinese lanthorns in the branches, a moon, a sweet-smelling tobacco plant, and nightingales. And all of us very late to bed.

More Americans came. Monroe Wheeler, and with him Glenway Westcott, very young, and solemn, and eager, in a long cape with a silver clasp, an exotic figure in our homely landscape. Ezra Pound came once, just before he and Dorothy migrated to Paris, and from London there used also to come two young men called Anthony Bertram and Dyneley Hussey, who were always welcome because they thought our view and our cottage quite as beautiful as we did. Alec Waugh and David Garnett and Edgar Jepson and the Clough Williams Ellis's and Edward Shanks also came, not to mention Margaret and Phyllis with their babies. Margaret's pram ran downhill by itself, and baby Jane was found pitched on top of the hedge below. Margaret was dreadfully shaken; Jane, not at all. Julie, now toddling, found a box of aspirin and crammed her mouth full. I was frantic; Julie, quite unaffected. Phyllis's Cordelia refused to put on weight until Phyllis was worn to a shadow, when she began to thrive. None of them were delicate at all, but we, their mothers, regarded them as the most fragile objects in creation, and their safeguarding through the dangers of babyhood, as a perilous kind of egg-and-spoon race.

After four summers and three winters in Sussex, we were forced to certain conclusions upon the subject of the English climate. In summer the life was ideal. But our steady stream of visitors made a great deal of extra work and was apt to destroy all our privacy and interfere with Ford's writing. My painting had of course, been hopelessly interfered with by the whole shape of my life, for I was learning the technique of quite a different rôle; that of consort to another and more important artist. So that although Ford was always urging me to paint, I simply had not got any creative vitality to spare after I had played my part towards him and Julie, and struggled through the day's chores. It is true that I painted a few little portraits, and did some illustrations for Ford, but they represented nothing but a hobby—an effort not to let go altogether.

Ford never understood why I found it so difficult to paint whilst I was with him. He thought I lacked the will to do it at all costs. That was true, but he did not realise that if I *had* had the will to do it at all costs, my life would have been oriented quite differently. I should not have been available to nurse him through the daily strain of his own work; to walk and talk with him whenever he wanted, and to stand between him and circumstances. Pursuing an art is not just a matter of finding the time—it is a matter of having a free spirit to bring to it. Later on, when I had more actual free time, I was still very much enslaved by the terms of my relationship with Ford, for he was a great user-up of other people's nervous energy. He had built his relationship with me on the lines he wanted and nothing is more nearly impossbile than to change one kind of relationship into another, by conscious effort. I was in love, happy, and absorbed. But there was no room for me to nurse an independent ego.

Any artist knows, that after a good bout of work one is both too tired and too excited to be of any use to anyone. To be obliged to tackle other people's problems, or merely to cook their meals, the moment one lays down pen or brush, is intolerably hard. What one wants, on the contrary, is for other people to occupy themselves with one's own moods and requirements; to lie on a sofa and listen to music, and have things brought to one on a tray! That is why a man writer or painter always manages to get some woman to look after him and make his life easy, and since female devotion, in England anyhow, is a glut on the market, this is not difficult. A professional woman, however, seldom gets this cushioning unless she can pay money for it.

But to return to the important subject of the English climate. In summer, as I have said, we had more visitors than we could manage, and in winter, we had almost none. The Londoner's horror of the country in winter meant isola-

tion for us during the long evenings and the days when our
out-door duties were a grim trial. It was the rain we minded
most. There was mud all around the back door, and the
path down the orchard from the road was a long, perilous
slide. The pipe which brought our water from the spring
would freeze and burst, the kitchen was damp and draughty
and it was always cold upstairs. We had no telephone, and
(in 1922) no wireless. We were too poor for a library sub-
scription and we never saw a cinema. Petworth was five
miles away and the only means of transport was the high,
open dog-cart. These thing did not matter particularly, but
the rain did. Day after day without any let-up at all. And
the darkness mattered, too. And the mud.

So that when Harold Monro came down for a week-end
and told us about the little villa he had bought on top of a
rock at Cap Ferrat, and described the sun and the view and all
the charm of the Mediterranean in winter, Ford was at once
filled with an immense nostalgia for his beloved Provence,
and I with a sharp longing to escape there also, away from the
cheerless murk of a fourth Sussex winter. Harold Monro
insisted that his villa was only a peasant's cottage, very in-
accessible, tiny, and with no conveniences, but he said that it
was probably going to be empty, and if so, we could have it
very cheap.

A few weeks later, the whole matter was arranged and we
laid our plans to winter abroad.

How dazzled I was by that phrase! But the difficulties
in the way before we could disentangle ourselves from Bedham
were formidable. Ford was just finishing the *Marsden Case*
and unless it was quickly sold, we should hardly be able to
raise the money for the fares. Julie was now just two, charmingly pretty, gay, affectionate, and quite managable, but we
wanted to take our little maid, Lucy, with us to look after

her, so that I might have some freedom to go about with
Ford. This was a very ambitious scheme, but the alternative
of being a day-and-night nursemaid on my first visit to
France was rather dismal.

We had to sell the animals. The market was glutted with
pedigree pigs, and ours had to go at bacon prices. They had
been an expensive enterprise. The old mare was turned out
to grass, and I forget what happened to the goats. Indoors
the cottage had to be left ready for a possible tenant, and all
our personal belongings packed away. We were planning to
come back in March or April.

Our clothes were the biggest problem. We simply had
nothing fit to be seen, and no money to re-stock our ward-
robes; yet we were planning to stay a month in Paris before
going south. For weeks I re-made, cleaned, and altered our
old things as best I could. I washed Ford's dress-trousers,
and put a gusset in the back; fortunately he looked impressive in anything. But having scarcely seen a well-dressed
woman nor a fashion magazine for three years, my own
appearance must have been pretty dismal. I think that Julie
was the only member of the party to do us any credit sar-
torially.

Ford's manuscript had gone to Duckworth, and in our
usual foolhardy fashion, we went right ahead with our plans,
trusting that the Lord would provide. The luggage was
packed, the passports obtained, and we were actually piling
into the dog-cart to drive to Fittleworth station, when the
postman delivered the manuscript—returned! This caught us
hard in the pit of the stomach. As we stood on the windy
station platform, Lucy and Julie and Ford and I, feeling that
it was the height of folly to have burned our boats and to
be leaving our blessed home, I managed secretly to undo a
corner of the parcel, in case there was a letter inside, for

Ford hated opening anything disagreable. The letter said that Duckworth would like to publish the book if Ford would make certain minor alterations, for which purpose he was returning the manuscript!

So we had a happy journey after all.

CHAPTER FOUR

The South of France

IF I HAD KNOWN, on that cross-channel steamer, that we should never go back to Bedham, it would utterly have broken my heart. For Bedham was still strongly with us; we were packed in its atmosphere and arrived in Paris like sleep-walkers from another world.

Ford and I were both slow people, and our natural slowness had been encouraged by our bucolic existence. Our nerves had been protected by the space and solitude of Sussex from the jostling noises of city life, and this physical calm had become to us almost a necessity. We were tired, jumpy and overworked, and I can remember both of us almost sobbing under the nervous strain of being buffeted along the narrow pavements of the clattering and screaming streets of the Left Bank. Just the noise—nothing else.

I love and adore Paris. I love the way its quick and brilliant life runs openly on the surface for all to see. Every face in the street, every voice, every shape, is hard at it, telling its story, living its life, producing itself. In London the faces in the street have the air of having been locked up before being brought outside, as though a flicker of life would give away a secret to the enemy.

Paris is good for me, because I'm a sluggard and can do with a great deal of stimulus. But it takes a long time to get keyed up to the necessary pitch of vitality. A month, especially if one doesn't speak much French, is nothing like enough, and

the four weeks we spent at the Hôtel Meublé in the Rue Vavin
before going to the Riviera, did little to prepare me for the
Paris life I was to know and love when finally we made our
home there.

Two or three pictures remain. First, the courtyard of
70 bis Rue Notre Dame des Champs, where Ezra and Dorothy
Pound had their studio. It was one of those quiet and secret
corners tucked away behind the street façade, whose narrow
entrance you might pass in ignorance a thousand times. It
was adorable, with tall, damp, black-boughed trees, a moulder-
ing plaster statue, a grubby goldfish pond, and not so much
as a dab of paint or a visible sign of repair upon any of the
ancient studios surrounding it.

I think that any foreigner who has lived in Montparnasse
leaves a little piece of his heart behind him, buried in a
courtyard such as this. His mind cherishes a vision of
summer greenery drooping down across the windows, dusty
ivy on a tattered trellis, some ornamental shrubs, a stone
bench, a few bulbs and the dark-stained façade of a shabby
pavillon. He will remember a stucco wall with rows of pale
grey shutters, some shut, some open, and some at half-cock,
with a peeping concierge within and a row of stockings
drying on a string. A picture to make him very homesick
for the most hospitable quarter of the most hospitable city
in the world.

The French are supposed to be less hospitably inclined
and less generous than Anglo-Saxons. They are certainly
harder-headed and closer-fisted. But in Paris you will never
feel shut out, starved for human contacts, and denied your
bit of life, as you easily may in London. In London you *must*
have friends, or it can be one of the cruellest cities in the
world, but Paris is the Heaven of all shy and lonely people
who want life to come to them of its own accord. I suppose

it is because the French are never ashamed to live. Being
realists, they accept their place in creation as ordinary speci-
mens of *homo sapiens*, dependent for survival upon their own
exertions. But they are determined to get their bit of fun and
bit of decoration on the way, so they bring their life out
with them into the boulevards and cafés, and it gets into the
air, and is soaked up into the houses, and into the soil of the
Luxembourg gardens. And if you go and walk under the
trees there when you are in a state of emotional ânguish,
let us say, and imagining in your Anglo-Saxon fashion that
your trouble is unique and insoluble, you will soon become
aware that these gardens have had a very large experience
of just your kind of malady, and that an understanding of
it is hanging all around you in the air. No problem is
too complicated for this long-established firm to deal
with Madame, and though quite indifferent to you personally, it does better than to offer you comfort; it offers comprehension, and the knowledge that although there is
generally no solution to the insoluble problem, it will have
ceased to exist by the time you have finished living through
it.

Imagine feeling like that in Kensington Gardens, the home
of the Boy who Wouldn't Grow Up!

I'm glad that Julie was reared in the Luxembourg.

Another of my early pictures of Paris was provided by
Marcel Proust's funeral. Ford decided that he ought to attend
it as a representative of English letters, and he sought to
illustrate to me the high esteem in which the arts were held
in France, not only by officials, but also by the man in the street
Calling the waiter of the café where we sat, he asked him
when and where Proust's funeral service would be held. The
waiter told him immediately, "And imagine," said Ford,
"if I asked an English waiter about the funeral of, say, Thomas

Hardy, I should discover that he had never heard of the fellow."

So we went to the church at the appointed hour, and it was lovely. Whole groves of candles, the church draped from top to bottom in black and silver, masses of flowers, rows upon rows of black-veiled widows, and Bach upon the organ. Beautiful singing and perfect stage-management. I had not yet read any Proust, but it was not necessary to know whose remains were underneath that amazing catafalque to feel the emotional importance of the occasion. The Catholic church certainly understands that side of its business.

After the ceremony, the audience began to file slowly forward towards a long row of mourners and Ford said, "now we have to kiss the next of kin." As this was indeed what appeared to be happening, I abandoned Ford and fled in a panic down the aisle, pursued by a Beadle who could not overtake me before I had made good my escape into a strange back street, where for a long time I was quite lost.

I had occasion to attend another French funeral when my aged landlord died some seven years later. I then occupied a studio in the Rue Notre Dame des Champs which belonged to the Académie Delecluse, and when M. Delecluse père expired, I was very anxious to do the correct thing—the more so since I wished to establish good relations with the new landlord, M. Delecluse fils, and remain in undisturbed possession of my studio. So I dressed all in black and hurried to the Eglise Notre Dame des Champs for the ten o'clock service.

There were no black drapes, no great catafalque, no flowers. Only a poor little pine coffin in a side chapel, with one row of candles and less than twenty mourners. "Is *this* the way the French reward a life-time devoted to the arts, after all," I said to myself, and I was all the more glad that I had come to swell the meagre numbers. When the service was over,

the mourners circled round the bier and each one sprinkled
holy water on the coffin before embracing the next of kin.
I managed the first part all right, but decided that a firm
handclasp, a deep bow, and "Mes condoléances, Madame,"
were sufficient for the widow. The tears were pouring down
her poor little face, but she seemed awfully glad to see me. . . .

A few minutes later, as I passed the Gare Montparnasse,
I noticed that the time was still only ten minutes to ten.
I then realised that I had not been to Delecluse's funeral at
all and headed back to the church. There I found that already
the big black draperies had been hoisted up, the great catafalque
with serried rows of candles placed before the High Altar, and
the organist was filling the church with lovely sounds. And
down the Boulevard Montparnasse I could see approaching
the nodding plumes and the mediæval trappings of a proper
well-to-do funeral which presently produced a mahogany and
silver coffin and whole masses of flowers. Greatly relieved,
I took a seat behind the female mourners, and this time everything went well. I knew how to manage the holy water, and
although there was an immense row of next of kin to negotiate,
I found that a bow and a handshake to the principal male
mourner, followed by a long scooping bend forward performed
during a crab-like walk past the lesser males and a repetition
of the whole business with the female mourners, was sufficient
to meet the case.

But to return to our first days in Paris, when I was still
an alien from the wilds of Sussex.

I can remember a crowd of people who had been invited
to meet us at the Pounds' studio, and the American wife of a
French man of letters who said: "Now do tell me, Mrs.
Ford, about all that is happening in the literary world in
England," and how I had to answer that it was no use asking
me such things because, being a rustic, I wouldn't know. I

had hitherto got through life quite well on a frankly low-brow basis, but on this occasion I got a good scolding from Ford. He said it was no use imagining that in Paris I should be able to get away with that kind of ignorance. It wouldn't be tolerated, and besides, it let him down. I must remember that we were no longer in England where the arts were always in disgrace, but in France where it was not considered funny to be an ignoramus about such matters. Quite the contrary.

We took the night train down south just before Christmas. In the winter of 1922-23 the rush to the Riviera was so great that for the privilege of sitting up all night in a second class carriage, we had to book seats a fortnight in advance.

I have made that journey many times since, but the thrill of finding oneself already in the landscape of Provence when dawn breaks gets sharper every time. At eight o'clock you are at Avignon, but ever since the first streak of light you have been beside the urgent, muddy Rhône and amongst the pale olives the dark cypresses, the grey rocks and the flat-roofed, flat-faced houses which in spite of their poverty and austerity seem to hold promise of a sweeter life within their dry old walls.

Dry, that is a great point! The sunshine meets no fog or mist as it pours downwards in that great radiant floodlight, which hits the ground and reflects upwards, to fill the shadows with a bubble-like iridescence, and turn Julie into a picture by Renoir. The pale houses, colour-washed in transparent water-paint, have an unsubstantial look to northern eyes as being a little out of date. They have an airy nonchalance about them as though not quite anchored to the ground.

I wish I could describe how magical Harold Monro's quite

ordinary little villa seemed to us when we got there. You climbed to it by a rough mule-track, or alternatively by long flights of stone steps of a giddy and exhausting steepness. All our luggage and all our provisions had to be carried up by hand; no wheeled vehicle could reach the place. But this steepness and slowness mattered nothing in comparison with the fact that the path was dry. It had been dry since the dawn of history! And the garden terraces which overhung Ville-franche harbour appeared to have been levelled and stoned up also since the same epoch. I thought pityingly of our efforts to level the orchard in front of the cottage at Bedham, and I thought of the rain and the mud and the darkness of Sussex and decided that climate is one of the few things in life that really matter. Other things, friends, fame, or fortune, may elude or disappoint you, but a good climate never lets you down. And really life is too short to be struggling perpetually with the weather when one is already struggling with so many other things!

The villa had three microscopic rooms in front and two behind. The only provision for cooking was the usual peasants' charcoal contraption, but since there was electric light and the water was laid on, my cup of bliss was quite sufficiently full. The front windows opened wide on to a great luminous sky with a Saracen fortress on the skyline opposite, and the transluscent blue-green waters of Villefranche harbour below. Down through the filmy tops of our own olive trees we could see a British man-of-war, floating like a child's toy above the sunny depths, and to our right the little dome of coloured tiles on the church belfry poked itself up amid the flat, huddled roofs of the harbour.

Behind the villa, the ground sloped more gently down-wards in the opposite direction. Here you looked over Beaulien towards Monte Carlo and Italy, a spectacular bit of coastline whose natural beauty somehow survives all the vulgarity with which it is bestrewn. I think that the small, haphazard, shabby aspect of the greater part of the Riviera—the casinos and the jardins publics and the grand hotels after all occupy only a small proportion of it—does much to save it from vulgarity. Most of the coast is perfectly unpretentious. The tourist industry is of course heavily catered for, but it is not the tourist industry which keeps the old town at Nice, seething with its multitudinous affairs. Even Monte Carlo is a cosy, unalarming little spot. I have stayed there in a shabby *maison meublé* and eaten in an Italian *bistro* along with Diaghileff's ballet dancers and felt beautifully superior to the rather childish splendours of the casino and the Hotel de Paris. I suppose it is this element of childishness that makes the Riviera, even at its richest and most ostentatious, so little oppressive to the humble wanderer. There is none of the solemn, overbearing offensiveness of Belgrave Square or Carlton House Terrace.

Soon after we arrived at Cap Ferrat we took Julie to Monaco to see the aquarium. We climbed up to that famous *place* in front of the dear little palace with the umbrella pines and the silly cannon-balls piled beside the ancient cannons that point east and west over the Mediterranean, and found it ornamented with a wonderful great canopy of fringed crimson velvet, supported on golden pillars bearing ornamental shields and garlands and streamers, and underneath, a richly draped daïs for the Prince who had returned to his loving subjects that morning from abroad. A pantomime designer couldn't have done it better, and it seemed to me that here was Sovreignty at its prettiest and most harmless. There were several beautiful soldiers standing at attention, each adorned with such a galaxy of medals, tassels, épaulettes, galons, bandaliers, scarlet and white cocks feathers and patent leather jack boots, that one trembled lest a breath should disturb their perfection. Julie, aged two, trotted slowly round and round the nearest with big eyes, murmuring, "Ooh! the loverly soldier," until the unfortunate hero could no longer repress a smile, which scared her away.

I used to take the tram to Nice with two enormous marketing baskets. Those baskets, when full, had to be carried back up the mule-track, but meantime I enjoyed a giddy hour in the maelstrom of the Nice marché. I never learnt to market well, for although I was soon able to reckon in sous, I was never any good at bargaining. But I improved my French and learnt my way about.

To my mind the best market on the whole coast is one which I came to know later at Toulon, in the Cours Lafayette. The booths come curving out of a shady street into a sunny boulevard which shows the waters of the harbour at one end and high mountains at the other. Immense symmetrical plane trees slant slightly forwards down each side of the old street, their trunks bisected by the tilted white canvas canopies of the stalls. Here, if you can make yourself heard above the clamour, you may buy garments or bandanna handkerchiefs or china, as well as all the fruits of the earth and sea. What flowers! What oranges, lemons, and tangerines! And what vegetables! Fennel, and pimentos, and courgettes and herbs and *salade de mache* and aubergines. And in the fish market, sea-urchins and octopus and langoustines and mussels, as well as all the serious fishes, and everything you could want for a bouillabaisse, even to the *rascasse*. A shop nearby sells nothing but olive oils, which you will taste from a row of taps, on a piece of bread, whilst next door is a noble selection of sausages and cheeses and a choice of olives. Daily life has richness and savour here, where a passionate interest attaches to the buying of even the humblest portion of food.　Lucky housewives, turning their leisurely steps into the crowded, sunny hubbub to choose, weigh, compare and haggle over the piled merchandise surrounding them ; little do they know that in other countries their sisters are huddled into mackintoshes and scuttling from the grocer to the butcher, who will serve them dourly with a fixed portion at a fixed price—a transaction calling for no skill and little judgment?

We had not been long at St. Jean Cap Ferrat before I had a letter from Dorothy Pound in Florence.　She said that she and Ezra thought it was about time that I. saw some real pictures, and invited me to join her on a tour of Assisi, Perugia, Cortona, Arezzo and Siena whilst Ezra went on to Rimmini— or it might have been Ravenna—to acquire a further store of that erudition which he was in the habit of extracting from old documents.　I was to join them first in Florence.

This tour was a very big event in my artistic life.　It was the first time that I had left Julie and Ford, but although I missed them horribly (and one can cram a good deal of missing into a fortnight!) this taste of freedom would alone have been sufficient to reawaken all my old excitement about painting.　Even the pictures I saw from the windows of the train were thrilling; and after struggling nervously through the hell that is Ventimiglia and being unexpectedly turned out of the train at 2 a.m. at Genoa and deposited at Florence twelve hours behind Cook's estimated time, I arrived with an already formed enthusiasm for the Italian landscape.　It had turned out to be quite unlike what I had imagined.　I had expected something soft and romantic, and behold! I had seen a hard country where everything had a lovely edge to it, and fell into marvellous formal patterns.　Trees in serried rows and rocks in sequence and rivers in the exact position

required to compose the picture. Old towns crowning symmetrical hills, with ramparts like a collar round the neck;
bridges and towers and churches, their yellow-grey stone
almost indistinguishable from the rocks upon which they
stood, until a second glance revealed their keen, austere, and
unblurred edges.

The pictures I had hitherto seen of Italy had vulgarised
the whole thing hopelessly, prettifying the colour and softening the shapes and missing the style and the symmetry. I
do not think that Italy is a subject for any sort of impressionist painting. The light is often lovely, but the important
thing is not the light, but what it falls on, which is always
something that cries out to be rendered with the greatest
precision. That is one reason why the primitive Italians are
such a joy. The Italy they painted was the real thing.

I had expected to be worried by the crudities of the early
painters and to find difficulty in understanding them, and
I knew that Ezra would not let me admire anything later than
1500. Actually, it was precisely the formal patterns of the
earlier painting which enchanted me as I had never before
been enchanted. It was like the first time I heard Bach—long
ago in Adelaide—and although I have come better to understand certain other forms of art since then, there has been
nothing to compare with these early loves for pure spontaneous
pleasure—nothing which so quickly rang my bell.

In 1923 I had the bad taste privately to prefer the crowded,
decorative murals of the lower church at Assisi to Giotto's
simplicities, but now it is the Giottos that I remember best.
And I remember the Piero della Francescas at Arezzo and the
Fra Angelicos at Cortona and Simone Martini at Siena and
Boteicelli when we got back to Florence. But what most
contributed to the impression of complete beauty that I got
on this journey was the harmony between the churches that

contained the pictures and the landscapes that contained the
churches. There is a very strong case to be made out for not
removing pictures from the country in which they were
painted. Fortunately when they are done in fresco, they
have to stay put.

Fresco itself seemed to me the most wonderful medium.
The texture was lovely and the narrow tone-scale which it
imposed eliminated those heavy effects of light and shade
which I knew were not what I was looking for. The pictures
of the fifteenth and sixteenth centuries—all high-lights and
anguish—were inexpressibly shocking after the formal and
pellucid serenity of those candid early masters. I did not get
on very well even with Titian, and Raphael was definitely a
back-slider.

When we got back to Florence I was able to compare the
fifteenth century Flemish oil paintings on panel with the
Italian, and for years afterwards I could not feel any virtue
in a picture done in thick, opaque paint, or with undefined
edges. Bonnard, for instance, I simply could not "see." It
shocks me now to remember how narrow was my view at
that time. But a narrow view, for a painter, has its advan-
tages. It concentrates his effort and his enthusiasm. A critic
or a teacher is obliged to understand the whole field and
expound it without prejudice, but I myself have never had
any highbrow understanding of art and am nonplussed before
the canvasses of certain modern painters through not being
able to understand what they are getting at. I can recognise
the hand of the master—the certainty, and the quality of the
paint. But I just don't see *why*, and this is to my very great
loss. But I would rather be that way than like the chap in a
drawing in the *New Yorker* who, "knows all about art but
doesn't know what he likes!"

Those early Italians who painted in a recognised convention were lucky fellows. The convention was such a good one, and while it lasted, was perpetually enriched by the genius of the great ones who did just a little bit better than anyone else, while even the smaller painters produced honourable work, since they started with their feet on a solid deposit of other people's experiments. *Any* convention or ritual has the advantage of being able to produce results beyond the scope of one man starting from scratch; it is as though the starter gets given a lift by train over the first part of his journey and is thus able to penetrate further than if he had had to walk all the way. Nowadays, every painter makes his own little law and starts out independently on foot—with the result that he seldom gets further afield than the suburbs! As Tchelichew once said to me: "Ce n'est plus nécessaire d'entrer par la porte de l'église. Tout le monde passe maintinant par la grand' route." And the confusion that this state of affairs exercises on the publc mind is such as to deprive art of any sort of popular support.

We live in a world where most of man's work is ugly and where ugliness quite obviously does not hurt most men. To be a person who suffers from this and who cannot settle down in surroundings which have no grace or charm and who needs a daily dose of beauty as a sick man needs his medicine, is simply to be at a great disadvantage in the modern world. It is to be in an uncomprehended minority, which makes for snobbery and preciousness and all sorts of vices. It means voting for and paying taxes to a system which will certainly never give you the things which seem to you to be the breath of life. It makes your citizenship worth less to you than it should be worth.

I do not understand how most people get along without the pleasures that the decorative arts can give. But then, I don't understand the attraction of football either, which claims far more devotees than all the arts put together. Popular taste is not bad taste—it is just negative. When my charwoman genuinely admires a Woolworth calendar she is admiring the sort of thing she saw in childhood and is sufficiently accustomed to for her to accept the convention it presents. That it is vulgar and banal is just too bad—the important thing is that she is registering pleasure in something visual, and if she had been seeing good designs all her life instead of bad ones she would register a higher pleasure. It is nonsense to talk about giving the public what it wants. The public will like what it gets, if it gets enough of it. But it won't discriminate. Not yet anyhow. It will discriminate much better where sport or even the cinema is concerned, because big money has been spent by producers and promoters in attracting the public to these shows and in educating its taste. Big money is not spent in this way on the decorative arts. If it were, we should get results. In Russia, for instance, they have apparently succeeded in creating a vast and enthusiastic audience for all the fine arts, the trouble is that they haven't yet been able to produce the artists!

When I returned to Cap Ferrat, full of ideas about formal composition and thin paint, I proceeded to wrestle with three or four small portraits on wood, done in great detail. These were subsequently shown at the Salon d'Automne and were described as "aimables petits portraits, fidèles et serrés." I don't think they were much good, but they marked the beginning of a long phase when I deliberately flattened out shadows and concentrated everything on linear design. I never began to paint until I had got a composition which I thought would stand up as a line drawing, and once started, I never altered anything.

It must have been five years before I got bitten by Greco and began to try and paint recession and space and a third dimension into my designs—and what a complication *that* made! I am still struggling with it.

We stayed at Cap Ferrat until Easter. Spring on the Riviera is spring *plus*, and we were quite unwilling to tear ourselves away. Besides, we had begun to see a few French people who treated Ford with great respect. I remember his receiving a note which began, "Cher et illustre Maître," which filled his heart with simple pleasure.

We had decided to stay in the south throughout the summer, but finally Ford said that he wanted to get away from the Riviera, and to show me the real Provence of the Rhône valley. He thought that Tarascon would be just about the right size and just about sufficiently free from tourists to make a good base, so we put up at a small hotel there where we were nicely treated, along with the commercial travellers who frequented the table d'hôte, and Julie learnt to sit up and eat properly in public. Lucy ate with us and was called "Mees." What she made of it all I don't know. She never learnt a word of French.

I acquired a passion for garlic sausage and black olives and cheap red wine, got used to lunching at twelve ("on peut vous faire déjeuner à onze heures et demie, si midi fait trop tard") and to being given the strangest comestibles—a flabby tepid omelette, for instance—to take with us on those good picnics when Ford and I were exploring his most beloved spots on earth.

Provence in spring must be seen to be believed. The soil is so fertile and so closely cultivated that the neat rows of green *primeurs* are flourishing in the warm earth before you have begun to expect their first shoots. The landscape is full of little, separate accents, white blossom, lettuce-coloured foliage, and rows of dark cypress, planted against the Mistral.

Grey olive trees with their black trunks rooted in the red earth; dark tufts of herbs amid the pale rocks, and more and more brilliant sprays of the new spring green. There is a little fruit tree with pink blossom which has its elegant trunk and slender twigs sprayed with a turquoise-coloured fluid against the blight. This little tree appears all over the south and is far too pretty to be taken seriously. I suppose it subsequently bears fruit, though its existence has already been fully justified without further effort.

In case the riches of nature should be insufficient for your delight, this landscape is also thickly studded with old, carved stones, old castles, arenas, cloisters and triumphal arches, some of which are tucked away nonchalantly in the little towns, some just planted in the sward beside the olive-fields, and others crown the rocky height above some huddled village.

It would seem that nothing has changed very much with the centuries. The lovely Romanesque churches are still in daily use, and you will find more peasants than tourists in their echoing, musty aisles. The lit candles, the votive offerings and the fresh flowers do more to render homage to the old stone carvings than all the tourists in the world ; just as the bull-fight and football fans who fill the Roman arenas at Nîmes and at Arles do more to reanimate them than any number of archæologists with their measuring tapes. Provence is neither sweet nor pretty. It does not greatly resemble the popular paintings that hang in the Salon or that English lady artists bring home. But the life that is lived there is quite alarmingly natural. Just as there are certain easy-going women with a genius for creating the atmosphere most favourable to the flowering of human life—an atmosphere where people feel safe, and inspired, and freed from self-consciousness, so in Provence life seems to run more freely in its channels than

elsewhere. The French are commonly supposed always to be
full of phobias and dark passions, generally connected with
money, but these they rather enjoy, and anyway they never
attain the grim intensity in the south that they do in the
north. There is gaiety and leisure wherever you go, and
always someone in the café, with whom to pass the time of
day.

We used to pass it in the café at Tarascon with the local
avoué and avocat. The avocat was a typical southerner with
a swarthy, spherical head and a big tummy. He lived with
his wife—who sighed perpetually for the elegancies of Cannes
where she was in the habit of visiting her sister—in a prison-
like house full of valuable provençal furniture, polished up to
the nines, with scrolly steel hinges shining in the dark corners.
He and Ford would discuss at length the proper use of the sub-
junctive, in elaborate French prose. Ford really knew French
perfectly but he spoke it badly because he never moved his
lips enough. I did not know it at all, but I picked up a certain
amount of colloquial slang from having to deal with shops,
hotels, and railways for the family, and eventually my highly
incorrect but fairly fluent French got more quickly understood than Ford's literary murmurings. At Tarascon, however, I had not begun to get my tongue.

The avocat's children used to take Julie to a cherry orchard
where she ate absolutely all the cherries she could stomach,
day after day. Ford said it would be better to let her be sick
and learn moderation that way, than to inculcate the idea of
Forbidden Fruit. But she was never sick at all, and so learnt
no moderation!

The avoué, who was a bachelor, offered to get seats for us
to see the first bull-fight of the season at Nîmes. I was in two
minds about going, but Ford said that one must see it once
anyway. The bull-fighters, looking just as they do in *Carmen*,

drove through Tarascon in open carriages before going on
to Nîmes, and the whole district seethed with hero-worship
and excitement. Nîmes itself was solid with a really formidable crowd and we were almost unable to reach our seats.

The sides of the Roman arena at Nîmes are much steeper
than a modern stadium. All round the rim at the top, the
people stand like a row of insects against the blue sky, and
below, the massed ranks are interrupted here and there by
perpendicular slabs and arches of the grey stone. The cheaper
seats are those facing the sun; ours were in the shade, but not
very close to the arena. If they had been, perhaps I should
not have had that sense of unreality all through the performance which made me unable to realise that I was seeing real
death and real danger. To begin with, the bull-fighter's
costume is like a ballet dancer's, and his movements have a
similar formality. He is a fairy being whose feet never quite
touch the ground and whose life could never conceivably be
in danger. Then there is the bull. He is rather slow, awkward
and puzzled. He does not really want to play. The god-like
creatures in spangled tights have the air of amusing themselves with this earthly booby for want of something better
to do. Horses come on, blindfolded and buttressed, and are
slowly and awkwardly gored. Very stupid and nasty, but
since none of the animals make the slightest sound, you are
persuaded that nothing much has happened. A horse falls,
is stabbed, covered up and dragged off. Dead? Of course,
though it all seems very unlikely. You notice that the bull
is all shining red across his shoulders, yet it is quite a while
before it dawns on you that this must be fresh blood, as he is
teased and tricked until he is finally in a condition to receive
the ceremonial sword-thrust.

We saw six bulls killed, Maëra despatching two—perfectly,
I believe, and the crowd gasped and raved at some of the

subtler points, which passed completely over my ignorant head. They called for music in the tensest moments, but when a nervous Mexican matador made a mess of his kill, they derided him with blood-curdling hoots and howls. The accuracy and brutality of judgment displayed by two young maidens in front of us was quite a revelation of connoissiurship. So was the analysis of the performance in next day's newspapers. My own eyes had registered many strange and beautiful pictures in colour and line and movement, with little appreciation of the significance of these movements. All the same, I *had* seen seven large animals slaghtered, and felt too shaken, when the avoué's sister asked kindly "ça vous a plû, Madame?" to give her any answer but a weak smile!

During the month of May, the heat in Tarascon mounted higher and higher. And the Foire de Beaucaire, with all its painted roundabouts and caravans and show-booths, moved itself across the Rhône bridge and settled under the four rows of great plane trees which flanked our boulevard. It also settled outside our bedroom windows.

Now a French provincial fair can be great fun. We had already visited this one in Beaucaire, where it filled the thickly wooded fair-ground between the river and Aucassin's Château, with the triangular tower perched above on its rocky crag. Julie was in ecstasies over the swinging boats and all the cockshies. There was laughter and music galore, and when the fair came to Tarascon, it woke up that sleepy little town in fine fashion. But Ford had begun to write "Some Do Not," and the shouts and howls and mechanical music which screamed under our windows until late into the night were death to the functioning of the creative mind. Also the heat had got beyond a joke, so that it became necessary to perform the always difficult operation of transplanting the writer in the middle of a book.

The avoué recommended us to go up to St. Agrève in the Ardèche, "un petit coin qui mérite d'être mieux connu." The distance did not look very great on the map, but it took us all day to get there, the branch-line mountain train having practically everything wrong with it that a passenger loco-motive can have. Lucy was sick all the way.

In my innocence, I had sent our winter clothes and heavy luggage by *petite vitesse*. We left Tarascon at noon, perspiring in cotton clothes (it was early June) and arrived after dark on a high, wind-swept plateau which at that moment suggested nothing so much as Haworth Parsonage. The little hotel had already laid off its winter heating, but we found that the summer season had definitely not begun. The place was empty.

For three weeks (it took that time for our big trunk to arrive) we shivered as I have never shivered before or since. Ford went down with severe bronchitis and I became acquainted with the local doctor of the French provinces. He is, perhaps, something that we do better in England. Unless you are dying, he can by no means be induced to visit you for at least thirty-six hours after you first call him in. It is unthinkable that he should get up in the night for any reason whatsoever. But when he *does* come, as though to give you your money's worth (he charges twenty-five francs) he prescribes some twelve or thirteen separate treatments, one of which is invariably "les ventouses," or cupping glasses. The others will take the more usual form of dark red potions, capsules, embrocations, purges and inhalations, each to be used four times a day, and elaborate dietic prescriptions. The soup that the patient may take to-day must be made with one potato, one and a half carrots and three leaves of cabbage, and to-morrow a slice of toast may be added. Raw milk is infinitely dangerous, and the discussion on the desirability of an egg, and, if so, how and when, is long and intricate. I have never had to nurse anyone in France with any kind of stomach upset. I imagine that no form of food whatever would be permitted, until starvation had brought the patient to the brink of the grave.

St. Agrève turned out to be a rather grim, stone-built village, the houses of which opened straight on to the cobbled streets, their ground floors consisting of stables for the animals in winter. There were no flower gardens, and no balconies—a cold-climate architecture, with thick walls and slate roofs, prepared to be under snow all winter. From the plateau where the village stood, roads wound downwards in all directions into the valleys below—spectacular switchback roads and deep luxuriant valleys with great mountains beyond—a great extravagance of natural beauty. The summer was incredible. It came with a rush and was over before you knew that it had started. The winter of June was followed by high summer in July and autumn in August. The meadows were filled with amazing flowers. The hay was cut, the meadows flowered again and were cut again, and the fruit and the corn, which you had just seen as blossom and green blade, were picked and harvested before you knew it.

"Some Do Not," had now got well into its stride. The Hôtel Poste, after the manner of its kind, provided spartan bedroom accommodation but excellent food, and by moving into an annexe, Ford was able to have a place for writing. I was painting out-doors, and between-whiles was being further educated by Ford on the subject of the Albigenses and the bitter religious wars that had once shaken the part of the country we were in. Presently we were joined by Phyllis and her husband, Harry Birnstingl, and with them we visited Le Puy, with churches and virgins perched on high sugar-loaf rocks springing straight out of the plain, and lacemakers

working in the sunshine up and down the steep cobbled street
that leads to the patterned face of the cathedral, built into the
solid rock and overshadowed by an enormous virgin made
of melted cannon. We also went to the source of the Loire,
and to all sorts of lovely villages where simple holidaymakers
stood all day fishing in the turbulent streams.

Then suddenly it was September, and going to be cold
again. We made tracks for Paris.

CHAPTER FIVE

Paris, 1924

SOON AFTER coming to France, we had succeeded in letting the cottage at Bedham for a year, and there was, therefore, no question of our going home until after the winter of 1923-24.

Paris—the Paris of the gay and glamorous nineteen-twenties was waiting to engulf us. To me, it meant painters and painting, and to Ford, people to talk to about prose technique. We were starved for human contacts and our wits were still rusty after more than four years away from any metropolis, although ten months in provincial France had done much to loosen the hinges of our minds. I was readier for Paris than in the previous autumn, and Ford was in that state of nervous fatigue which follows any big creative effort, and which craves outside stimulus. I guess he knew that his power was coming back to him; but he needed refreshment.

When, just after the war, I had begged Ford to start a new book, he had said that he never wanted to write another word. He wanted just to grow vegetables and raise pigs and sink into a peaceful obscurity. He said that if I made him write, I should have to put up with having a nervous, cross, and ailing man on my hands instead of a quiet and happy one. This was to some extent true, but of course he had to go on writing. He was such a good writer, and such a bad farmer! Besides, I believed firmly that his books were of the highest importance.

The trouble was that I never managed to build a structure of security for the protection of our little family and the monumental writer himself. If I had been a Frenchwoman with the right traditions, I should have managed 100 per cent better. A Frenchwoman would have kept him in the country, and cooked and scrubbed and sewed and made him extremely comfortable, and Julie a pattern of health and *sagesse* without any help at all. She would have known how to furnish up her personal appearance without spending money, and how to join the group at the local café, and entertain Ford's literary friends, without any suggestion of the stuffy-minded housewife. She would have had the spending of all the money there was, and have given Ford his *argent de poche* every Saturday. That is the kind of wife that a poverty-stricken artist needs and (in France) usually gets.

She would have balanced the budget. And since economy would be in her blood, Ford might conceivably have accepted to be dragooned and rationed by her. But I was nothing but an amateur in domestic economy, and I never in my life wanted to dragoon anybody. Besides, I wanted to paint.

We never had any arguments or difficulties about money at all. When necessary, I withdrew small slices of my capital from Australia, and considered that I was investing it in a promising career. Ford, in recognition of this, subsequently made over his English royalties to me.

On one of our first days in Paris, we bumped into another large, pink-faced blue-eyed gentleman on an island in the Place Médicis, and Ford said, "do you know who this is?" I looked and said, "it must be brother Oliver," and sure enough it was Ford's brother, Oliver Hueffer, whom he had not seen for many years. We went home with him to his cottage, which was behind a group of shabby old studios—*style rustique*

—in the Boulevard Arago, and met his delightful wife, a keen-faced writer with a twinkling smile and thick, wavy white hair. She was just off to America and said we could have their *rez-de-chaussee* for two hundred francs a month. This was a godsend. Nothing could have been cheaper, and since Lucy was homesick and had to be sent back to England, it seemed possible to economise on domestic help as well. I thought there was a chance that we might be able to afford our winter in Paris after all.

Of course the cottage was extremely picturesque, and of course, it had no comforts at all. Our usual achievement! Oliver and Muriel were already tired of it and pointed out that it was damp, shabby, and without gas or electricity. The cooking was again on charcoal. But in front of it there was a great deal of bowery green, and behind, it had its own little walled garden, with a tree in the middle, nasturtiums all around, and virginia creeper dripping over the French windows of the living-room. It was not until the winter set in that we noticed that the curtains were always wringing wet and the damp-marks on the walls had begun to darken and expand. The rooms were built straight upon the earth, and in London they would no doubt have been condemned. Later, we all developed chest colds.

But in those warm early autumn days, when we first began to feel the exhilaration of being in Paris, it was fun to lead people down yellowing greenery of the little winding path behind the studios and give them tea in the tiny room with the shabby divan and the big French windows, and the sun pouring through the hanging sprays of creeper. They all thought it charming, and we thought it quite delightful to be making so many new acquaintances. For Ford had begun to go to the Dôme and the Deux Magots with Ezra, and presently Hemingway began to visit us with his immense grin and tough-seeming bonhomie, and James Joyce, the most courteous and unassuming of guests—and others of a more lawless and exuberant temper, including two painters called Cedric Morris and Lett Haines who, in beautiful B.B.C. voices, were pleased to regale us with tales of their more lurid adventures. They were all very nice and I also began to meet—and rather to like—the type of woman whose façade of glacial correctness conceals a private life of that far-from-glacial incorrectness which, when all is said and done, requires a deal of courage and dignity to carry off successfully. I felt that to these folk I must appear as very ordinary, sentimental bourgeoise, and was flattered when they were nice to me.

Lucy having been dispatched to England, I had to stay at home to mind Julie when Ford went to the café in the evenings. But on Sundays we budgeted for déjeûner at a restaurant for all three of us, and would sally forth in gaiety to eat at the Nègre de Toulouse in the Boulevard Montparnasse, or at the Restaurant Cécile. We would stop first for an apéritif on the terrasse of the Closerie des Lilas, facing the trees which surround the statue of the Maréchal Ney, with the old Bal Bullier opposite and the clipped chestnut avenues of the Petit Luxembourg stretching away in formal perspective to the left.

I think that in France the apéritif before lunch is the real high spot of the day. In England, there are seldom any high spots until after tea. That means cocktails, the children out of the way and a different frame of mind. It was otherwise in Paris. Julie, in a new little green coat and flowery dress, would imbibe her *sirop* composedly through a straw, and presently we would be joined by Hadley and Ernest Hemingway who lived just round the corner in a timber yard. Their baby was relatively new, but they had the right sort of con-

cierge and were sometimes able to leave Bumby with her.
Hadley was a gay and pretty soul and an excellent pianist,
and in those days it was fine to see how she and Ernest would
brighten up to each other, and how little their lack of money
seemed to matter to them. (Hemingway had not yet published
a book, but Ezra thought very highly of the work that he
was doing. He had been rather portentous about it.)

After lunch we would proceed slowly home, along the
wide boulevards, under the trees, in the autumn sun; and
Julie, prancing and laughing, delighted to have us both at
once all to herself, would raise a smile from those other
parents who were also promenading with their offspring on
the Sabbath. Our bosoms would swell with pride at the sight
of ourselves as *bons bourgeois* and *gens sérieux* amongst so many
other *bons bourgeois* in this exhilarating town. And our spirits
would rise, also at the prospect of the tea-party we were going
home to prepare for some of our new friends.

It was at about six o'clock one Sunday, with the level sun
shining through the plane trees and under the awnings of
the great cafés and with the crowds milling around more
than usually *en fête*, that Ford and I suddenly turned to each
other and said together, " Do you want to go back to Bedham?"
I don't know who spoke first. Then we said, "don't lets." It
was decided just as easily as that!

So we wrote a letter and offered the cottage for sale.

No doubts entered our heads but that we should be able to
buy ourselves a new home in France when we sold Bedham.
To own the roof over your head is the best insurance in the
world against the lean years. We feared to be saddled with
rent to pay all our lives, nor could we bear the idea of a city
flat. In any case, Paris flats and studios were already practically unobtainable on unfurnished lease, and what we
wanted was something with a garden, outside the town.

The story of my life during the next three years is of a long, unequal struggle to get together another permanent home. It overshadowed everything. A great many amusing and exciting things happened during that time, which seem better worth recounting than those hopeless journeys in suburban trains, those trampings in the rain from one *agence de location* to another, and the ignorant struggle with the most astute rogues in the world, gérants, propriétaires and concierges, but our homelessness was what chiefly coloured my existence.

On the morning that we got a letter to say that Bedham was sold, lock, stock and barrel, for a price that just about covered what it had cost us, I wept at this final burning of our boats. But the same mail brought a notice from the Salon d'Automne that my three little pictures had been accepted; and Ford was beginning to hatch a great new idea.

I am rather vague as to how the *Transatlantic Review* actually began. I think brother Oliver sought to install Ford as editor of a review that was to be started, or revived, by some friends of his in the city. Ford's name as an editor was one to conjure with, since he had been the founder and first editor of the *English Review* and had there published the early work of a whole galaxy of writers who afterwards became famous. He could judge the quality of a manuscript by the smell, I believe! "I don't read manuscripts," he said, "I know what's in 'em." Naturally the idea of editing a new review in Paris which was then crammed with young writers from all over the world, was just jam for Ford, and naturally the city people were interested in acquiring his services. But I think he was quite misled as to the conditions that were actually being offered—maybe there had been some wishful thinking involved!—and by the time he discovered that the proposition was quite insubstantial, the word had gone round that a new literary review was afoot, and Montparnasse had begun to hum.

Ezra was particularly excited about it. With his passion for promoting the sort of writing he approved of, he had a whole line-up of young writers waiting for Ford, with Hemingway at the top. Between them all, it would have been hard to announce that there would be no review, after all.

I was profoundly alarmed. We had the money in hand from the sale of Bedham and I was trying frantically, by combing the *banlieu* each day, to find a little *pavillon* with a garden and a reasonable train service, which we could buy. All the agencies of Meudon, Vaucresson, St. Cloud and the Valley of the Chevreuse knew me well, and my French was improving fast. Twice I nearly clinched a bargain, but owing to my ignorance of business, it slipped through my fingers. Meanwhile Ford was more and more absorbed in his scheme and I could not help seeing how lovely it would be for him if he could have his review. And then Mr. Quinn of New York turned up and offered some money, if we would double it. . . .

That was the beginning. The *Transatlantic Review* ran for a year, and I never got my house! So I joined that sad army of Paris wives who spent their days following up vague clues of flats to let, and planting pourboires in the palms of likely concierges, hoping that they would bear fruit—when the next vacancy occurred. In those days of the post-war housing shortage, with Paris crammed to capacity with foreigners, there was no such thing as a "to let" board visible anywhere, unless it were for an "appartement meublé" at four times its unfurnished rent, or a flat in one of the palatial new buildings that were springing up everywhere to accommodate Americans at New York prices. When the big black draperies went up at a house-door for a funeral, it was already too late to inquire about a possibly empty flat. It was said that in order to be the first applicant, it would be necessary to know a doctor or a priest who could tell you of an expected demise! An outgoing tenant could always make a tidy pile by refusing to stir until he had found someone to pay a "reprise" for his fixtures at five times their normal value, and the concierge always stuck out for 1000 francs for smoothing your way with the land-lord. Even if you were lucky enough to find an apartment, you had to reckon on paying out several thousands of francs before you got your agreement with the proprietor, who would then demand a deposit of six months' rent, as well as the first quarter in advance!

The early days of the *Transatlantic Review*, before it became apparent that by no conceivable chance could it be made to pay, were great fun. The whole thing was run in conditions of the utmost confusion. Everything that could possibly go wrong with regard to the printing, paper, packing, forward-ing and distribution, did go wrong. An elegant White Russian colonel offered his services for a pittance, and was sent to make all sorts of arrangements with printers, bookshops and for-warding agents. All his arrangements fell through. A nice young man called Basil Bunting also offered his services—in exchange for his keep. He slept in a damp little store-room beyond our kitchen and was kept on the run by Ford for eighteen hours a day. He endured much in the cause of Litera-ture, and indeed everybody seemed ready to be overworked and underpaid in the good cause—rather in the same fashion as in a theatrical production. Then Bill Bird—a friend of Ezra's who was mad about printing and ran the Three Moun-tains Press on the Ile St. Louis, said that Ford could have the little gallery over his printing press for an editorial office. Topped by a handsome iron eagle, the press itself occupied most of the ground floor space, and in Ford's six-foot balcony there was just room for his desk, some improvised pigeon-holes, and a chair for visitors. When he stood up, his head touched the vaulted roof and onlookers below trembled for the safety of the whole structure.

Confusion became worse confounded until a real American secretary, called Margery, arrived upon the scene and said she would put everything straight, only she must have a proper salary. She got her salary, and she had the whole thing under control in no time. She became, in fact, the backbone of the concern.

On Thursdays, the *Transatlantic Review* was at home, and I made tea for all and sundry at the office, which opened straight on to the Quai d'Orléans. Bill Bird did not print on that day, so we could spread about downstairs. Ford would first be observed aloft at his desk, narrowly framed by the semi-circle of the arched roof, and talking to a new contributor. Presently he would descend and spread geniality amongst the faithful.

He really enjoyed himself superbly.

He survived all the troubles and set-backs, which ordinarily would have bowled him over, with an amazing buoyancy, so deep was his pleasure in the enterprise.

He published Ezra and Hemingway and Gertrude Stein and James Joyce, also Bob McAlmon and Phillip Soupault and Jean Casson and Paul Valery and many unknowns.

Soon a lot of Americans began to appear upon the scene, mostly from the Middle West, and all with their pockets bulging with manuscripts. Paris at that period was not only the nerve-centre of the arts, but the happy meeting-place of all those questioning foreigners who had succeeded in throwing off the shackles and prejudices of their home towns and had not yet wearied of an aimless freedom. People who have lately escaped from something that has been cramping them for a long time, whether war, or wage-slavery, or an em-bittered marriage, are the best company in the world. They are reaching out feelers in every direction to find new subjects for self-expression. They are gloriously egotistical and at the same time madly interested in their surroundings. Finally the tentacles close seriously upon a new object and the egotist retires with his prey for the un-social business of assimilation. If he doesn't manage to digest what he has eaten, he usually disintegrates into one of those attractive, or unattractive, wrecks in which Montparnasse abounds. Generally speaking, the wreckage is only temporary, and the wrecks themselves are very nicely treated by those of their comrades who are still afloat. There always seems to be someone ready to pay their bill and take them to their lodgings and put them to bed. Someday, they no doubt go home to resume impeccable rôles in the bosoms of their families.

Of course there are also the real Wild Ones, who by no conceivable chance can be re-absorbed into respectable society. Sometimes they have great gifts, and indeed it has often seemed to me that an intense struggle with artistic creation doesn't leave a man with much energy or interest to spare for the setting of his house in order. His private life becomes a mess, and his only notion of dealing with a mess is by a series of explosions or evasions.

The danger for the order-loving people is that they get grabbed at by the messy ones, who suffer from an inter-mittent but rather pathetic longing for respectability as exemplified by clean linen, paid bills, and regular meals. But as soon as the Wild One has someone to look after him, he generally becomes more unmanagable than ever, and ends by exhausting the resources of the Orderly Person with-out getting any benefit himself.

But artistic achievement is by no means confined to the Wild Ones. Ford, looking for manuscripts, would find them just as often in the pigeon-hole of a "monsieur sérieux," alongside his cheque-book, income-tax receipts and identity card, as in the salvaged suitcase of the bad hat who had been chucked out of three hôtels meublés in a week !

It took me a little while to get used to living amongst people who, on the whole, had replaced all their moral pre-judices by æsthetic ones. They did not consider themselves as having any particular duties to society, nor were they interested in world affairs. They were all busy developing their egos and having sensations and producing works of art. It was quite all right to be dirty, drunk, a pervert or a thief or a whore, provided that you had a lively and an honest mind, and the courage of your instincts. What damned you, was social snobbery, bourgeois ideology, smugness and care-fulness.

This kind of freedom certainly gives results. You might almost say that you cannot know much about human nature unless you know how people behave when they have stopped obeying the social taboos, and that a period of lawlessness is almost a necessity if you want to qualify as an adult human being. People who have spent their lives accepting the con-ventions of their group or caste hardly ever attain to this status. It's the old business of being born again, and this may just as easily follow a period in the gutter as a period on the mountain top!

Of course, a good many of the weaker brethern stay in the gutter far too long.

After about three months in the Hueffers' cottage, we moved up into one of the big studios in the Boulevard Arago, which was temporarily vacant. This cost rather more, but the damp of the cottage was making us all ill.

The studio was immense. It had neither gas nor electricity, and its kitchen was a black underground dungeon, reached by a perilous flight of narrow, slippery stone steps. There was a gallery at one end, filled with stacked canvases, and here the unfortunate Bunting had his shakedown. The place was well heated by an ancient and leaky anthracite stove, the fumes from which were my constant anxiety. Huge gold frames containing gloomy, indecipherable pictures hung on the walls, which were bursting into large white pimples of damp through the grey distemper. Long serge curtains, once red, hung dustily over the gallery stairs. We liked the furniture. It consisted chiefly of heavy carved chests and antique cupboards, one of which had glass doors and contained four shelves of fragile etruscan remains. This was locked.

When the studio was lit by a couple of dozen candles, in bottles, or stuck on to saucers, it looked very dramatic. You could not see the roof, it was filled with gloom and blue smoke, but the people below had the air of being grouped upon a stage, and it was here that we began to have our parties.

In Montparnasse, if you gave a party, you could not hope to know more than half the people who came. You catered (in vin rouge ordinaire and hot dogs) for twice the number you had invited. This made it ever so much more exciting.

I have always thought that the charm of a railway station is that you never know who will be there. And I always considered that the great drawback to the old dances in Adelaide was that you knew, only too well, exactly who would be there. Paris had no such drawback.

There were gardens back and front of our studio, which was the last in a long row, and as the weather got warmer, the folks would overflow outdoors and walk along to where the concierge lived under the archway, and out on to the boulevard.

Once at midnight as I was coming up from the dungeon with a dish of hot dogs, I saw through the open front door that Maitland was in the garden with his face all covered with blood. Now Maitland was a young man who was said to be always trying to commit suicide, and Mary Butts, who had brought him to the party, was usually able to prevent it. Imagine my annoyance when I saw what I believed to be another attempt, and at my party! I foresaw the police and what it is usual to call "des ennuis." So when I found that it was nothing worse than a bloody nose, inflicted by a hefty American who had been brought by an English girl who had just come through a particularly sensational divorce with a long list of dazzling co-respondents, I was mightily relieved, and took no further notice. It appeared merely that a person called Pat had smacked Mary unceremoniously as she danced past him, and she had demanded that Maitland should avenge her. But Pat's friends pointed out that he was much too drunk to defend himself, so the American stepped forward and offered to take Maitland on instead.

Why they elected to settle the matter under the concierge's windows, where the blood spattered her rose bushes and the flagstones for all to see, remains for me one of those lapses in tact which alas! were all too frequent on the Left Bank.

Next morning, I was accosted by a wild-eyed Madame Annie (recently engaged to look after Julie) who asked, "What, Madame, can have occurred last night?" She had seen the blood and heard the concierge's story, which by then had become a legend including a duel, possibly a death, with crowds of wild women rushing out into the Boulevard. I never was so mortified in my life!

The only other mishap that I remember was Cedric Morris pulling the Etruscan remains down on his head. The glass doors were not damaged, but all the little objects were thrown down, and some broken, and we could not open the doors to set them straight. Fortunately, the amiable landlord never reproached us.

The acquisition of Madame Annie to look after Julie was one of my mistakes. For three years she ruled me with a rod of iron, and at the end of that time, when I had achieved reasonable domestic conditions, and knew I could command the services of someone more congenial, it was all but impossible to get rid of her.

She was a lively little widow of forty with a formidable temper, but since the temper was reserved exclusively for the purpose of forcing her wishes on me, and never made its appearance in her dealings with Julie, I put up with it as best I could. Bad temper has always troubled me out of all reason, I suppose because I never had any experience of it in childhood. I recognise that a great many people enjoy a good blow-up and feel all the better for it, but if I am made angry to the point of having a scene, I am apt to feel ill all next day. So I generally resort to a policy of appeasement, and people like Madame Annie get the maximum results from their tantrums.

What made her valuable was that she was ready to put up with our ramshackle way of living at a quite small salary, and that she was completely devoted to Julie. Julie was now speaking French rather than English and had acquired a disconcerting Gallic realism, as I found when a visiting English publisher of haughty mien, asked her, "Tu es une petite fille sage, alors?" and she replied promptly, "Moi, je suis très sage. Ce n'est qu'une très mauvaise petite fille qui fait pipi dans ses culottes!"

My efforts to find a home—to rent, by now, not to buy—led me in ever-widening circles around Paris and finally, at the suggestion of Gertrude Stein, to a village called Guermantes, near Lagny, on the Chemin de Fer de l'Est.

Gertrude Stein and Alice B. Toklas then lived in the Rue de Fleurus, where the walls of their studio were hung with priceless early Picassos which had been bought cheap when he was unknown. There were also lots of other cubist and post-impressionist pictures, from Cézanne onwards, and charming bits of metal, glass, and carved wood from Spain and Africa. The studio was large and light and warm, the deep-sprung chairs shabby and comfortable, and it felt, then, like a friendly place. We first met Gertrude Stein through Hemingway with whom she had not yet quarelled. In fact she had just become Bumby's godmother. I found her a very commonsensible person, of a robust and earthy disposition, ever ready with domestic advice. She said that she and Alice Toklas were in the habit of motoring through Guermantes on their way to Meaux and that there was an attractive house there to let or for sale. I found the house in question to be far too big for us, but discovered near by an old stone labourer's cottage with four rooms and a small orchard, to let at five hundred francs a year. We took it as a kind of insurance against complete homelessness, since our tenancy at the Boulevard Arago was coming to an end and I had to have somewhere to put Julie and Madame Annie. With the help of an aged villager, I got the place cleaned out and the walls papered. I painted the woodwork and scraped together enough second-hand furniture to move in, and installed an un-coperative and suspicious Madame Annie with her small charge. Madame

Annie, however, quickly made this cottage her own personal home, and greatly resented our presence there at week-ends, when she insisted on going up to Paris. I think she was jealous of the pleasure Julie took in our company; but in spite of this, Guermantes became something like a home to Ford and me as well. We kept it for nearly three years, and presently acquired a primitive kind of annexe with a beamed ceiling and an open fireplace, which made a good study for Ford.

The whitewashed, slate-roofed village was typical of *le Brie*, and the surrounding country, if a trifle bleak, was not without a charm of its own. It was, of course, far more "real" country than anything at the same distance from London. There were no Parisians and no commuters in Guermantes, which was three kilometers from Lagney and one hour by train from town.

When I had got Julie and Madame Annie settled, I began to think that I might be able to paint again. Since coming to Paris I had had a lot of fun, lots of cafés and restaurants and parties and good talk, but my real time had been all taken up with house hunting and domestic complications. Ford, for the first time since I had known him seemed able to take care of himself, or rather the *Review* was taking care of him, and I wanted to feel that part of my life belonged to myself.

I was lucky to get the use of Lett Haines' studio during the summer of 1924, since the studio at the Boulevard Arago offered no peace or privacy. It was rather a horrid studio, with an opaque window giving on to a narrow courtyard, but to me it was like Heaven. To arrive in the morning with the key in my pocket, to be able to lock the door behind me and to know that I should be absolutely undisturbed all day, was the most exhilarating sensation I had had since that first fine moment when Ford and I decided to live in France. I do

JULIE, 1940

AU NEGRE DE TOULOUSE

TUSNELDA'S INTERIOR

EDITH SITWELL

EDITH SITWELL'S HANDS

FROM THE RUE NOTRE DAME DES CHAMPS

JULIE, AGED 12

RAMON GUTHRIE

CARL VAN DOREN

DOROTHY THOMPSON WITH HER SON

EMBANKMENT GARDENS

THE MITCHISON FAMILY IN MADEIRA

MARGARET I. COLE

LADY CRIPPS

ROBERT LYND

JOHN, ELDEST SON OF RAY AND DAISY POSTGATE

CLIFFORD BAX AT HOME

TUSNELDA

not think that the work I did in that studio was much good, but it got my painting faculties into regular play.

When our tenancy at the Boulevard Arago expired, we moved into a poky little apartment in the Rue Denfert-Rochereau. There was of course no bath, and one of the beds was in the kitchen; but there was both gas and electricity. When Julie and Madame Annie were with us, it was impossible to turn round, and we missed being able to have our parties.

I have always had a passion for parties if they are given with no ulterior motive but that of enjoyment. The nice thing about most of the scallawags of Montparnasse was that they had no respect for people of importance and there was none of the snobbery and log-rolling that was rife amongst the more established Parisian careerists. Nobody suffered bores gladly because they were rich or well known, and if somebody was described to you as "simply wonderful," it would quite likely turn out to be an ugly old woman nobody had ever heard of, who was as mad as a hatter, but who had somehow preserved the flame of her curious personality unspoiled.

This is the right spirit for a good party. A good party is a time and a place where people can be a little more than themselves; a little exaggerated, less cautious, and readier to reveal their true spirit than in daily life. For this, there has to be an atmosphere of safety from exploitation—a sense that you are all amongst friends, and that nothing you say will be used against you. Social ambitions are death to such an atmosphere, and so is the presence of even one person who won't play, and remains coldly aloof.

A good party is a splendid tonic. It warms and quickens the wits and comforts the heart and stimulates the brain. To a person cramped by work and worry, it is as good as a hot bath to someone cramped by cold. I have been to many gatherings quite unworthy to be called parties where people circulate in coldly cautious groups, collecting recognitions, attempting to improve useful acquaintanceships or to attract the attention of the principal guest and snubbing other people whom they deem un-useful.

I should admit at once that I have never mastered the technique of the French drawing-room reception, and that I do recognise that this is a skilled game, giving interesting results. Your hostess advances towards you with a well-balanced opening remark, which shows that she is thoroughly aware who you are and what subject is likely to interest you. To this there is always one completely correct reply, and only one. I have never found it. I have tried a deprecating kind of bluff, which does not do at all, and I have tried to strike a different note, which is even worse. The next move is that you are introduced to someone who is obliged to talk to you, for good or ill, for ten minutes, when your hostess removes him, and brings up someone else. After another five minutes she reappears and takes away your second partner and this time you are left to fend for yourself.

Fending for yourself is sometimes amusing, as you hear things which would otherwise escape you. Once I was standing near a group of people in a house on the Ile St. Louis, when a sudden spate of departures disclosed a dark little lady and Monsieur André Chamson seated on a sofa. The lady was saying, "Alors, Monsieur, vous ne pensez donc jamais à Dieu?" Monsieur Chamson said, "Non, Madame, franche-ment, ça ne m'arrive pas." The lady insisted that surely the gentleman wished to cast his cares upon a Higher Being in moments of storm and stress, and asked what he did in the face of an insoluble problem? "Alors, Madame, je cherche la solution." "Tout seul? Tout seul." The lady then expounded the joys and comforts of union with God, and just as I was thinking that a Catholic evangelist was a strange person to find in that particular drawing-room, and Monsieur Chamson had gallantly said that almost the lady could persuade him to join her faith, the lady replied that he couldn't possibly do that, because you had to be born into it. She was a Parsee! Well, that was fun.

We used to go to several houses where French and English and Americans were successfully mixed together, amongst which was the Bradleys. William Aspenwell Bradley was an American who had known Ford long ago and was now established as a literary agent in Paris with a French wife of the *haute bourgeoisie*. Jenny Bradley is still one of the great admirations of my life. To begin with, she is the finest conversationalist I have ever known. But beneath the brilliant wit and capricious fancy which make her the best company in the world, there lie a vast courage and a scope of vision which only serve, eventually, to isolate their possessor. Jenny has always been festooned about with weaker people, feeding on her strength, which is as unlimited as her willingness to accept responsibility. Everything she touches is properly done, on properly laid foundations, even if it is only a matter of giving the right introductions to people in distress, or furnishing *renseignments*. To me, she very quickly became the wise woman. She did much to civilize me, and at the same time exploded the remains of those Adelaide prejudices which still fogged the corners of my mind. She understood, and accepted and despised, convention as only a socially entrenched Frenchwoman can. She gave me a new slant on the confusions of Montparnasse.

Bradley was an extremely cultivated and sensitive person with a kind of whimsical gaiety that could create the party spirit at any dinner-table where he sat. We sat at a great many tables with him and Jenny, for they soon began to share with us their unparalleled knowledge of how to eat, and where. They did all the research, i.e. tried out unfamiliar *bistros* and restaurants until they found something special and then we were invited to join them. It was they who introduced us to the "Mariniers," where the Seine fishermen used to eat on the Quai d'Orléans, and which we all frequented until it became spoiled by tourists. It was they, also, who found the Maison Paul in the Place Dauphine on the Cité. Here at noon came chauffeurs and employés from the Belle Jardinière and the man who wound the clock of the Palais de Justice. But in the evening it was emptier and M. Paul liked to be asked for special dishes. It was a nice, steamy little place with sawdust on the floor and a zinc bar and a pot of flowers between the spotted lace curtains and M. Paul, when on his mettle, was a marvellous cook. He was kept pretty closely in the kitchen by madame, but after cooking us a special *plat*, he would creep out and hang around the doorway, shyly twisting his apron in his hands until somebody spotted him, when he would come forward to receive our congratulations.

Under the tutelage of Ford and the Bradleys, I began to acquire a palate. As regards wine, I had expressed a profound indifference to it when we first came to France which annoyed Ford, who said he couldn't take a woman around who wouldn't drink—it wasn't civilised. So by dint of having a great many kinds of liquor poured down my throat, I gradually acquired quite an expensive taste and I daresay Ford came to rue the day that he ever educated me in this direction!

I can see Ford and Bradley now, sitting side by side, warming their glasses, circulating them beneath their noses, glancing at each other with an affirmative nod, before imbibing the first sip and breathing out through the nostrils. All very solemn, very happy, very convivial.

For everyday eating, we used to frequent the Nègre de Toulouse in the Boulevard Montparnasse. There was a little back room here with only two tables which we colonised with our friends and which M. Lavigne discouraged his other clients from penetrating. Here we had the fun of eating in company without having to entertain. We made another such arrangement with a certain *Bal Musette*, in order to satisfy our desire to dance. A bal musette is a little café where there is an accordion player, sometimes with cymbals tied between his knees and bells upon his ankles, sitting above the dance floor on a raised seat or gallery. Chauffeurs and *petits commerçants* bring their girls to dance and drop two sous into the proprietor's cap each time they take the floor. There is always a policeman sitting just inside the door. That is the law.

Now a really good accordion player can compel even the lame and the halt to dance. He can work up a rhythm that positively lifts you off the floor. But most *Bals* were too crowded to be enjoyable.

We found one, however, that was always closed on Fridays and we persuaded it to re-open for us at ten o'clock. The proprieter said he had no licence for a "bal privé," but his regular clients were not accustomed to come on Fridays and we could have the place pretty well to ourselves. Sometimes a few of the local inhabitants drifted in and always we had the policeman, who used to enjoy it; but on the whole the tactful proprietor, in response to a weekly tip, was able to give preferential treatment to the friends of Monsieur Ford. The two sous per dance was dropped.

The Bal du Printemps was a charming little spot. It showed a row of electric lights across an angle in the Rue du Cardinal Lemoine, a steep and twisting old street behind the Panthéon. Inside, the rough tables and wooden benches were painted scarlet and the walls around the dance floor were set with mirrors and painted pink, with garlands, all done by hand! Here the charm of the railway station prevailed with a vengeance since you never knew who would be there. It was a public spot and the word went round. . . .

You would find yourself dancing with someone. Nothing but the coat sleeve to indicate whether he should be addressed in French or in English. You decide to try English.

"I love an accordeon," you say.

He, "So do I. I have a beauty at home, in carved ivory and pink silk. My wife gave it to me the first time she was unfaithful to me." Dare you ask if he got a piano the second time? Perhaps not.

Lett Haines and Cedric Morris and their friends were the life and soul of the bal musette, but they were disapproved of as decadent artists by certain 100 per cent efficient and clean-living Americans who wanted to organise the whole thing as a club, with members who should be chucked out if they did not sign an attendance register and pay subscriptions. I knew that it would be quite impossible to extract subscriptions from most of the people and that the main charm of the thing was its informality, but the schism grew. Then journalists began to drop in who wanted to write us up, which made Ford very angry, especially when one of them asked him if he was "making a good thing out of it!" And the journalists would bring Englishwomen in evening dress, who thought it fun to go slumming in Paris, to see how the artists amused themselves in their lairs. So eventually the whole thing died.

Towards the end of 1924, Nina Hammett told us of a vacant studio in the Rue Notre Dame des Champs. She really needed it herself, but couldn't afford it. The studio was enormous, but without conveniences or living accommodation of any kind, having until lately been part of Delecluse's Academy of Art. However, there was a water-tap, and electric light, and some heavy, movable screens.

We decided to convert it into some sort of a dwelling and got permission from M. Delecluse to install an enclosed gallery which should serve as bedroom and *cabinet de toilette*. Madame Annie and Julie, when in Paris, would have to be accommodated on two divans, behind the screens.

The *Transatlantic Review* was coming to an end, having absorbed all the money we had, together with certain supplementary donations from outside. Ford felt very badly about closing down and we both went through a deal of anguish before finally accepting the fact that by no possible means could it be continued. It ran for twelve months.

But *Some Do Not* had appeared, and *No More Parades* was being hatched, and the loss of an editorship could not inflict a mortal wound upon a man who was just embarking upon the best creative work of his life. He had something else to think about.

I, too, was full of hope and joy at getting a studio at last, after flat-hunting for nearly a year. Its rent was more than it should have been and we could not get a lease and the balcony cost twice the architect's estimate. Also, there was no plumbing save the tap and a large zinc sink. But it had immense windows and a lovely light and a small outside balcony and it overlooked the trees of a convent garden. I made a bet with myself that somehow I would convert it into a real home, refusing to realise that though it might be grand for working in, or playing, it could never really serve for family life.

We had given up the nasty little flat in the Rue Denfert-Rochereau and had spent the summer at Guermantes. In the autumn, when the affairs of the *Review* were being wound up, we were camping in the studio whilst the workmen were still there and we had practically no furniture. We were both very tired. I had installed the family in three furnished and two unfurnished domiciles within a twelvemonth, none of them with *confort moderne*, and Ford was worn out by the fluctuating fortunes of the *Review*.

So we decided to go south for the winter, leaving the final shaping of the studio until the spring. The recent devaluation of the franc made this just possible.

We chose to go to Toulon because of Juan and Josette Gris. We had met them at Gertrude Stein's and Ford had asked them to come to the Bal Musette. Gris afterwards said to Gertrude, "C'est épatant—ce Monsieur Ford, il a son bal musette à lui, et il m'a invité d'y aller. Je trouve ça très gentil." He was a person nobody could help liking, a sturdily built Spaniard with a childlike grin and not a thought in his head but for his painting. Desperately poor and in delicate health, when we met him he had just rented a tiny, glass roofed annexe to their appartment at Boulougne-sur-Seine in which he could paint undisturbed. It was the first time he had ever had anything resembling a studio!

Josette was the perfect wife for an artist—as pretty as a picture and as stout-hearted as a lion. Naturally she had no domestic help, and naturally, being French, she was a wonderful cook, as we found when they asked us to dinner. Besides all this she had an open and generous mind and an excellent head and could hold her own in any company.

Well, Juan and Josette were going to Toulon and Josette offered to find rooms for us, and to bargain for the best prices, a good offer at which of course I jumped. She also very sweetly lent herself to a small deception on my behalf concerning our dog Toulouse. Toulouse was a nine months Alsatian puppy who had been given to us by M. Lavigne and who, so far, had been accommodated at Guermantes and mismanaged by

Madame Annie. He was imperfectly house-trained and extremely turbulent and absolutely enormous. Ford adored him. But Madame Annie didn't, and I was in great hopes that we might be able to leave him behind when we all went south. So when Josette—who was in the secret—wrote that she had found very nice rooms for us in the Hôtel Victoria, which for a séjour would make us a more advantageous price than any of the other hotels, she added that, unfortunately, they absolutely refused to take a dog! *All* the hotels of Toulon, she said, refused to take dogs. But it was no use, Ford just said "nonsense," and instructed me to engage the rooms and say nothing about the dog, who spent a miserable journey avoiding the over-heated footplate on the carriage floor and the over-zealous guard who would not allow him in the corridor.

Of course, the hotel accepted him without a murmur!

CHAPTER SIX

Toulon

I FELL IN LOVE with Toulon at first sight. I wished I could to be born again as a native of that enchanting little town and I observed with distress that the natives themselves appeared to be insufficiently aware of their good fortune. Never having lived in an ugly place, or a cold or dark or lonely place, they took for granted such things as light, warmth, picturesqueness and social liveliness and never troubled to look backwards from the ferry-boat that carried them to their work or to their Sunday pleasures, to observe the highly ornamental stage-set which their home town represented.

Seen from the harbour, Toulon consisted of a long row of tall, shabby and colourful old houses, unmarred by any intrusion of modernity. This shuttered and balconied façade, topped by bunches of crooked chimneys, reared itself like a cardboard cut-out in front of a drop-cloth representing an impressive circle of rocky, fortress-capped mountains. In between, the whole town lay concealed.

Backwards and forwards on the broad pavement of the quai, between the bobbing motor-boats and the awnings of the shops and cafés, there strolled a crowd at ease. In 1925, this included sailors from all over the world, skins of all colours, travellers of all denominations, as well as sundry artists and writers. In the quai-side shops, you could buy those childish red pom-poms and blue and white striped vests with which France adorns the manly persons of her seamen.

And very nice the lads looked, too! You could also buy a clasp-knife with a garland of flowers adorning the handle, and on the blade the pious inscription, "When I strike, may it be fatal!" and a shell-encrusted, satin-lined souvenir casket for your love letters. Or you could invest in some highly-coloured post cards and install yourself for a morning's correspondence at that water-side café where the French naval officers made *rendezvous* and the glittering water reflected arabesques of sunlight underneath the awning.

Behind the *rade* there lay the old town, where you might lose yourself completely in the smallest possible area. It was dotted with modest and gracious little *places* which were shaded by fat plane trees and decorated with mouldy, ornate fountains and the gay booths of vociferous flower-vendors. It was seamed with winding, cobbled canyons framing glimpses of the mountains and criss-crossed by lines of coloured washing, hanging quietly between the upper windows. Down in the street, dim and varied avocations were pursued. In caverns, under vaulted ceilings, behind curtains and in open door-ways, strange objects were being fashioned of leather, wood and metal. Precious junk was repaired. Hammers, bellows, lathes and sewing machines were busy; sails, nets, lines, awnings and tents were fabricated; most of all, the buying, storing, cooking and selling of food was practised with all that personal fervour and faith in the importance of the job in hand which hold the secret of France's invincible sanity.

I once knew a very sick poet in Montparnasse who had a nervous break-down and spent many dark months in a clinic. His window looked down on to a baker's shop and he told me afterwards that his convalescence began on the day when, noticing a woman going in to buy bread, he suddenly felt unutterably envious of the interest she was taking in the choosing of a loaf. It seemed to him to denote a miraculous state of bliss, a birthright that he had somehow lost and must recapture; a birthright, I still believe, that belongs especially to France and will surely survive . . .

In the market under the plane trees of the Cours Lafayette there throbbed the most articulate and ebullient life that I had ever seen. It was also a very good market for finding strange foods, although the finest sight I ever saw there was a large wagon-load of quite ordinary oranges, spilled in a flaming stream, right down the street.

The delights of Toulon were not confined to the water-front and the old town. There was a large modern boulevard, a Grand Place with tall palm trees and a guignol for the children, a Théâtre Municipal, a Museum and a Place d'Armes where the band played. There was also a very rewarding rag-market outside the ramparts. And the cream-cakes of the Palais des Délices had no equal anywhere, unless it were those of Chez Phillips; while the crystallised fruits which were sold all over the town reached their brightest manifestation on Palm Sunday when they were arrayed dangling from branched *rameaux* to be held in the hand and taken to church and blessed with the rest of the palms, before being eaten. And at Christmas, in front of the Cathedral (very dark, very full of bogies) stalls were set up for the sale of *santans*, those rough, brightly-painted little clay figures made in the region and representing the Virgin Mary and all the Saints. These were for your *crèche* at home.

Toulon was not concerned with the tourist trade. There was no casino, no promenade, and no fashionable cocktail bar. The social life of the town circled round the officers of the navy whose slender purses and civilised requirements kept amenities high and prices low. The merchandise in the shops was cheap and attractive and as Josette said when she met us on our arrival, "Il y a cinq cinémas et deux dancings. Ça fait juste la semaine!"

We found Josette and Juan Gris installed in rooms with a garden outside the ramparts. Josette said that it was quiet and airy and cheaper than in the town and that the outlook pleased them greatly. She had hung a white curtain against the sun and tacked sheets of brown paper on the walls so that Juan's canvases should not mark the landlady's wall-paper, and she had completely subjugated that formidable personage and persuaded her to sweep and dust their rooms. I daresay it was the first time Josette had ever had a hand's turn done for her. She gave us an exquisite lunch, with new potatoes no bigger than cherries and *petits pois* no bigger than barley and declared that with nothing to do but the cooking, marketing and mending, she had become a real lady of leisure! When Juan had done painting for the day, he used to bring her, fresh as a daisy, to the café where we all decided which cinema or which "dancing" merited our patronage that evening. Our preferred "dancing" was very charming, with a Russian balalaika band and several nicely-behaved ladies of the town who could be relied upon to provide the party spirit. It was a little awkward when a British man-of-war was in the harbour, because the sterling exchange rate enabled our sailors to over-crowd these haunts of the French officers. There were not enough girls to go round, so the boys began dancing together until the proprietor displayed a hastily-inscribed notice to the effect that, "Mm. les clients sont priés de choisir une dame pour danser." Ford, in whom some latent snobbery was aroused by the sight of the British Navy (we had just been to a tea-dance on board the *Warspite*) whispered to me, "Dance with a seaman if you like, but not with a petty officer!"

Our group at the café was frequently joined by M. and

Madame Georges Duthuit and a painter called Latapie. One day we found there also a powerful-looking personage with a piercing blue eye and a lot of hair who turned out to be Othon Friez. He at once invited Ford and me to visit his home at Cap Brun, a charming old *mas* which had been restored and developed as a background for his attractive wife, his pictures and his collected treasures from Africa and China. Squat archways cut in the thick, whitewashed walls led the eye inwards towards these precious objects, and outwards to a sunny doorway where a sinuous aloe set in an oil-jar pointed long fingers at a marvellously pink judas tree flowering between a grey olive and a dark cypress. We found the aloe and the judas tree also on an easel in the studio in a fine, rhythmic composition which I recognised as the work of a familiar painter whose name I had forgotten. It had all those qualities of airiness and freedom, dashing manner and sensuous movement which so far I had been slowest to recognise, and which helped me to see a new aspect of painting. Friez had another studio on the quai at Toulon, a long narrow attic in a warehouse which commanded the busiest aspect of the port. There were battleships on the left, the old house fronts on the right, the dockyards opposite and the foreground packed with yachts and dinghies. In this attic, bare save for his painting kit and a colossal Chinese umbrella, Friez painted many of his most characteristic harbour pictures. He told us of a similar room below this, the rent of which would be about £10 a year. We took it immediately, and I used it as a studio during the two winters that we spent at Toulon. It had neither water nor electricity and was reached by a grand, rough old wooden staircase which mounted in a kind of primitive scaffolding round four sides of a square. There was always a queer smell on this staircase which puzzled me until one day an open door revealed a great vista of onions piled in mountains on the floor and hanging in festoons from the roof, a landscape of tiny, copper-tinted globes, each one bearing a highlight from the distant window.

My studio had an uneven brick floor, a roof supported by twelve great beams and the harbour view. Furnished with a trestle-table and a pot of flowers, it had a wonderful atmosphere for work. Later, when I could no longer afford to keep it on, I handed it over to Willie Seabrook who wrote his book *Jungle Ways* there.

In Paris I had sat at hundreds of café tables with Ford, listening to talk about literature and "le mot juste." In Toulon, I was able to listen, at last, to talk about painting. Juan Gris was no great theoritician. "J'aime composer," was all he would say, and I never heard him talk about his work beyond admitting to a dislike of highly-detailed work as "trop prétentieuse," and an indifference to the fate of his own pictures, once they were finished and disposed of. ("Peindre, pour moi, c'est remplir ma fonction. Quand j'ai fait un tableau, je n'y pense plus. Je commence un autre.") Friez, older and more successful, was more aware of his own methods, and more talkative. Francis Carco was staying with him at Cap Brun when we were there, and they both had plenty to tell of the early struggles of "les fauves," of milk bottles stolen from doorsteps in the early hours, of knives and forks chained to the table in the lowest eating-houses, and their first very young enthusiasm for the Impressionists before the post-impressionist movement was born, and their excitement whenever one of their group—Braque or Picasso or Modigliani, made painting history with a new experiment. I was fascinated when Friez—who can paint water so liquid that it would run away out of any picture less well composed than his, described a great day in his life when he first asked himself, "Why should I fill all that in with blue?" and decided not to. This fitted in with something I had been trying to work out for myself.

Beside these giants I was miserably conscious that my notions about painting were extremely embryonic. It was natural that I should be regarded chiefly as a wife-and-mother, who did a little painting as a hobby. Five years later, another painter said to me, "Je crois que vous êtes très encore jeune dans la peinture," and it was still lamentably true. I have always been late with everything I have learned and everything I have become. Faint yet pursuing, with greying hair, I am still learning, still "becoming," still trying to understand my surroundings!

It is platitudinous to say so, but being a woman does set you back a good deal. You begin longing for a satisfactory emotional life even before you are grown-up, and this occupies an unreasonable amount of your thoughts and energies. When at last the emotional event comes, you put into it everything you have got. Afterwards you begin to grow up and to see more of the sky than can be filled by one person, but if by then you have given your life into that person's keeping, you will have become bound and entwined in every detail of your being, and will have developed simply into a specialist in ministering to his own particular needs. Perhaps you never intended to devote your life to this kind of specialisation, but society, and your own affections, and the fear of loneliness that besets us all, may keep you at it. And you will very likely find that it suits you well enough. But beware; unlike other specialists, you will receive no promotion after years of faithful service. Your value in this profession will decline, and no record of long experience, or satisfaction given, will help you if you want to change your job. By the time you are forty, you will probably have got your children through babyhood and provided your husband with all the emotional excitement he is going to get out of being in love with you. Teachers will step in to educate your children, and sirens to educate your husband, whose own career will be just beginning to expand. There remains the housekeeping, your social life, and possibly a profound friendship with your spouse, but this is definitely less than what you have been accustomed to. Can you make a life of it?

If the home and the children were unconditionally your own, and the social structure of your life did not depend upon the most fragile of bases—a human relationship—one might demand that you should make a life of it. One can't have a home that is safe and sweet and comfortable without some woman devoting herself to making it so. Perhaps it's a luxury trade, but even so—it deserves a safer foundation than can be provided by tying some poor devil of a man to the domestic wheel by all the traditional trickery of virtuous womanhood. A desperate plight for both, with a bad money system at the bottom of it, which leads to the clumsy and humiliating absurdities of the divorce laws.

No. If you are a woman, and you want to have a life of your own, it would probably be better for you to fall in love at seventeen, be seduced, and abandoned, and your baby die. If you survived this, you might go far! Otherwise, emerging from a love-affair into the position of a middle-aged housekeeper, you may suffer the most desperate sensations of constriction and futility which your situation will give you little chance to surmount.

I have been very lucky to have escaped both these sad fates. I have known both attachment and freedom. But whether attached or free, I find that wherever I am, I invariably start to dig in and try to make a home. Four times in my life I have gone away with two suitcases, leaving all behind me, never to return, so that my home-making activities are always having to start again from scratch. Sometimes I think this is just a pathetic manifestation of ineradicable femininity!

Ford was another rolling stone with domestic instincts and a steady longing for a house, a garden and a view. When we found ourselves again in Provence, which had always been his spiritual home, and was fast becoming mine too, the cottage at Guermantes appeared by contrast no better than a makeshift, and the studio in the Rue N. D. des Champs just a *pied à terre*. Ford had a little money in sight, so his notions of the future became very grandiose, and I lent myself willingly to the building of castles in the air. We never admitted that, having financed the *Transatlantuc Review*, we had nothing left to buy a house with, nor that it would have been an act of folly to jeopardise my small but precious Australian income by blueing the remainder of the available capital. Neither would we face the fact that, given Ford's temperament, his earnings would never, by any conceivable chance, be set aside and saved. So we began looking for a "little place" in the country surrounding Toulon and actually made an offer for an old five-roomed house on a hill with a shady *terrassed* garden. Luckily for our finances the offer was refused.

Whilst we were talking about a permanent migration to the south, Ezra and Dorothy Pound had already achieved this feat. They too had decided that a climate was one of the things best worth following in life, and their chosen land being Italy, they had burned their boats in Paris and settled in Rapallo.

Their studio in the Rue N. D. des Champs had in any case become untenable for persons of their nervous and privacy-loving temperament. Being on the ground floor, they were at the mercy of anybody who chose to stroll in and knock. Hordes came. So when they got back from their winters in

Italy, they would beg us to keep their return a secret for as long as possible. But in Rapallo, when we went to visit them from Toulon, we found them in a sixth floor flat with a big *terrasse* overlooking the harbour, and although the house was new, the lift was permanently disabled. Anyone who wanted to see them had six long flights to climb and no guarantee that they would find anyone at home when they got to the top. This eminently satisfactory arrangement enabled Ezra to write his Cantos undisturbed and to devote himself to his immense correspondence, which consisted mainly of the wildest abuse of everyone who did not agree with him, conveyed in highly impressionist typescript. This gave him immense satisfaction, and meanwhile Dorothy applied herself to the composition of abstract water-colours. When disposed for conversation, Pound would place himself on the quai-side *terrasse* of the café above which he lived, and conversation would come to him. It was an excellent system, which included one meal a day at the café-restaurant and the minimum of household cares.

Dorothy walked me up the hills and through the olive groves above that beautiful bay, whilst Ezra and Ford discussed the world of letters in general and their own careers in particular. Ford was convinced that Ezra ought to pay a visit to his native America, if only for the sake of his prestige; but Ezra was violently averse to doing anything of the sort. He was looking to Italy to provide him with all the future he wanted.

We hired a carriage and drove to Portofino, whose overwhelming picturesqueness was lovelier than anything I had seen on the French Mediterranean coast. But the background was alien. I did not understand Italian and I did not like coming upon Mussolini's heavy features stencilled all over the walls and glowering at me from every corner.

Ezra admired Mussolini and had already made contact with him. I suppose that the dictator appealed to his orderly nature and passion for organisation.

I have known other artists who supported Fascism under the impression that it would provide the social stability essential for their survival. They feared that under true Socialism they would be forced to earn their living by doing something "useful" unless the State happened to approve of them as artists. Having a well-founded mistrust of official-dom in matters of taste, they would prefer to remain dependent upon the patronage of individuals of the leisured classes, which Socialism sets out to destroy. As creators of something entirely without material usefulness, they have sought the protection of the Strong Man, in the hope that he would calm the only waters in which they have, with difficulty, learnt to swim. They have reckoned without the Strong Man's hatred of their liberal and independent spirit, which causes him to poison those waters, and finally to stir them into the inevitable final storm in which their individuality is submerged.

Ezra, however, had more definite reasons for liking Mussolini. He, too, was in rebellion against the poverty and insecurity of the artists' lot, but he had become a convert to the principles of Douglas Credit System. In Mussolini's domestic finance, he claimed to see most of these principles in operation.

The gay twenties had given place to the anxious and poverty-stricken thirties before I saw Ezra again. Ten years after the visit with Ford to Rapallo I was invited to go on a painting holiday to near-by Portofino by an English friend, Dolly Osler. We found Ezra in the middle of his yearly musical festival. Starting from scratch, a foreigner, and with no money at his disposal, he had built up a regular winter concert season for the performance of very ancient and also very modern music at which the artistes, some of them of international reputation and all bitterly hard hit by the economic crisis, gave their services for the pleasure of playing the kind of music they enjoyed and seldom had an opportunity to perform at popular concerts. The Fascists had given Ezra the free use of a hall (he said it was because the Mayor chanced to overhear his quartet practising and said, "Such music must be made available for the town of Rapallo," and Ezra, as swaggering and flamboyant as ever, would stand at the door and hold out the hat to the arriving audience. The proceeds were divided equally amongst the artistes.

It was nice to find that Ezra's violinist and chief stand-by was an old friend of mine, Olga Rudge, a very fine musician, whom I had known as a young hostess at musical parties in Paris in more affluent days. Now she was broke like the rest of the musical world and lived in a tiny villa on the hills above Rapallo.

She asked me to spend the night with her after one of the concerts. She warned me to wear stout shoes and to bring the smallest possible luggage. We left the lights of Rapallo at midnight, and as soon as we were outside the town, Olga changed her slippers, hitched up the skirts of her evening dress, and slung her violin-case on a strap over her shoulder. Then we began the slow, steep ascent of a cobbled, zig-zag mule track through the pitch-black olive terraces, losing our way, stumbling on invisible steps, and bumping into someone's silent cottage. It was a long way up, lonely and ghostly and dark, but Olga, who made that journey by herself twice a week, declared that she had long ago stopped being nervous.

Her home was the upper floor of a peasant's house, every room of which seemed to be surrounded by windows. They looked out into a huge black silence, with stars above, and festoons of lights defining the harbour below. My room had a domed ceiling, painted pink, with garlands. It was furnished with an iron bedstead covered by a patchwork quilt, a bent-wood chair with a candle on it, and a peg for clothes. As soon as it was light, I got up to see if the view was as marvellous as I expected. It was.

The house had no water-tap and no electricity, and the cooking was on charcoal. Olga preferred pine-cones, and used them with as much success and precision as most people achieve with a gas-tap. She had almost no material possessions, but her well-proportioned rooms furnished with big rectangles of sunshine had a monastic air which was highly conducive to the making of music. Her rent was seventy-five lire a month and she supported herself by the sporadic sub-letting of a charming little gondolier's house which she still owned in Venice.

Another of Ezra's artistes was a young German pianist who lived at Capri on £5 a month ; he also managed somehow to scrape together the fare to come to play at the Rapallo concerts. They all of them practised madly and I could not see any of that artistic rotting-away through non-success that seems to assail poor artistes in London and New York. Ezra obliged me to recognise that this was all happening in Fascist Italy—but I preferred to think that what made it possible was not Mussolini, but the heaven-sent climate.

To return to Toulon and the nineteen-twenties. Owing to the success of *No More Parades*, Ford and I were able on our second visit to hire a room with a bath. We were very impressed by our own affluence, for until then there had been no bath in any of the places where we had lived. This second winter, however, was less happy that the first, owing to the death of poor Juan Gris. There were no longer the old café

gatherings, and in 1927 the town seemed less gay and prosperous than in 1925, when there had been all manner of interesting passers-by. Madame Duthuit had brought her
father, Matisse, to dine with us; we had given Walter Rummel
a hasty meal between a pianoforte recital and the night express
to Paris, and on another occasion a high voice in our hotel
restaurant had startled me with, " Oh, you are Mrs. Ford,
aren't you? I've just seen Ford and we are going to dine
together." That was H. G. Wells with Madame Odette Keun,
motoring through Toulon, and we duly dined *á quatre*, Wells
and Ford sparring together as they had been in the habit of
sparring on and off during the last thirty years. All of this
was fun, and good for my education. I was learning to be a
reasonably fearless mixer.

In the spring of 1925, when we went back to Paris to
occupy our new studio, the spell of Provence lay heavily upon
us, and coloured all our hopes for the future.

It lies upon me yet. It is something to do with the light,
I suppose, and the airiness and bareness and frugality of life
in the Midi which induces a simplicity of thought, and a kind
of whittling to the bone of whatever may be the matter in
hand. Sunlight reflected from red tiled floors on to whitewashed walls, closed shutters and open windows and an air
so soft that you live equally in and out of doors, suggest an
existence so sweeetly simple that you wonder that life ever
appeared the tangled, hustling and distracting piece of nonsense you once thought it. Your mind relaxes, your thoughts
spread out and take their shape, phobias disappear, and if
passions become quicker, they also lose their powers of slow
and deadly strangulation. Reason wins. And you are released
from the necessity of owning things. There is no need to be
cosy. A pot of flowers, a strip of fabric on the wall, and your
room is furnished. Your comforts are the light and warmth

provided by nature, and your ornaments are the orange trees outside.

We broke our journey from Toulon to Paris at Tarascon, leaving Julie and Madame Annie at the little hôtel, whilst Ford and I pushed on to Carcassonne, and from there hired a ramshackle car to take us into the Montaignes Noires and also to Castelnaudary to eat the cassoulet. I remember that day well; it was at Easter, and the first heat of the year lay upon the white roads and white houses of the little town. The Hôtel de la Reine Jeanne, where the cassoulet has sat on the fire without a break for the last three hundred years, was one of those unpretentious but excellent establishments where the commercial travellers sit round a big table in the middle of the room, and private clients at small tables round the walls. The sun blazed outside the screened windows, the flies buzzed, and we partook of one of the most stupendous meals of our whole gastronomic experience. After finishing our second bottle of admirable wine, and sampling the *fine maison*, Ford said that we really ought to send p.c.'s to all our friends to commemorate the menu. He was very unwilling, however, to stir from his chair, so I said I would go in search of picture post cards. The distinctly vague feeling from which I was suffering was enhanced by the blazing emptiness of the provincial noon-day. But when I observed a shop full of antique furniture plainly marked in very low figures, I remembered that we were on our way to Paris, where an empty studio awaited us. A notice on the door of the shop said that the proprietor, *en cas d'absence*, was to be found at the café, so there I sought him, and announced that I would buy the *armoire rustique*, the grandfather clock (it was a pot-bellied thing that did not work but looked nice), the walnut knee-hole writing table, and the antique flap-desk. These come to some eight hundred francs altogether, and I then sought

Ford to obtain the cheque-book from his pocket. He was extremely sceptical about the whole transaction, and was convinced that the goods would never reach Paris—but I carried the day. Later, I discovered that I had been given no receipt, and Ford almost persuaded me that (*a*) the purchase had never taken place, and (*b*) that the shopkeeper would pocket the money and keep the goods, or that (*c*) they would take six months to arrive and there would be hundreds of francs to pay for carriage. But I had faith, and when all the things turned up in Paris safe and sound, with almost nothing to pay and looking lovely in the studio, he generously admitted that I had had good judgment, even in my cups!

CHAPTER SEVEN

The Rue Notre-Dame-des-Champs.

WE LIVED for more than a year plying backwards and forwards between the cottage at Guermantes and the Rue N.-D.-des-Champs. In the studio I at last had light and space in which to paint, and Ford had his desk and all his books in the little upper room we had constructed. We ate our meals at Lavigne's restaurant, and encountered domestic cares only at the week-end, when we relieved Madame Annie at the cottage and resumed family life with out delightful daughter. Julie was five by now, well-grown, blonde and pink, laughing perpetually, and lavishing kisses and affection upon us as soon as we made our appearance on Friday evening. What was even more consoling, was that on Monday mornings she waved us good-bye with equal equanimity, and showed no objection to being left alone for another five days with Madame Annie. This relieved us of worry on her account, but not on our own. We wanted to have her with us all the time and chafed at the lack of accommodation in the studio.

Julie never had any nursery life. She travelled with us wherever we went, ate in our restaurants and was perfectly accustomed to mixing with all our grown-up friends. She had an extraordinarily happy temperament and showed no more than a mild distaste for the dame's school at Toulon and the Sisters' school at Guermantes where she got her first rudimentary instruction. She got no serious education until she came finally to Paris and we sent her to the École Alsacienne, where she accepted the rough-and-tumble of a large co-educational day-school remarkably well for an only child.

Ford at this time was in the middle of the Tietgen's books and there was money to buy some decent Algerian rugs for the studio, and a gramophone for dancing. We were also "at home" on Thursdays, and Ford's American admirers would come early for a cup of tea, and our intimate friends would turn up later for a glass of vermouth before pushing off to a restaurant. We continued to have lovely meals with the Bradleys—cosily in winter, with steam running down the window-panes and the aroma of cooking in our nostrils, whilst in summer we sought the fresh air and greenery of the restaurants in the Parc Montsouris or the Buttes Chaumont. I never saw the Buttes by day. But at night, after traversing certain queer and quite unknown quarters of Paris, its effect of being part of a Wagnerian opera was as unexpected as it was fascinating. Great rocks rose in pinnacles above lakes and streams. Suspension bridges spanned chasms, and luscious sloping green-sward and giant trees showed aniline green by the artificial lights, which with the moon and the stars were reflected in the dark waters. Under feathery green branches, one was served with *grenouilles provençales* of a remarkable succulence, and after dinner one wandered by the Styx or mounted to Valhalla with the rest of the proletariat.

The restaurant in the Parc Montsouris was more elegant. I can remember being in the second of two taxis which were taking us there with the Bradleys and an American publisher and his wife whom they had in tow, and the publisher saying, "How happy all you people seem to be together. You like each other quite a lot don't you?" I explained that it was partly because we like the same things and also because we were all exceptionally nice people!

Another American publisher bought the first picture I

ever sold in Paris. It was a nude of the concierge's daughter and I was much heartened by the sale. When he said he would like to dine somewhere "out of the way," we ordered a special meal at the Maison Paul, and were obliged to laugh when he turned up in the sawdust-strewn bistro in white tie and tails. But he was enchanted with everything, and got the dinner of his life.

We began to meet folk with money. I felt awkward with people whose ways of living enabled them to ignore the *soucis* which governed the lives of ordinary people, who skimmed the cream and knew nothing of the dregs, and who dropped whatever bored them at a moment's notice. It was as though they belonged to a different race to whom the law of gravity did not apply, for they never came down to earth. But Ford, bitterly aware that his best suit was nothing but a poor old has-been, and that standing his share of the drinks meant that he could not have the shoes he needed, nevertheless talked the jargon of the rich as to the manner born. He presented a wonderful appearance of a bland, successful gentleman whose shabbiness was mere eccentricity and who regarded a preoccupation with the relative merits of Foyot and Larue, Vionnet and Poiret, the Ritz and the Hôtel George V, as very natural and necessary. He was not conscious of any incongruity, having had his moments of glory as well as of poverty long before I ever knew him. He was now fifty, his work was getting some recognition, and he could never tolerate that anyone might be in a position to patronise him. At the least hint of patronage, his pride would flare up, and he would metaphorically double the stakes. I found this a strain, and rather unreal, for my natural position was to remain seated firmly on the ground. This is an ungraceful attitude to assume amongst people who are not obliged to notice that the ground is there, and that it was possible to fall down upon it rather hard; people who, like Alice, float down the stairs with their fingers just touching the balustrade. But my vanity was not of the same kind as Ford's. It had to be indulged in a different way, and it drove me to insist on being more than usually down-to-earth when Ford wanted to do a little fancy window-dressing. I expect I was very tiresome. It was easy enough for me to escape Ford's feelings of humiliation at being poor and anxious and insecure, for I had never had a position to keep up, nor a reputation at stake; nor had I bound up my thoughts and feelings into publicly-printed books and offered them in the market-place.

I think that women are often unimaginative about the vulnerability of Man the Protagonist. Even in the ordinary businesses of bread-winning and love-making, his active rôle exposes him to a detached appraisal of his performance that he often finds intolerable. Masculine vanity is one of the biggest motive forces in the world, and if it suffers deflation, the result is often a moral collapse. And if this is true of ordinary people, it is much more true of the artist who exposes himself to the public in such peculiarly intimate fashion, and cannot shelter behind the idea that it is other people's fault if he is misunderstood. It is his business to make himself understood. That is what art is for.

So artists are a thin-skinned lot. Ford was no exception, and for this reason often found it necessary to disguise himself as something very splendid and successful. I was but a poor-spirited supporter of his efforts, in spite of his charming habit of urging me always to buy more and grander clothes than we could afford.

It was necessary, all the same, to come to terms with what luxury and glamour came our way. You cannot allow a lack of money to cut you off from all the experiences which the

world of pleasure has to offer, without feeling hopelessly
worsted. So you learn to walk on thick carpets with the head
held high—to concoct an appearance which gets a bow from
the flunkey at the door, and to treat the favourites of fortune
with a bluffing casualness that deceives them into thinking
that you are one of them at heart. Your poor feet are still
set shamefully upon the ground, for you have never learnt
to fly; but nobody notices, and you enjoy the party more,
perhaps, than the fairy acrobats themselves. Besides, there is
always the chance that it will turn into a real good party
with no barriers and no pretentiousness, and your own
feet off the ground at last!

Amongst parties of this sort, I remember best those given
by Bill Bullitt and his wife, Louise Bryant. Louise afterwards
changed a great deal and there were troubles and finally a
divorce, but when we first knew them they were a gay and
vital couple with a new born baby girl. They seemed terribly
rich. They would turn up in Paris—generally from somewhere in Eastern Europe—and take a house for the season.
Once it was a house of Elinor Glyn's, all decorated in mauve
taffeta and green brocade as a background for red hair. When
you sank on to a divan in an alcove, you really sank completely in, until you found yourself looking up at your own
back teeth reflected in a ceiling mirror. When we teased Bill
about the frilly-boudoir, amorous-intrigue atmosphere of
the house, he said, "I don't care, it's darned comfortable,
she's done a good job of plumbing and we took it for the
bathrooms." We were told that Elinor Glyn had gutted and
re-decorated something like eleven houses in thirteen years,
at incredible expense, and had finally landed in Hollywood
where she was doing the same thing for the movies, but in
perishable materials, which seemed more sensible.

The Bullitts had brought with them a Turkish butler of

great beauty who wore the old Imperial uniform of pale blue cloth embroidered all over in silver. They used to run into him at all the best night-clubs in Paris on his night out, somewhat to their mutual embarrassment. Not so was the butler they had when they inhabited an elegant, old-fashioned house in the Rue Lascases. This one looked like an arch-deacon and I can still see the meagre, drooping lines of his frigid old face, the chin propped up by a three-inch collar, as he cast down his eyes disapprovingly upon Louise doing acrobatics on the floor in a silver Vionnet gown, just to show everybody that she could!

Afternoon parties of a more decorous and intellectual kind were given in the Rue Jacob by Miss Nathalie Barney, who lived in a delightful old *pavillon* with tall trees and a little Greek temple in the garden. The gatherings in her drawing-room were always held in honour of one or other of the arts, and from a semi-circular alcove hung with an antique embroidery, French verse would be spoken, or modern music played. I remember four harps, and how exquisitely they looked and sounded in that setting. I also remember listening with respect to Mm. André Gide and Edmond Jaloux and Paul Valéry and admiring the sangfroid of certain lawless and exotic young American women who, rushing in where angels feared to tread, obtained an excellent response from *ces messieurs* and also from those older ladies in tailored black and excellent pearls who were without visible nationality and who seemed to me much more formidable than any *homme de lettres*.

Miss Barney herself, "l'Amazone," was not, however, unduly formidable. I was once looking down on our studio from the gallery at an evening party which had not yet got going, and wondering what I should do to warm it up. Then Ford, a tall mountain of a man whose dancing was never more than an amiable shuffle, took the floor with Miss Barney, short, plump, all in dripping white fringes, and the sight warmed the cockles of all hearts. Both had pink faces and yellow hair. Neither was young, both were stout, and gay, and completely unselfconscious. The party was launched!

Alas! there will never again be anything like the Paris of the nineteen-twenties in our life-time. Those were the days before international finance collapsed and the depression pulled us all into the mire—before the dictators had begun to threaten their neighbours and refugees to flee from their fatherland. It is difficult now to remember how completely we were without political preoccupations, but such was the world we lived in, and from England in 1940 it looks like a remote and unbelievable Heaven.

We were all ex-patriates, and very few of us earned our money in France. The rate of exchange made us richer than we should have been at home, but that was not the chief reason why we lived abroad. We lived in France because the French understood how to live far better than we did. Behind our irresponsibility was the background of French shapeliness and realism. We tried to absorb and imitate these things, and to educate ourselves in the French way of life. We were alive to all its beauty, all its excellence of craftsmanship and precision of expression. We admired the Frenchman's realism in knowing his place in the world, accepting his rôle and filling up to its outlines without going beyond, and above all we admired this quality in the Frenchwoman. The feminine rôle is so much better understood and honoured there than in England, and there is much less offensive masculine patronage to resent. Woman have so much real and actual power that the political shoe pinches less hard than it does in a country where wives have to account to their husbands for their expenditure, instead of vice versa, and where billiard-rooms and smoking-rooms and clubs are filled with able-bodied males, schoolboys in all but years, who simply don't like women very much, except when feeling amorous; and even then, they don't acknowledge their debt with very much grace.

The Frenchman not only acknowledges his debt handsomely on the amorous side of things, but he also admires a feminine quality of mind since, to some extent, he possesses it himself. Perhaps this is what makes France such a happy place to live in, psychologically; for what is more boring than the 100 per cent male? or the 100 per cent female for that matter?

The Americans and the English and the Danes and the Swedes who lived on the Left Bank in the 1920's were divers enough, bound only by their love of all things French, and their precarious dependence upon a supply of foreign currency. Some of them meant to go home, some day. But with many of us, our hopes and plans for the future were all woven thickly into the fabric of France. It was like a marriage, believed indissoluble. We did not know that we were building castles upon sand. It is true that we had to pay complicated taxes and occupy ourselves with obtaining *Cartes d'Identité* and that any foreigner could be expelled from France without an explanation, and was usually debarred from working for a wage. It is true that anyone whose papers were not in order or who had no visible means of support had to dodge any contact with the police. But on the whole, life was made very pleasant for us foreigners, if not always very easy. We brought money into France and the French saw to it that our living cost us more than it cost them. They devised a thousand ways of making us pay.

And the only refugees were the White Russians, and they had already been there for some time. They drove taxis and they ran restaurants and snack-bars. They sold their heirlooms and they made amusing things of glass, and silk and leather. They designed clothes and stage-sets and they sang haunting songs to the balalaika. They added greatly to the decorative side of life.

We began meeting them through a young couple called Ann and Carlos Drake who were running a small travel agency *de luxe* which appeared to be entirely staffed with Russian princesses. We asked these to our Friday dances.

They came and they brought their friends. They were mostly completely penniless, and they shared what they had amongst themselves quite communistically. They had lovely manners and were so gay and charming that they were a real asset to the parties. The Americans loved their titles and they themselves loved to escape for a few hours from their lowly avocations or, worse still, from their lonely idleness. There was always a row of taxis outside the studio, whose chauffeurs were dancing inside!

They had a certain song. They would collect in a corner of the room and fill an immense goblet full of drink. Then they would advance slowly, *en bloc*, singing in unison, towards their chosen victim. If it was yourself, you didn't realise what was afoot until they were quite near. There was no escape. You were surrounded and given your potion, which you were made to drink without a pause for breath, whilst the song went on.

I got the idea that the Russians are marvellous people to play with after 6 p.m., but before that they are best left alone, because they are certain to be in a Russian gloom, or in a mess.

The most brilliant Russian that I knew was a young painter called Pavlick Tchelitcheff. Several dealers and collectors already had their eye on him, and with his irregular and chancy earnings he contrived to support his invalid sister and also to send money to his aged parents in Russia.

He had a still more impecunious boy-friend living with him, and also his sister Shoura in the intervals between her banishment to various cheap and remote mountain pensions where the air was good for her lungs.

They lived in a little black hole of an apartment in the Boulevard Montparnasse and they were never for an instant free from the acutest money worries. For a Russin, Pavlick had a remarkable sense of responsibility, and laid out their meagre resources with prudence. But he was a genuinely important painter and he would have broken all ties and chucked every responsibility to the winds if his freedom to paint had been threatened. He lived—they all three lived—in a perpetual haze of nerves, emotions, far-sightedness, blindness, silliness and wisdom.

We were able to render them one small service by handing over to them our cottage at Guermantes, with a nucleus of furniture and the improvements that we had made. The rent was neglible, and we were giving it up ourselves because we had had the luck to find a tiny attic in the Rue de Vaugirard which served for Julie and Madame Annie and for domestic life in general, leaving the studio free for work and for parties. Julie was able to go to school at the École Alsacienne in the Rue d'Assas, and we ourselves gloried in the possession, at long last, of a bath tub and a gas cooker.

Whence comes the longing in one's heart for permanency? There is no justification in nature or in history for the expectation of any such a thing. It is certain that everything in life changes all the time and wisdom would appear to consist in learning to ride the change; and yet one keeps on trying to make time stand still, saying, "There! now I've got things as I like them and I'm going to make them stay put." Of course, they never do, and a whole piece of one's life is swept away with the little structure one has built.

I actually imagined that, between the attic and the studio, I had got a permanent home together at last, which would frame and shelter our family life and the deep-rooted and absorbing relationship that I had with Ford. That relationship still governed every particle of my life—except when I was actually standing at my easel—and I was so conditioned to its furtherance that I had never questioned the solidity of its structure. Nevertheless, there was a crack.

Why are people allowed—and women encouraged—to stake their lives, careers, economic position, and hopes of happiness on love? Why did not my godfathers and godmothers in my baptism, and my copybooks at school, and my mother when she tried to explain the facts of life, all tell me, "You must stand alone?" How dare parents encourage their girls to remain in a state of receptive idleness so that they may be ready, at a moment's notice, to follow the dictates of a love affair? How can the nations afford to waste the immense volume of women's energy that is left over after the emotional life has taken its toll? How dare society allow those women who don't find a partner, or who lose one, to rot away as unskilled, unwanted "superfluous women". How *dare* they use that phrase?

Every day I see dozens of middle-aged, dowdy, deprecating, slightly daft females pottering about in shops and in buses, every lineament depicting a fatal sense of inferiority. They are utterly incapable of effective independent action. I see others, more intelligent, and more embittered, who on emerging from their private world seeking independence in work find all doors closed against them. Only the girl who was trained for a job and has never stopped working has the privilege of continuing to work when she's mature.

I am not speaking merely of the money side of it, but

just of the longing to be needed and used by the community and to express one's self in a job of work.

Women are eating their hearts out, and rotting away right and left, because love and domesticity have been inadequate to fill their lives. They are sobbing on sofas by the thousand, now, at this moment. Men don't. And why? They haven't time. They are needed elsewhere. Their lives are held in shape by the framework of their vocation, and if they sometimes go to pieces inside, it hardly shows.

I am told that there is enough water-power running away in England to give us all free electricity, if the influence of vested interests did not prevent its being harnessed. I believe that woman's powers—her two eyes, her two hands, her ears and her brain—are running to waste because vested interests have got a mortgage on love. And I am not going to agree that it's woman's own fault, for not being quicker to emancipate herself. I didn't blame the Chinese women whose feet were bound up for so long. They were no more easily enslaved than others—of both sexes—are to-day. Men as well as women have shown themselves to be sheep who can be bred to any pattern, who will accept any conditions on the promise of a meagre security.

Why did not my copy-book say, "There is no security?"

The landscape of love is extravagantly rich and varied. It holds its own havens and its own battlegrounds for the enactment of its own story. The life lived therein is blindingly vivid and touches the quick both of spirit and body. But woe betide the travellers who get lost in that invisible domain and who have neglected their contacts with the outer world of fact. They discover that the passing of the trance has left them lost indeed, without identity and without hope. The landscape of love and the landscape of fact cannot possibly be made to correspond. It is ridiculous to decree that two people should keep their clothes in the same chest of drawers all their lives, because they once fell in love. Falling out of love is as delicate and important business, and as necessary to the attainment of wisdom as the reverse experience. The chest of drawers, saturated with associations, may well be the cause of an intolerable extra pang and hold up the whole process! Away with it! And away with all interlocked roots and inter-twined branches! They are enough to make any gardener give up his job in despair and leave the two plants to go on stran-gling each other.

Ford was a much larger and more luxuriant plant than I. He required to be well entwined around the support of his choice, but in due course the roving tendrils began to attach themselves to other supports, without showing any dis-position to release the first one. This created a situation which I found too difficult. It brought me into relationship with new elements which I was too tired to cope with.

Ford *was* tiring. Like most other creative artists, his personal atmosphere was always charged with a highly emo-tional egotism. He also had a genius for creating confusion and a nervous horror of having to deal with the results. I had become pretty adept at living in this atmosphere, but it was a constant strain because he never allowed me to escape from it, even for a moment. It meant being on duty twenty-four hours a day.

Millions of women know what that is like. They know that other jobs mean harder work and fewer amenities, but that none makes the same perpetual demand on one's nervous reserves.

It is true that since getting the studio I had been much better able to paint. But even when working at my easel, my head was conscious of Ford's needs and wishes and states of mind. This would not have been so if I had been bored by him, but I was not. Nobody could be. They might be exasperated and antipathetic, but never bored.

He always believed in my painting and encouraged me to go ahead. And he also made me very conscious that whereas *he* went on writing steadily through thick and thin, weal or woe, and every kind of crisis, *I* lacked the determination to stick at painting in the same way. I allowed myself to be deflected by the crisis of the moment and was always trying to set my poor house in order before getting down to work.

I don't think it ever occurred to Ford that if I had been a 100 per cent professional artist like himself I should have been very little use to him. He would say, "I can finish my book this month if you can manage that I am not worried by *anything*." That meant that no one must speak to him and no mail be shown to him until after he had finished his morning's work. Silence must be created, but he could not bear whispering. Then there were his admirers to be talked to and stage-managed and there was a great deal of waiting about until he should be ready to walk, or to eat, or whatever it might be. And when there was bad news — as for instance an expected contract falling through, or a publisher going bankrupt, or any of his multifarious negotiations with the world of letters going wrong—the air would be so filled with pain that we could neither of us do any work at all. I would far rather bear a worry alone than shared with Ford. It was easier.

He would send me on errands. "I wish you'd go and sound so-and-so about such-and-such. I don't want to do it myself, but it should be quite easy for you. You can represent me as being a Grand Panjandrum who can't be approached personally." I never believed in the usefulness of these schemes and was a quite unsuitable emissary. I was both too timid and too downright.

Ford thought that I was hopelessly puritanical—not to say provincial—in my liking for factual truth. I had always admired the saying, "Things are what they are, and the consequences will be what they must be. Why should we seek to be deceived?" But Ford could take a fact, any fact, and make it disappear like a conjuror with a card. All his art was built on his temperamental sensitiveness to atmosphere, to the angle from which you looked, to relative, never absolute values. When he said, "It is necessary to be precise," I used to think that he meant—precisely truthful. Of course, what he really meant was that you must use precision in order to create an effect of authenticity, whatever the subject of your utterance, in the same way as the precision of a brush-stroke gives authenticity to an image on canvas, and need have no relation to anything seen in fact. Words to Ford were simply the material of his art, and he never used them in any other way. This created confusion in his everyday life, for words are not like dabs of paint. They are less innocent, being the current coin in use in daily life.

Poor Ford! His own kind of truth was something that he lived in his life, in his tremendous humanity, his taste for all things living and growing and modest and un-selfconscious, and his knowledge of the aches and pains of the human heart. It was not in any logical viewpoint, but the vivid and poignant images which he could create, and which carried their own conviction, having the stuff of life inherent in them. Precise and effective he could be. Pronounce upon matters of fact, he could not.

And why should he? There are plenty of efficient little clerks running about with busy measuring tapes. And when the fact is past and forgotten—an object once seen from a railway train—the image that it helped to inspire remains, bright and living.

And Ford's images build up into a harmonious and authentic picture—the picture of his idea of the good life; a life of frugality, of modest individualism, of trustfulness and gaiety and goodwill, unregimented, local, unambitious but full of savour, the kind of life that the Fascists of the world are now destroying; the kind of life that he found in Provence.

So he had a message, after all, that was important. And his devotion to everything that was excellent in literature was important, too. He had a real, consuming passion for letters, and this was the mainspring of his life.

I don't think his personal relationships were important at all. They always loomed very large in his own view, but they were not intrinsically important. I don't think it matters much from whom the artist gets his nourishment, or his shelter, so long as he gets it.

In order to keep his machinery running, he requires to exercise his sentimental talents from time to time upon a new object. It keeps him young. It refreshes his ego. It restores his belief in his powers. And who shall say that this type of lubrication is too expensive for so fine a machine? Goodness knows, female devotion is always a drug on the market!

I happened to be the "new object" at a moment when Ford needed to be given a new lease of after-the-war life. The new life was a success. For the whole nine years of its duration, we were never bored and I don't think anyone ever heard us utter an angry word. Even when we were on the brink of separating, we could still go out to dine together and have a grand argument about Lost Causes, or the Theory of the Infallibility of the Pope, or some such theme. But by that time our real relationship had become quite a different thing from what it had once been, and my education had received a big shove forward.

Four years before this, Ford had fallen in love with a very pretty and gifted young woman. He had got over it in due course, but the affair had taught me many new things. It cut the fundamental tie between himself and me, and it showed me a side of life of which I had had no previous knowledge. The girl was a really tragic person. She had written an unpublishably sordid novel of great sensitiveness and persuasiveness, but her gift for prose and her personal attractiveness were not enough to ensure her any reasonable life, for on the other side of the balance were bad health, destitution, shattered nerves, an undesirable husband, lack of nationality, and a complete absence of any desire for independence. When we met her she possessed nothing but a cardboard suit-case and the astonishing manuscript. She was down to her last three francs and she was sick.

She lived with us for many weeks whilst we tried to set her on her feet. Ford gave her invaluable help with her writing, and I tried to help her with her clothes. I was singularly slow in discovering that she and Ford were in love. We finally got her a job to "ghost" a book for someone on the Riviera.

She had a needle-quick intelligence and a good sort of emotional honesty, but she was a doomed soul, violent and demoralised. She had neither the wish nor the capacity to tackle practical difficulties. She nearly sank our ship!

She took the lid off the world that she knew, and showed us an underworld of darkness and disorder, where officialdom, the bourgeoisie and the police were the eternal enemies and the fugitive the only hero. All the virtues, in her view, were summed up in "being a sport," which meant being willing to take risks and show gallantry and share one's last crust; more attractive qualities, no doubt, than patience or honesty or fortitude. She regarded the law as the instrument of the "haves" against the "have nots" and was well acquainted with every rung of that long and dismal ladder by which the respectable citizen descends towards degradation.

It was not her fault that she knew these things, and the cynicism they engendered had an unanswerable logic in it. It taught me that the only really unbridgeable gulf in human society is between the financially solvent and the destitute. You can't have self-respect without money. You can't even have the luxury of a personality. To expect people who are destitute to be governed by any considerations whatever except money considerations is just hypocrisy. If they show any generous instincts as well, it is more than society has any right to expect.

Ford's girl was by no means without generous instincts, and her world had its own standards of *chic*. What I did not then realise was that this world, which has since found an impressive literature in the works of writers like Céline and Henry Miller, stood often for a rather feeble and egotistical kind of anarchism without any of the genuine revolutionary spirit which would seem to be the logical outcome of reflective destitution.

Life with Ford had always felt to me pretty insecure. Yet here I was cast for the role of the fortunate wife who held all the cards, and the girl for that of the poor, brave and desperate beggar who was doomed to be let down by the bourgeoisie. I learnt what a powerful weapon lies in weakness and pathos and how strong is the position of the person who has nothing to lose, and I simply hated my rôle! I played it, however, until the girl was restored to health and her job materialised, since we appeared to represent her last chance of survival. But it was not here that the shoe pinched most.

The obvious and banal business of remaining in love with someone who has fallen for someone else is anybody's experience and no one will deny that it hurts, or that it creates an essential change in the original relationship, however well it may afterwards appear to have been mended. And to be suddenly called upon to change one kind of relationship into another is rather like changing boats in midstream—a difficult operation, though not necessarily impossible.

To realise that there can be no such thing as "belonging" to another person (for in the last resort you must be responsible for yourself, just as you must prepare to die alone), is surely a necessary part of an adult's education! How trite it sounds, how not worth mentioning. But what a discovery it makes!

After being quite excruciatingly unhappy for some weeks, I found on a certain day, at a certain hour, that for the first time, I was very tired—not to say bored—with personal emotions, my own no less than Ford's. This feeling recurred with greater and greater frequency, until it became perpetual.

I think that the exhilaration of falling out of love is not sufficiently extolled. The escape from the atmosphere of a stuffy room into the fresh night air, with the sky as the limit. The feeling of freedom, of integrity, of being a blissfully unimportant item in an impersonal world, whose vicissitudes are not worth a tear. The feeling of being a queen in your own right! It is a true re-birth.

The eventual waning of Ford's attachment to his girl had its distressing side. A man seldom shows to advantage when trying to get rid of a woman who has become an incubus. When Ford had disengaged himself from what he called "this entanglement," he announced that having weathered the "pic de tempète" nothing could ever upset us again. But of course he was wrong. The desire for freedom was already beginning to work in me, and what he really needed was another mate.

During the winter of 1926-7, and also the following winter, Ford made two visits to America, the first to lecture, and the second to straighten out a tangle with his publishers. He had a great personal success and was feted and flattered as indeed he deserved to be. For me, these periods alone in Paris served as dress-rehearsals for the time when I should be permanently alone.

After the second trip, Ford announced a sentimental attachment to an American lady whom he proposed to visit every year. He thought that our Paris ménage could go on just the same in between-whiles, but I did not. I wanted to belong to myself. I wanted to slip from under the weightiness of Ford's personality and regain my own shape.

So, with Ford's consent, I went to see a lawyer. . . .

Julie was now seven. I told her, after Ford had finally left for America, "Il ne sera plus mon mari. Mais il sera toujours ton père. Alors il n'y a rien changé pour toi." She did not appear to be in the least perturbed, since I had agreed with Ford that he should return from time to time and see her in a second attic in the Rue de Vaugirard which I had taken and fixed up as an independent study for him during his previous absence. It was, indeed, a separate, if tiny, *appartement*.

I imagined that facing Paris without Ford was going to be full of difficulties. There were none. I felt chilly and forlorn at one moment and like a million dollars the next.

I went to stay at Bandol with Jenny Bradley. It was the first time I had been in the south without Ford and I remember very well feeling that I loved it more than ever and that it had now become my own.

I also paid a visit at Antibes, and from there went along the coast to see what Pavlick Tchelitcheff was doing at Monte Carlo. He had been given a ballet to design by Diaghilieff, which, if approved of, would be included in the Paris and

London seasons. In May, Monte Carlo was filled with members of the ballet. Scene-painters, costume-makers, designers, orchestra, electricians and technicians of all sorts were working for it, for each year the Prince of Monaco placed the Théâtre du Casino and all its staff at Diaghilieff's disposal. Dancers were practising, artists were painting their back-cloths and composers were rehearsing their score with the orchestra.

Pavlick's décor was not to be painted. It was to consist of a cinema projection of pale geometric shapes on a misty blue ground, moving in time with the music. The cameraman, the electrician, Pavlick and the composer were working day and night to get the timing right and the lighting. Of course, they said, we are young, we have ideas, and *le père* Diaghilieff is nothing but a stupid old man who battens on *la jeunesse*. It appeared that he had taken to his bed and removed his false teeth, which was a very bad sign, and it was considered that he would be quite incapable of appreciating the pearls that were about to be cast before him.

Nevertheless, the young men were extremely chastened, not to say nervous, when he arose from his bed and demanded to be shown the results of their work, in the theatre. I was allowed to sit at the back of the elegant, darkened little auditorium on a sunny afternoon, and watch Diaghilieff waddle in, smothered in rugs and coats, and sit impassively before the curtain whilst Pavlick poured excited explanations into his inattentive ear. After the costumes and the cinema projection had been shown, the old man still said not a word, but rose slowly to has feet and gathered his wraps around him. He then precipitated himself silently upon Pavlick's bosom and embraced him on both cheeks and we knew that everything was all right. Everybody felicitated everybody else and Pavlick and I and the composer took Serge Lifar to a tea-shop and fed him with all the cream-cakes that Diaghilieff did not allow him to have. And, "Il n'est pas bête, quand même, le père Diaghilieff," the young men said.

At that time, Pavlick owed a good deal to Gertrude Stein's patronage. They may have quarrelled since, but in those early days, when he was so poor and his sister so ill, she certainly helped matters by passing round the word that he was "worth watching." "He *knows* he can paint," she said, "and he knows what he wants to do."

I knew that Gertrude Stein was a great puller of strings and a great arbiter of artistic fashions with a taste for intrigue, and I knew that she was considered very formidable. But during the period in which I was encouraged to "drop in after dinner," I never saw her in action because when I went round it was just for a spot of cosy low-brow conversation. She and Alice B. Toklas and I would sit beneath the Picassos and the rest of the collection and discuss methods of dealing with one's concierge, or where to buy linen for sheets, or how to enjoy French provincial life, or how I could best get rid of Madame Annie.

She once wrote a little book called *As a Wife With a Cow*, which she sent round to the Rue Vaugirard with a dedication to Julie to which Juan Gris (who had done the illustrations) had added words of his own. I hastened to thank her, with a bunch of black tulips, but spoilt everything by failing to recognise an incident in the book concerning some pink cakes, of which Julie had been the heroine, at one of her tea-parties. I had never read a word she wrote.

She was charming to Julie and sent her a pail of ice-cream when she had her tonsils out, and a gold-embroidered eastern head-piece full of chocolates on her birthday. You would have said that she was just a dear old Auntie with a taste for plain speech. But, of course, she was nothing of the sort. She was a very great careerist, skilfully stage-managed by Alice Toklas.

It was she who produced Edith Sitwell. "I've got an Englishwoman for Pavlick to paint," she told me, and whilst the portrait was in progress, murmurings began to emanate from the Tchelitcheff ménage about the "*grande poète Anglaise*" who was so tall, so gracious and so "*vraiement extraordinaire.*" It was evident that she was making a terrific impression, not only on Pavlick and Shoura and Allen, but on all the rest of the Russians and Americans who drifted in and out of that cramped little flat which sheltered so much life and talent. "You must meet her. Absolutely. I tell her all about you." And so a lunch was arranged at Lavigne's.

I think the most extraordinary thing about Edith Sitwell is the big gap that exists between her quite wonderful but alarming façade and the soft and flagrantly human woman whom it conceals. The English aristocrat, six feet tall, aquiline, haughty, dressed in long robes and wearing barbaric ornaments, was a strange sight in happy-go-lucky Montparnasse. But the sweet voice, the almost exaggerated courtesy and the extreme sensitiveness to other people's feelings, were so immediately winning that we all took her to our hearts at once.

It really was a matter of taking her to the heart. There was a great deal of affection all round and she became the good angel of the Tchelitcheff ménage and a close friend of mine. And in spite of the fact that each of them has the temperament of a Prima Donna, she and Pavlick have maintained an intimate, if somewhat stormy friendship, ever since.

Pavlick could not read a word of English but he understood very well the shape and the quality of Edith's poetry. "*Je comprends ce qu'elle veut faire.*" And although she didn't see why Pavlick should want to paint her without a mouth, or model her in patches of brown wax on a netted wire frame, nevertheless she admired his genius so sincerely that she and her brother Osbert gave themselves a great deal of trouble to get him successfully launched in London. But that came later.

In Montparnasse, we scolded her for having brought across the channel the prejudices of an English gentlewoman. Pavlick would tell her that an artist had no business to be a lady. I would tell her that no one was going to behave as well as she expected them to and that she had better resign herself. She was very sweet about it, but from time to time her native arrogance would assert itself against some unfortunate offender. "I think he must be taught a lesson," she'd say and the lesson would be administered with the alarming façade and the deadly wit in full operation. No one could have guessed at the vulnerability concealed behind that mighty shield and buckler.

Pavlick in his way was fragile too. Indeed, they were each of them a packet of nerves, infusing therefrom a palpitating and sensuous life into their respective work. The shape and texture of Edith's words were like surfaces felt with the fingertips, and Pavlick's sombre paintings had the organic, breathing kind of life, stilled but vital, of a fish whose gills are just kept moving.

He had never studied in an art school. He would come round to my studio and scold me roundly and brilliantly for all my painting faults, and then say, "Brown; how do you get that colour? I don't know anything about it." He painted in greys for a whole year, then in greens, then in blues. "Some day," he said, "I shall dare to paint a tree."

Well, he has become fashionable now, and famous. Last time I saw him he was housed *en prince* in the London home of a rich patron of the arts who had placed a studio at his disposal, and he was putting the finishing touches to an immense canvas, "Phenomena," before its sensational exhibition at Tooth's in Bond Street. Princesses were inviting him to go

sailing on the Adriatic, the Ballets Russes were begging him
to do a décor for Covent Garden, dealers and hostesses were
clamouring, but Pavlick, unshaven and paint-stained and
labouring in his old stripy blouse was precisely as he had
always been, distracted yet concentrated, fussy, unmanageable
and capricious; deadly intelligent and at the same time
wildly irrational. He had the mournful eyes, mischievous
grin and nervous gesticulations of old days, but when he
shaved himself and put on his beautiful London tailor-made
and went downstairs to greet the world he assumed an authority that was new. He had also acquired a picturesque command of the English tongue that was all his own and that
London found enchanting. His caprices had become the
idiocyncracies of the master and even the friends of his youth
had become duly respectful. But I don't suppose he had the
smallest sensation of security. He was always peculiarly aware
of the cold winds that blow around the heads of people who
have to sing for their supper, and I could not help being reminded of those tight-rope dancers whom he loved to paint.

In Paris, I was under the happy necessity of crossing the
Luxembourg Gardens each day between the Rue de Vaugirard
and my studio. I would go back to the flat for lunch, and
Julie would often come to tea with me in the studio after
school.

Working conditions were perfect. Still full of enthusiasm
for the early Italian paintings I had seen long ago with
Dorothy Pound, I had embarked on a tryptych of the proprietor and personnel of the restaurant "Nègre de Toulouse"
where I had eaten so many happy meals. This was a perfectly
formal pattern done on a gold background with M. and Mme.
Lavigne in the middle surrounded by appropriate decorations
and the waitresses grouped at the sides like a chorus of angels.

They all went to see themselves at the private view of the Salon d'Automne where the picture was spotted by an Australian journalist who asked for an interview and gave me a big write-up in the Australian press, to the astonishment of my Adelaide cousins. I had seen nobody from Adelaide since my brother Tom sailed back there after the war, and I had written no letters, except a yearly budget to him. It must have been sixteen years after I had left home when I received a message that three of my cousins were passing through Paris on a Cook's Tour, and I was quite touched when they expressed a wish to visit my studio. I told myself that of course they would be unrecognisable—that I myself would be quite unrecognisable to them—that in sixteen years I had transformed myself completely, and that I must remember that the same years had passed over their own heads. I desired to impress them, and to counteract their probable view of me as a queer bohemian, so I invited Edith Sitwell to come and help me do it.

She did not come alone. "My dear Stella," she said, "I find that Georgia and my brother Sacheverell have long desired to call upon you and I thought that to-day would be a good occasion."

Now the Sitwells are all about nine feet high and of extremely haughty mien, and Mrs. Sachie is a glamour girl straight out of Vogue, so I felt that the impressiveness was perhaps overdone, and I began to feel rather mean. I said to myself, when there's a knock on the door, I must open it with a smile of welcome, even if the cousins look completely strange. The knock came and I opened the door to the identical figures—in no way changed—that I had left behind in 1914, except that there was now a large additional son.

They were (momentarily) taken aback by the Sitwells, which was excusable, but also quite unimpressed by any-

thing so alien to their lives and interests. I need not have
bothered!

I had a cosy time with them and got the impression that
Australia was the one thing that remained the same in a
changing world. It was rather comforting!

But later, when two young painters turned up in London
with an introduction from Adelaide, my heart sank at the
prospect of having to find a common ground on which to
talk about art. I feared they would ask me to take them to
the Academy and would want to know what I really thought
about "all this modern stuff." Instead, it was they who put
me through my paces concerning the entire course of European
painting since the war. There was no name in modern art,
however obscure, with which they were unfamiliar, and no
reputation whose growth they had not followed with attention.
And it had all been done by dint of enthusiastic reading and
the study of reproductions. I was abashed when I remembered
my own awful ignorance when I first arrived in Europe, and
have thus become quite confused in my idea of the Australia
of to-day.

In the studio at N.-D.-des-Champs I had a very handsome
coal-box. It was an old inlaid chest which I had discovered
in a peasant's barn at Guermantes and it stood under a big
mirror at the end of the room. Edith spent a great many
hours seated thereon whilst I did her portrait. She was a lovely
subject for a painter and gave me all the sittings I wanted.
We talked hard all the time and when the picture was finished
we knew each other very well indeed. Then I invited a party
to meet her and she had to sit on the coal-box again because
it was the nearest approach to a throne that I could manage.

Just then Ezra turned up in Paris so, of course, I invited
him to the party too. I did not know how the two star turns
would get on in the same arena, but the studio was large and

Edith said that Ezra was a great poet, so all was well. Ezra held his own court on the model-throne, whilst I led Edith's admirers to the coal-box one by one. I had just left Genevieve Taggard standing in front of her when someone pointed out that the latter's petticoat was falling off. I had never met Genevieve Taggard before, but I put my arm right round her and led her lovingly and carefully to the balcony door nearby. Once outside, we removed the petticoat in full view of the street (very preferable to the full view of the studio) and after hiding it in the dog's kennel, returned nonchalantly to the party.

George Seldes was always my barman on these occasions. When the time came to change from a tea-party into a cocktail party he got very busy and worked devotedly at the drinks for as many hours as people cared to stay. Most people knew better than to make a dinner-date when they were coming to my place for tea. They could get food at the Coupole at any hour.

Sometimes Edith would herself invite people to the studio. We had a supper there, for her friends, after the first performance in Paris of *Façade*, where her verses were spoken through a megaphone to William Walton's music. Cecil Beaton came, and Constant Lambert and Walton himself and of course the Tchelitcheffs and several lovely ladies. On another occasion we decided that she ought to give a poetry reading, and for that we had an evening party and I had to hire a lot of little gilt chairs. Pavlick had designed some clothes for her and her appearance in a full-skirted red velvet gown with large renaissance ornaments was really splendid. Indeed, the whole occasion was quite impressive, and I found myself entertaining a great many handsome strangers. A very polite party.

A much less polite party was the one when the Bradleys

asked if Claude Mackay might bring the Black Birds round after their performance at the theatre. Claude Mackay was a negro writer and a friend of the Bradleys who thought that many of their Paris friends would love to meet the Black Birds, but they themselves lived in a very bourgeois house on the Ile Saint Louis where noise after midnight would have been unthinkable. In my studio, on the contrary, I had only to keep quiet until the art school downstairs went home at five o'clock. After that I could do as I liked.

So I invited some of my friends and the Bradleys invited theirs. Stiff French ladies in black and gentlemen with goatee beards and ribbons in their buttonholes, the like of which had never before been seen in those shabby purlieus, sat around on my divans and refused to be comforted. I thought that nothing would melt them; but I reckoned without the Black Birds. They arrived soon after midnight, black, brown and golden, some with their mammies, and all so bursting with life and gaiety, that you would never guess that they had just come off the stage after a strenuous three-hour show. They couldn't keep still and they couldn't keep quiet and you should just have seen the French folk melting like wax in the sun! All the ladies wanted to dance with Snaky-hips, the blackest and slenderest of them all, whose performance at the theatre resembled that of a miraculous marionette to whom the ordinary laws of gravity did not apply. But Snaky-hips was not there. Adelaide Hall was there and the tap-dancer with the wooden leg and all the others, but Snaky-hips, they said, was not refined—and so they had not told him about the party. Nor the pianist. Of course, there was another pianist (we had hired a piano) and those ecstatic negroes began doing their whole show over again in the centre of a tight-packed semi-circle round the piano. In the middle of "I can't give you Anything but Love, Baby," in walked the slippery and sinuous Snaky-hips and his friend, to the joy of all the Europeans. After that everybody danced together and was very happy indeed.

And then, suddenly, it became frightening. There came a thunderstorm, and the lightning flashing through the great windows and skylights and the thunder crashing into the rhythm of the music whipped everybody to excitement, and the rhythm became even more tremendous. Negroes don't dance like ordinary folk. I had had crowds of people shuffling round the studio many times before and an architect had said that the floor was solid enough for ordinary parties. But it was a jerry-built place and the studio below us was twenty feet high and our immense floor was unsupported. When those negroes really got going, it began to heave and bounce like a spring mattress, and quite suddenly I found that several of us were creeping towards the walls and casting scared eyes upon the big old stove, which was roaring its head off, with red-hot sides. What a crash that would have made!

Of course it all subsided safely. The storm died down and the people got tired. At dawn, the pianist with a girl across his knees was banging the piano and the girl with impartial regularity, and at six, it was time for breakfast at the Coupole.

That was almost the end of the good old times. I can remember one more party, just before the summer holidays of 1929. I had invited half a dozen Americans to dinner at the studio on the fourteenth of July, and since there was no kitchen it had to be a cold meal. I set the table in the middle of the room with candles and soup and cold chicken and salad, and after that there were raspberries and cream. Katie and Willie Seabrook were in the party, and an American Judge, and John Goss the singer. When it began to get dusk, I lit the candles, and when the chickens were finished, I fetched the great platter of raspberries. I perceived to my horror that these were permeated with those little white grub to which raspberries are prone and I had nothing else to offer, not even a bite of cheese. So I hastily blew out the candles. "It looks so much more romantic in the dusk, don't you think, with the sky such a wonderful blue?" And I smothered the raspberries heavily with cream, and everybody said they were the most delicious they had ever tasted.

After supper (it was a very hot night) John Goss took off his shirt and sang "Randall my Son," so affectingly that Willie Seabrook went out and cried on the balcony. Then we sallied forth and joined in the dancing on the street.

Hard times were drawing near. Ford had come back from America—alone—and had re-installed himself in his own little *appartement* in the Rue de Vaugirard. We found him there when we returned from our summer holdiay and at the same time I was told that the Academy Delecluse, which contained my belovéd studio, was scheduled for demolition. It became evident that I must find another home—a *studio-appartement* where Julie and I could live and work and where a *gouvernante* would no longer be necessary. It would then be possible for me to hand over our old *appartement* in the Rue de Vaugirard to Ford, who besides being very hard-up, was inadequately lodged.

I turned once again to the business of flat-hunting with a leaden heart. The first three years of my life in Paris had been poisoned by the lack of a proper home and now it was to start all over again. Only this time I was alone.

I had £400 of free capital left, which though likely to become quickly diminished by current expenditure, would, I judged, see me settled into a new flat, if I could find one. Once there, I must at all costs manage to earn money by my painting. I must get commissions for portraits, and I must have an exhibition. Playtime was clearly over.

But what a good playtime it had been! The tall roof of the studio in the Rue N.-D.-des-Champs had been filled with the fluttering of little birds (*becs-de-corail* they were called, and they obediently re-entered their cage on the wall at feeding time) and at Christmas there had always been a great tree which nearly touched the roof, in which they had loved to perch amongst the tinsel and the shining gew-gaws. The Christmas tree would be bought on the quai, and brought home in a taxi with its top reaching far out behind and sweeping the street in great circles as we turned the corners. The chauffeur and the concierge and the rest of us would carry it up the stairs and lay it on the floor. Then we would fasten the big star on to its topmost spike and fix the ends of the long tinsel garlands, before hoisting it into position. Every year I bought more and more ornaments and on Chirstmas Eve half a dozen of us would spend an ecstatic afternoon with Julie, doing the decorations. I can remember Pavlick, more serious and concentrated than any child, stepping backwards and announcing critically, "Il faut un peu plus de mystère à gauche." He would then proceed to create the *mystère*, with *cheveux d'ange*, silver snow, fairy lights and a little ballet-dancer doll on an elastic who pranced every time the old floor shook. Then we had a crêche. An American called Bill Widney modelled charming little figures in coloured wax of all the personnel, and we made a ruined cowshed out of sticks and felt, and with a mirror, we directed a beam of light through a hole in the roof, which fell straight upon *le Petit Jésus* on his spun-silk straw. Some twigs provided a group of trees and the background was a paper cyclorama on which Pavlick painted a blue night sky with gold stars pasted on and "in peu plus de mystère" done with gold dust. It all went into a large gilt picture-frame.

The père Noël always arrived by the roof and entered via

the balcony. The children of our friends and of all the *concierge's* and *femmes de menage* with whom we had ever been connected would be seated around the lighted tree with their backs to the balcony, until the Père Noël cracked his whip, and they looked round and discovered him gazing benevolently down upon the scene and preparing to descend the stairs with a sackful of presents for everybody. He always praised the tree and he always wore the same beautiful red gown and fur-bordered hood and fuzzy white beard, but whereas in Ford's day he would be tall and soft-voiced, in later times he might just as easily be short or he might be loud of speech, so that one Boxing Day Julie addressed me thus: "Mummie, dites-moi, est-ce que c'est *vraiment* le Père Noël qui vient, ou est-ce que c'est bien un de tes amis en travesti?" To which I replied, that unfortunately the Père Noël was so fearfully busy at Christmas that we could never be sure whether he would have time to come himself to every party, so we always had to have an understudy ready, in order not to disappoint the children. . . .

CHAPTER EIGHT

The Rue Boissonnade

AFTER WEEKS of tramping the streets in search of a new home, I at last found a large and a small studio to rent as one *appartement* in the Rue Boissonnade. They were tied up with more than the usual demands for *reprises, pas de porte*, etc. etc., and they were shabby, inconvenient, and in dire need of money to be spent to make them habitable.

I ought never to have considered taking them, but I was desperate. I still thought that my pleasant Paris life could be salvaged, if I could work and sleep in the same *appartement* and look after Julie with the aid of a *bonne* to replace the *gouvernante* and *femme de ménage*. Above all I wanted to get out of the Rue Vaugirard so that Ford could re-occupy my little flat there, instead of his own small attic on the other side of the landing.

I must have been one of the last of the thousands of foreigners to be despoiled in a big way by a French landlord. The depression which presently engulfed us all soon brought the artificially high rents tumbling down—but not until after I had signed a six year lease at a price which bore no relation to the legal rent, paid an enormous *reprise* to the out-going tenant, and undertaken extensive repairs and alterations which a cynical architect had assured me would cost less than half the amount that I was eventually made to pay. A deposit of six months rent over and above the first term due was demanded, also a large fee for the drawing up of the lease. I

obtained the lease with difficulty, for the landlord would
have preferred a three-monthly contract by which he could
have given me notice to quit at any time without compen-
sation. When I refused these terms, the *gerant* screamed and
shouted at me as though I were making a criminal suggestion.
He had also been screaming and shouting at the other poor
frightened tenants who had come to see him that morning,
as I had very well heard from the waiting room. That was
what he was paid to do—to "protect the interests" of landlords
who were honourable gentlemen and did not care to do their
own dirty work.

There is nothing much harsher or better versed in sharp
practice than a French *homme d'affaires*. I was no match for
him, and was even induced to undertake outside repairs that
were legally the landlord's affair. I was naturally very troubled
and frightened by the whole business, and by the size of the
committments I had undertaken, and I am now heartily
ashamed of my lack of business acumen. But the bit was
between my teeth and the determination to achieve a permanent and suitable dwelling had become an obsession. It
was to symbolise the new independent life I was building out
of the ashes of my life with Ford and provide the necessary
background for an ordered existence. Besides, if I was to obtain
portrait commissions, a studio was a necessity. And Montparnasse was still full of people who had been living in *hôtels
meublés* for years whilst waiting to find one. I still had £125
a year from untouchable capital in Australia. If I could have
foreseen that the various exchange rates would collapse and that
this would presently buy only half as many francs as formerly;
if I had known that poor Ford's publishing affairs would go
from bad to worse, and that presently Paris would become
emptied of its ruined Americans and with them would go
all my chances of selling portraits; if someone had told me

that my beautiful studio into which I proposed to pour all my available resources and more would presently be un-lettable at any price, I should no doubt have packed myself and Julie back to England then and there. It would have broken my heart, and Ford would never have forgiven me for taking Julie away from Paris. But it would have removed us from the menace of exchange fluctuations and the hope-lessness of being a foreigner trying to earn money in France.

But I could not know what was coming and in conse-quence we had over three more years in my adored Paris—three years of ever-increasing worry, but also of lovely moments and happy friendships and of progress in my painting.

I did one very sensible thing. In converting the studios I arranged that they should be capable of being divided into two separate *appartements*. So when the rascally architect presented me with bills amounting to 250 per cent of his "approximate estimate" (which he had assured me would prove correct to within 10 per cent—a statement which turned out to have no legal significance whatever) and I was faced with a supplementary debt of £200 which I had no means of paying, I was able to sub-let the smaller studio, furnished, at a profit. I had put in a bath-tub and a gallery, and there was a kitchen and a separate front-door opposite mine. My tenant was Katherine Johnson of *Vogue*, and she was a perfect neighbour and became a dear friend. I used to provide her with meals and service, and the arrangement was excellent for me both financially and socially and gave me the pleasantest company on lonely evenings. Sometimes we would throw a party together and open up the whole place, and sometimes we entertained separately.

The studio where Julie and I lived was the nicest home we ever had. It was lofty and well-lighted and Julie's tiny be-flowered bedroom, with a huge window and a small balcony, led straight into it. Above was the erstwhile loft, now my sleeping quarters and reached by a gallery into which I had put a bath-tub. Fortunately it was quite possible to take a bath without being seen from the studio!

My bedroom was nothing but the inside of the centre gable of the main building, and it had sloping sides like a tent, and a little window right on the floor which was exceedingly dangerous until I had some bars fixed. I dressed up this window like a Victorian mantelpiece—such being its position and dimensions—and put a shelf above with rounded corners and fitted it with a fringed mantel-border of crimson damask, and tasselled curtains to match. On the "mantelpiece" stood a large artificial bouquet under a glass dome, flanked with ornaments made of shells and a couple of flamboyant candle-brackets. Above, in the peak of the roof, hung a horseshoe-shaped painting of a sentimental landscape surrounded by a beautiful border, which must once have adorned the outside of a shoeing forge, and which with the rest of the ornaments I had found in the *marché aux puces*. In the middle of the roof there hung a contraption arranged by Pavlick of shining red and gold globes, representing a bunch of grapes and lit from within with multi-coloured electric bulbs from the Christmas tree. Red damask covered the divan and the dim green of the walls was repeated in the satin stripes of two exquisitely ridiculous Victorian chairs, low, tufted, armless and heavily fringed, which Jenny Bradley had unearthed for me and which added much to the gaiety of the small scene.

But although this little attic was arranged as a joke and filled with all sorts of shining bits of nonsense, I myself took a keen secret pleasure in its old-fashioned look which seemed to stand for safety and permanence and a comforting sense of familiar things used and understood. I had also bought an immense mahogany chest of drawers with a marble top at a junk shop—a really solid and worthy piece of furniture which gave me a lively confidence in myself as an established citizen—a feeling I had never before enjoyed.

To-day that chest of drawers stands beside me in a Tudor cottage on the coast of Essex. This roof slopes just as steeply as that other, and this dormer window is also nearly on the floor. The black oak beams set sturdily into the walls and the ancient bricks of the lovely chimney-piece would seem to hold an even greater promise of permanence than the chest of drawers, or the heavy oak table that must be as old as the cottage. Yet as I look down over the red and white roses on the porch to the neat rows of vegetables that I have planted in the garden, I am wondering how soon we are going to be invaded by the German hordes—how soon the chest of drawers and all the rest will have to be abandoned, and homelessness begin all over again.

From here, in the gathering darkness, the studio in the Rue Boissonnade looks like a distant but brilliant peep-show, framed in black. It has the precision and the homeliness of a Dutch interior. Its faint yellowish walls and warm grey paint are the colours of sunshine and shadow on a plaster wall. Beneath the skylight there runs a gathered white awning which catches the sun and creates a shadowless radiance all over the tall room. The big stove has little mica windows all round, like a lighthouse. The books are set into a wide recess and the old coal chest is still there with the big mirror above, and the same low divans invite conversation. But there is no room for the model-throne, so I have a tall chair to perch my sitters on.

I was once painting a highly decorative person called Jean Wright (now Mrs. Carl Van Doren) who was sitting on this chair in a great fox fur out of which her long neck rose with excellent effect. Suddenly behind her I saw our cat, crouched far above on the gallery railing, eyeing the fur with a strange intensity. Before I could shout a warning, the animal had leapt through the air and landed violently on the back of Jean's neck, inflicting two enormous scratches. Jean's sangfroid was impressive. She neither flinched, nor dropped her cigarette. She just said, "I suppose this *is* a cat?"

I got other portraits to do. An Australian who wanted to send her picture to her fiancé—a girl-writer who wanted one for her old home in Virginia, the wife of a rich tourist, and various children whom Julie learned to keep distracted by working her little model theatre just in the spot where I wished them to look. The lawyer who was trying to extricate me from the toils of the wicked architect allowed me to settle my account with him by painting a friend of his, and I traded another picture with a tailor for a good spring overcoat.

I painted Edith Sitwell's extravagant hands with their huge Victorian ornaments holding the African mask from Timbuctoo that Willie Seabrook had brought me. I painted various interiors, which always turned out to be pictures of windows. I loved painting windows and I loved painting hands. I daresay Mr. Freud would have seen some peculiar significance in this, though I have no idea what it might be.

The depression was well upon us by now. It was evident that the time had come for me to hold an exhibition, though I was warned that no one was buying pictures any more. Nevertheless I arranged for a show in a gallery in the Rue de Seine for the spring of 1931 and set about working for it. Then Julie caught the measles and when she was recovering, I went down with it too. Never having had this ridiculous complaint in childhood, I took the precaution of laying in an extra stock of the necessary medicines, etc., and set everything in order for my own possible retirement. On my first day

of fever, the boiler burst in the kitchen. A heavy-handed old
ignoramus came for an hour each morning to look after me.
She wore a nurse's uniform, but considered that any ablutions
would be most dangerous and confined herself to giving me
injections to stimulate the heart, which it did not require,
but which bruised my poor limbs dreadfully. There is nothing
like a high fever for making you feel degraded, especially
when you are in debt and are trying to work for an exhibition
and are anyhow quite unaccustomed to being ill at all.

One day when the stiff mask of my face seemed softer and
more normal, I asked for a mirror. What I saw was an immense round disc of fiery red with two little eyes embedded
in the middle like currants in a bun. When I expressed my
horror at this apparition, the nurse said: "But oh, Madame,
ça va beaucoup mieux maintenant. C'était plutôt grotesque,
avant."

I think it was at about this time that the Australian £ fell
to 16s. and I began to get properly frightened about the future.
On the day of my *vernissage* I was told to bring my pictures
to the gallery at 8.30 a.m. where the unshaven dealer, a cigarette hanging from his lower lip, stood them around the
stained and empty walls and cocked a cold eye upon them.
In the grey light of that rainy Monday morning they looked
absolutely awful. I could not imagine how I had ever had the
effrontery to try to take up painting as a profession and I
helped the dealer hang that show in a mood of the blackest
despair I had ever known.

At midday I got home to find that Aylmer and Phyllis
Vallance had arrived from London and they comforted me
with drinks and with love. At three we were back at the
gallery and there was a big bouquet of flowers from someone and all of my friends turned up and were lovely to me.
By the end of the day my morale was sufficiently restored to

enable me to listen with profit, humility and pleasure to the serious criticisms of my painter friends. Pavlick, Marcoussis and Picart le Doux all gave the work their detailed attention, with an absence of flattery which made me feel almost important. Pavlick, saying "Vous avez quand même une certaine honnêteté," was more flattering to me than any jam, and what is more, I sold one-third of all my pictures, despite the slump, which enabled me to send another good cheque to the architect.

The night of the *vernissage* we had a grand party in both studios. For the moment, everything was fine and dandy.

But the foundations of all our lives were cracking. That summer, I sent Julie to stay with Ford and Janice at Toulon. Ford had met and fallen seriously in love with Janice quite soon after Julie and I moved into the Rue Boissonnade. He had sent her to call on us and since we liked her very much, we were pleased when Ford asked for our blessing on his approaching union with her. She was a young Polish-American painter who made him very happy until the day of his death, and she developed a strong affection for Julie.

Whilst Julie was with her father in Toulon, I went and stayed in the Haute Savoie with an English friend who had hired a villa where we had the use of a fine studio. We painted hard and never saw a newspaper during the whole of August. But before returning to Paris, the cold winds of fear began to penetrate even to our mountain retreat. There were rumours of war and rumours of financial collapse all round and the political atmosphere was appalling. On the morning after my return to the Rue Boissonnade, I opened my *Herald Tribune* to see in the right hand corner, £1 sterling=frs. 103. That sentence had read £1 sterling = frs. 125 for months and years, and when it quickly sank to 86, I knew that I was ruined.

I had the studios, but I still owed money on them. I saw that I should have to sub-let both and go away somewhere with Julie and live as best we could on the proceeds.

Everyone was panicky and unsettled, but Katharine Johnson's job on Vogue still kept her in Paris, and she agreed to remain at the Rue Boissonnade at a reduced rent, and share the housekeeping with a spoilt child of fortune whom I found to take my own studio for six months. This was the charming young daughter of a tenor of the Metropolitan Opera of New York, who was well furnished with funds and chaperoned by a stalwart Italian maid.

I proposed to take Julie to my old attic studio at Toulon, which Seabrook would have given back to me, and to camp there as best we could. But Ford, who was living in a villa along the coast at Cap Brun, rightly stressed its unsuitability for Julie and urged us to use his little place instead, since he and Janice were coming to Paris for the winter. I found it difficult to enter again into Ford's life in this way, but it was clear that Julie would be better in a house with a garden than in a noise-some quay-side slum; so I accepted.

We arrived at noon and Ford and Janice left for Paris that evening. I had never felt so sharp a pang of desolation as when, alone with Julie, I looked around and took stock of the domestic difficulties which confronted us.

Ford had, of course, acquired a home that was picturesque but entirely without amenities. The Villa Paul stood high above the sea, towards which there sloped a long garden with fig trees and oranges and a water cistern. It was reached from the Toulon bus route at the rear by a long, steep and stony path, and from the sea by a confusing labyrinth of lanes. The shutters of its upper windows were always closed. They concealed the domestic life of M. le Commandant and Madame, who lived a dim but passionate existence on the upper floor, sub-letting the *rez de chaussée* and the garden to Ford and Janice.

The ground-floor shutters were always open. They had once been painted palest grey, and were folded back against the pinkish stucco walls whose flaking surface discovered patches of a previous periwinkle blue. Through the windows you stepped into two small rooms with rough grey walls and red tile floors. Behind these, on one side was the kitchen, dark and primitive, and on the other a sleeping alcove and *cabinet de toilette*. The parlour walls were painted with crude but charming bouquets of flowers, which Ford had discovered under a peeling modern wallpaper—a black and silver monstrosity which Madame la Commandante thought very handsome and forbade her tenants to destroy. Fortunately, Janice had by then removed it all. Before the house was a wide *terasse* whose comfortable balustrade served as a sideboard for outdoor meals. There was a shady tree and a fountain with goldfish and a great view right across the harbour to Saint Mandrier. It was indeed a most delectable spot. But whereas Ford and Janice had been living entirely in the garden, when we arrived in October the weather broke, and we had to live indoors. Here cobwebs hung in black festoons, and broken windows admitted rushing draughts, and the three of the five electric lights were out of action. The glazier had broken all his promises to come, so had the electrician, and likewise the *femme de ménage*. There were almost no kitchen utensils, household linen or china—for Madame la Commandante's notions of "*méublè*" were frankly unworthy of the name. Cooking was on one charcoal burner. Fortunately I had brought a primus.

I had not any money but I did buy some red check napkins and some candles and a lot of polish. I decided that a *femme de ménage* was out of the question, and it was some time before I got things homelike. I used to sleep in the alcove, looking across the polished tiles of the floor, over the sill of the open door, over the balustrade and the tops of the distant trees, across the dim blue water and into the vast starry sky. It was a lovely last minute sensation before going to sleep, and it was extra lovely in the early morning. Julie went to the lycée at Toulon, and had to leave at seven-thirty and I had a very slick system for producing coffee on the primus and toast on the charcoal and a nice fire of sticks to breakfast by. She got a lift home at six o'clock in the car of an aristocratic Frenchman who was running an *agence de location* in Toulon, following the loss of all his investments in the slump. This gentleman and his wife lived but a stone's throw from the Villa Paul and were without exception the most innocent and the least practical people I had ever known. They had but lately returned from coffee-growing in the tropics and seemed all unfitted to struggle in the modern world. Each summer they paid a round of visits to "la famille" which included some of the most famous names in France, but nothing would have induced them to disclose the straits to which they were often reduced. Even when there could be no petrol for the poor old car, "la famille" was never allowed to guess it.

Our other neighbours were a French painter and his blonde young wife and two children. They, too, were tenants of the commandant and their little villa was an adorable spot with a charming garden. But their poverty was quite unlike that of the drifting, fatalistic aristocrats who would rather starve than ask for help. They worked and fought and cheated and borrowed and would cheerfully do a midnight flit if such a move would cut the Gordian knot of their entanglements. Monsieur was always full of plans, plots, irons in the fire and slightly shady projects. He was a big, vigorous, and intelligent man who treated his small boy with extreme brutality, and the child, who was violent and clever and highly sensitive, had become the most circumstantial and accomplished little liar I had ever known. He was always heavily punished, but since no one in his home ever spoke the truth, he was not convinced of the necessity to reform.

His young wife was fortunately blessed with an excellent physique. Not only did she provide her husband with a splendid model, but she was an admirable cook, an experienced laundress and a capable nurse to her fretful two-year-old daughter. She had no outside help in the house or garden ; her kitchen was stocked with every imaginable condiment, her coffee was a dream, and her temper was appalling.

Her husband would explain to me that there was absolutely not a *sou* to be made any more out of painting, nor yet out of sub-letting a Paris studio. For him, as for me, these had hitherto been the most hopeful sources of income. He told me that people were giving away all their furniture to any one who would relieve them of their leases, and he told me that the canvasses of the great X—— were selling for five hundred francs apiece.

I could not see any future for Julie and me. My studios were let for six months, but after paying their high rent, there was only just enough left to keep us both at the Villa Paul. There was nothing to look forward to but a return to Paris, in the spring, with empty pockets. And I still owed money to the architect.

I felt I'd done all that was possible to cope with the situation, and for the moment there was no further effort that I could usefully make. Each morning, as I carried food and water to Ford's chickens and occupied myself with the *ménage*, I used to see a plane take off from St. Mandrier and do exercises in the tranquil sky. He's just obeying orders, I used to think, and how easy and uncomplicated that must be. But when necessity issues orders which you must accept, that, too, is easy and uncomplicated. I was not discontented.

Of course, I was in a very beautiful place. That helped. Indeed, that made everything possible. I was living on the view !

Then suddenly I had a letter from America. It was from a good friend of mine called Ramon Guthrie, and it simply said, "How many portraits at $300 would you need to make it worth your while to come to America?" I replied "three," and waited in a state of breathless suspense which degenerated into a calm hopelessness as many weeks went by without an answer.

Meanwhile, the mother-in-law of the neighbouring painter became ill in Paris, and his wife was called to the bedside. Then the painter, left to cope single-handed with the housework and his obstreperous offspring, fell down and sprained his ankle. He did it properly, so that it swelled up like a ham, and when he struggled up my garden path on two brooms for crutches to beg for my help, it was obvious that half-measures were useless. Julie and I moved down into the Villa Florida, and for two weeks I cooked, washed and cleaned for the two families. I did not do it as easily as Madame. I made foolish and ill-received efforts to keep the children clean and to get their breakfasts on time for their various schools. The boy went off first. Then Julie. Then the baby had to be struggled with for half an hour with a patent food. Then the painter —prone upon his sofa—must be fed. Then the house must be cleaned, and the marketing attended to. I would find myself still washing up at 11 p.m.—out of doors where the tap was —because I was too inefficient to get through sooner.

Still, they liked my cooking.

When madame returned, she wept with gratitude and presented me with a handsome glass bowl.

Soon after this I got rather sick myself. Little Julie was

marvellous. Before going off to school, she would put beside
me all the things I needed for the day, including a spirit lamp
and food. I had given up all hope of America by now;
nevertheless, when one morning the bell rang on the outer
gate (Madame la Commandante would never allow it to
be left unlocked) I got out of bed and went out in the rain
to see if it might be a telegram. It was. It was from Carl
van Doren and it said there was work waiting for me in New
York amounting to $1000. I wept.

CHAPTER NINE

America

I LEFT JULIE with our aristocratic French neighbours at the Villa Paul until Ford and Janice should return to take charge of her. Saying good-bye was terrible.

I was frightened in my very bones of this American trip. I was frightened of the consul who gave me my visa and asked about my resources and my political views. I was frightened of the steamship officials who demanded a guarantee that I had a substantial sum of money at my disposal. I lied about that, but cabled to my friends to come and bail me out at the docks, supposing they insisted on searching my handbag and discovering my penury. Of course, nothing of the sort occurred,

I had borrowed the single fare from good-natured Peggy Guggenheim, who was willing to wait many weeks for re-payment. My two studios were still sub-let, which would provide the wherewithal for Julie later on to spend the summer holidays in Normandie with her bosom friend, Madeleine Marcoussis.

It was Easter when I sailed. It was a German boat, because there was no other at the moment when I wanted to go. I spoke to no one on the voyage. I was sick. I lay in my bunk and comforted myself with going over the list of the good friends whom I would see on the other side.

First there was Katie Seabrook. She was lending me her flat on West Eleventh Street, complete with a daily negro maid, and confiding me to the care of her friend and neighbour,

Lyman Worthington. She herself had gone to Mexico with Clare Spenser.

Katie was just about the nicest person in the world. Ford had once lent her his flat in the rue Vaugirard during one of his absences in America, and I had enjoyed having her for a neighbour. Willie who had taken another flat in Neuilly, would drop in to see his wife with "How sweet of you to ask me to tea, Katie," and she would reply tranquilly, "Why, I think it's very nice of you to come, William." In my foolishness I imagined that Katie was being brave, and putting a good face on Willie's quite obvious absences from home, but I soon found that I was mightily mistaken. Katie did not care a hoot about Willie's private life. She hadn't the remotest spark of envy, jealousy, or curiosity. She was sweet right through with an easy generosity, and she went about her own affairs with a grace and gaiety that filled her little rooms with adoring visitors, of whom one of the most frequent was her husband.

They had been married for fifteen years and there was nothing they did not know about each other. They appeared to have a warm and unshakeable understanding. You would have said that they were the perfect example of an indestructible marriage because, the bonds of possession having been loosened, there was nothing left to break.

Katie had a natural happiness all her own. She never fussed. She was warm-hearted, unsentimental, rather elusive; and there were absolutely no penalties attaching to her friendship. In a world where women are fond of clinging all too closely, elusiveness—when it's real and not just manœuvring —can sometimes appear as the greatest of virtues. When, later, she and Willie were divorced, it was as though a scientific experiment, on which one had set the highest hopes, had gone wrong after all.

Another thing about Katie was her surprising toughness. She would cheerfully accept all manner of risks and hardships in the desert or in the jungle; sleeping on boards in the midst of predatory beasts and still more formidable insects; making herself responsible for all the camp equipment when she and William went on their famous expeditions into Darkest Africa or wherever it might be, and nothing, absolutely nothing, ever caused her the smallest surprise. And the surprise element in some of her adventures must have been very high indeed!

She had turned up in Paris the second time with a slightly-bewildered air, however. She was collecting the equipment to go to Africa with William who wanted to write a book about Black Magic, and she had been pursued on to the ship in New York harbour by a publisher who wanted her to sign a contract to do a book herself, for young people, about the kind of life the black children lived in the jungle. Having lived all her life amongst people who yearned to write books, often without any encouragement to do so, Katie had automatically signed. But upon reflection, she was appalled at what she had done. " I have never written a word," she said, "I can't possibly do the darned thing. What a fool I have been."

Well, when they came back from Africa, Willie entrenched himself in my Toulon studio and prepared to write his Great Work, but Katie, who had been attacked by all sorts of tropical bugs and microbes which defied analysis and were making her very ill indeed, went home to the Rockefeller Institute to see what could be done by way of a cure. They did a very good job on her, but it took a long time. Nevertheless, Katie's book was written, published, and chosen by the Junior Book of the month Club, long before Willie's was ready for the press.

That was Katie all over. With her soft Southern voice and picturesque hats and flowery dresses, she had all the airs of a spoilt woman, yet she was always doing the most astonishing things, without appearing to lift a finger.

Carl van Doren was another friend who would be waiting to give me a welcome in New York. He had liked the portrait I did of Jean Wright Gorman (she whom the cat had scratched) and had commissioned me to do one of himself and obtained another client for me. He was a large and helpful person who had a wonderful way of soothing out one's troubles and difficulties, and had given me my first taste of being spoilt in the American fashion when I was spending the summer with Julie on the Riviera in 1927. I had engaged rooms in an isolated farmhouse pension on the Island of Porquerolles, and Carl, together with Jean and Herbert Gorman, motored all the way from Cannes to meet us at Toulon and then stayed to help me with the hot and difficult journey from Toulon to Hyères by crawling train, and thence by bumping bus and seasick ferry and broken-down car to our destination, which turned out to be extravagantly lovely, but hopelessly dirty and uncomfortable. When I found myself alone there with Julie I fell into a black *cafard*. It was my first summer without Ford and it was far too beautiful and far too lonely. Then Julie fell sick and Carl and Co. insisted upon transporting us—again by car—to Cannes, and administering large doses of comfort. That is the sort of thing to warm the cockles of the heart.

Then there was Ramon Guthrie, whose portrait I had done in Paris and who was now teaching French at Dartmouth College. It was really his idea that I should come to America to paint portraits, and he had got Sinclair Lewis interested enough to commission a picture of his wife, Dorothy Thompson. That meant going to Vermont.

Ramon was a poet who had served in the last war, first in the French Army, and then in the American Air Force, and

he had fallen 1000 feet out of the sky without any visible hurt.
No one knows how it happened. He reached the hospital alone
on his own feet far from the scene of the crash, but he has no
recollection of so doing. After the war he married all the
Gallic virtues in a girl from Nancy called Marguerite, who
turned out to be just the decorative, unpretentious, staunch
and capable wife that a war-shaken poet needs. She used to
sing naughty old French songs at my parties in Paris, but by
now she was quite adapted to having become a professor's wife
in America.

Then there was my old crony, Ruth Harris. She used to
have a minute *appartement* up six flights of stairs on the
Boulevard Montparnasse which was flooded with shunshine
and looked down into a beautiful convent garden. She wrote
Art criticisms for the *New York Times*, and cooked the most
delectable little dinners which she served to select parties on
square plates. She was small, dark, and bursting with energy.
We liked doing the same things in the same way and had been
fast friends for years, and she, too, was in New York.

And there were others. Cecil Goldbeck and Irita van
Doren and Irving Fineman and Lyman Worthington and of
course Jean Wright. I counted them all up and began to realise
that sea-sickness was not a permanent condition, that we were
very near the end of the voyage, and that the chances were
heavily in favour of Providence permitting me to land
and to proceed to Katie's welcoming flat. Queueing up for
the immigration officer and the medical officer and all the rest
of it takes some time on the last morning of the voyage, and
when I was released, I ran up on deck and suddenly saw the
whole famous skyline bang in front of my eyes. The sun was
shining through the prettiest little drifts of smoke which
trailed across that magnificent silhouette. I think I must have
squealed, because the three business men at the rail turned

round and smiled at me. I wanted to tell them it was the first time I had seen New York—I wanted to tell everybody!

I was met. And the people who could not meet me sent telegrams and flowers and long-distance telephone calls. For two weeks I did not eat a meal at my own expense. I was silly with excitement.

I started work with the portrait of Carl van Doren. He was an excellent subject and a good sitter and he had a fine, light apartment to work in. As he posed, the telephone would ring and he would stretch out his hand for the receiver and conduct his literary business in a suitably high-handed manner which fulfilled all my imaginings of American business methods. At one o'clock he would cook poached eggs on muffins which we would eat at a low table with a peach-coloured mirror top.

When I had painted Carl I did a picture of the small son of another publisher. This gave me my first introduction to the American child to whom you cannot give any direct orders. I found that if I wanted him to look to the right, it was better to ask him to turn to the left. But just when I had decided that he had taken too violent a dislike to me to be manageable at all, he suddenly remarked, "You know you are my darling love!" and I realised that he had no idea that he had been exasperating me ! That is modern education. He was a nice kid, really.

Later, when I left New York, I picked up quite a number of commissions for small heads of children. I did whole families—three little pictures to hang in a row, for instance, with the full face one in the middle and the others composed accordingly. They were unpretentious and precise, and painted on panel. What I had in my mind were the choirs of angels of my first loves, the early Italian masters—but that did not mean that I was able to produce the conventional flattery required. When a rich old man, who was ordering pictures of his second batch of grandchildren, said, "And we want you particularly to be sure and give the children *a happy expression*. We think you have made my other daughter's eldest boy a little sad," I answered coldly, but with terror at my heart, that I was afraid I couldn't guarantee any particular expression. I couldn't tell how the pictures would turn out, and I thought to myself, "If only you knew, my good man, how lucky you are to get a likeness at all. *I* don't know how it happens!" By the time I had done eight or nine of these little pictures, I had developed a pretty good technique for snatching a few minutes pose here and there, and working between whiles from memory. I would set up my easel and invite the kid to come and talk to me and help me make a picture. I took care to dismiss him very quickly and tell him to come back later on, when he felt like it. He generally came back of his own accord, and I worked as hard conversationally as at painting, so that he should not be bored. I used the most shameful flattery, I told the tallest possible stories, and I played one child off against another. "Do you know," I'd say, "the last little boy I had to paint was not like you at all. He was such a *naughty* little boy! When I wanted to see what colour his eyes were, he'd turn his back right round on me, so of course his picture came out awfully ugly." The small person would be extremely interested and feel very self-important in having a grown-up woman poring over his looks and hanging on his lightest word, and I got a surprising amount of co-operation. The three and four year olds were generally the most difficult. At two, a child will sit on its nurse's knee for ten minutes at a time, and at five he is already amenable to flattery and conversation. He—or more often, she —is also very interested in the choice of what she is to wear. As one small girl remarked with displeasure, "You haven't put in all the tucks in my dress. If you don't put them all in, my mother won't pay you!"

This business of being paid, by strangers, for goods received which are required to give satisfaction, was both stimulating and frightening. To find that one has a market value is highly reassuring, but the knowledge that the client expects to be pleased is really paralysing. It was salutary for the character and necessary to the making of any career, but whether it is good for one's painting is another matter. I myself incline to think that although the nervous strain of painting in full view of a strange household and parrying premature criticism and silly suggestions, and being exhibited to visitors as Our Tame Artist at Work, is intolerably heavy, I doubt whether it really affects one's work very much. Mostly that comes just the way it wants to come, and there is not much you can do about it. There is, however, a real danger of a loss of freshness if you begin fussing. And you do get fussed by clients who think that ordering a portrait is like ordering a coat-and-skirt, and are determined to get a good fit. It is absolutely necessary to grow a protective crust against these. The English critic Wilenski once told me that in his opinion it was impossible for a professional portrait painter to remain honest as an artist. He might start out well enough, but would be bound to succumb to the pressure of his sitter's wishes. It is true that I have always found this pressure heavy even when —as is usual—it is exercised unconsciously; but it was partly my own fault that I suffered by it so much whilst in America. I was still a very immature painter with absolutely no self-confidence in my ability to carry out the commissions which, to my astonishment, I continued to receive. I would set out for a new destination with all my painting kit and a feeling of high elation that I had got a new job. In the train I would tell myself that it was something, after all, to be the kind of

person who is met with a huge limousine and installed in the
best guest-chamber with a pink porcelain bathroom and paid
quite a lot of dollars for painting a bit of flesh, when painting
a bit of flesh was just what I liked best to do. I knew that
besides the dollars and the wonderful plumbing, I should be fed
sumptuously and cocktail'd liberally and taken to parties and
given swims in blue-lined pools or bowery lakes. But the
elation did not usually survive the railway train. Once in the
limousine, I always got the same old pang of cold fear. Here
I was putting myself once again at the mercy of the unknown.
I was to be a hostage until I had given satisfaction; I could
not escape, even for an hour, to be comforted by my cronies. I
was alone in the enemies' camp.

They were charming enemies. They were mostly quite
delightful to me, accepting my unflattering versions of their
offspring with a good grace, and professing to recognise the
authenticity of all sorts of characteristics which I had unconsciously incorporated into my pictures. But the world of
money was nevertheless enemy country. It always will be
and must be to workers who have to snatch, wangle or extort
a wage from its inhabitants. I was fortunate in being able to
fraternise with them as well as I did.

Most of my jobs were in country homes in New England
where I was handed on from one family to another. In one
house I was astonished to find that a fine collection of first
editions had been bound in uniform calf bindings, and in
another that the sagging line of the olde-worlde roof was
meant to be a faithful—if costly—reproduction of a Normandy
farmhouse! Once you got the idea, you saw why there were
so many rough-hewn benches and chests and three-legged
stools set about amongst those deep-sprung chairs and sofas
that were so hard put to it to preserve a rural character. But
it needed some explanation.

I never could stomach this faked simplicity. The phony
rustic furniture was immensely expensive, and I could see
nothing appropriate in spending a lot of money in trying to
imitate a style whose forms and colours had been shaped by
poverty and necessity in a wood-producing country with a
completely different way of living. I thought the French
efforts towards grandeur on insufficient means were more
honest. If you are a real millionaire, with the courage of your
convictions, why not go the whole hog with yellow brocade
and crystal chandeliers? or chromium and streamlined glass?

Another thing which at first worried, but afterwards
delighted me, was the lavish installation of all the gadgets and
equipment which are designed to take the horror out of housework. They seemed at first sight to have killed a great deal of
that interest in domestic craftsmanship that made life in
France so satisfying. One of the first houses where I stayed
was a charming clap-board dwelling with old Colonial furniture and frilled muslin curtains and a perfectly genuine
homelike atmosphere. But the real pride of the family was in
the basement, where I was taken almost before I had had time
to admire the living-room. Here, in a series of white caverns,
ran a network of pipes, some pink, some delicate green, some
blue. They were attached to the roof by gold bands, and they
led to three large white mounds which contained three fur-
naces, one fed by oil, one by coal, and one by electricity. You
could heat your house and your water by whichever system
you fancied. You just manipulated a switch. In the living-
room there was a gadget which you set to the temperature
best suited to your mood, and the furnace automatically leapt
into flame and roared away until the thermometer registered
correctly. Then the furnace died down, until the temperature
began to fall again, when it re-ignited itself.

The kitchens and pantries in this house were equally perfect.

They had rows of pastel porcelain sinks, glass-fronted cupboards, drawers which slid in and out with the ease of a
dentist's cabinet, and towel-racks which sprang towards you,
ready loaded, at a touch. What a marvellous laboratory, I said,
for the production of exquisite meals! I thought of Toulon,
with its one battered saucepan on a charcoal burner; but when
the dinner turned out to be rissoles, stewed prunes and cereal,
I thought longingly of the culinary standards of the Villa
Paul, and was ready to condemn an over-attention to means,
at the expense of the end in view. When I got to the Guthries'
little house in Norwich, Vermont, however, I became more
than reconciled to American domestic arrangements. I saw
that in the right hands they meant freedom and leisure for
people like me. When I knew Marguerite in Paris, she had a
dark, shabby and highly inconvenient apartment, but in
Vermont she had a neat little white house with a sun-parlour,
a breakfast alcove in a commodious kitchen and all possible
amenities. She had no maid, but she had plenty of leisure and
when she said with her Frenchwoman's pride: "Ramon et
moi, nous avons toujours tenu bonne table," she was not
boasting. She had learnt all about American food, now spoke
American with a charming French accent and there she was,
sitting as pretty as possible in the middle of a lovely landscape
and only twenty minutes from Ramon's classes at Dartmouth,
surrounded with delightful and cultivated neighbours of the
college faculty.

I liked the college, with its good red and white buildings
and square windows facing over the green campus. Later,
when I had seen the fake Gothic of Yale, I appreciated it even
more. I wished I could have seen Princeton.

There was an Art Gallery in the college and Ramon had
obtained an invitation for me to hold an exhibition there.
For this purpose I had brought over a crate of pictures, and

when I arrived in Norwich in Ramon's car, there it was sitting on the grass beside the railway station. Hanging this show in the college was much less harrowing than hanging the show in the rue de Seine. It was a lovely gallery and the pictures looked much better in it. Also it was not a commercial occasion. Ramon gave a sort of lecture about me on the opening day, but I felt too abashed to attend, and went and hid in the library until it was over. I do not know what he said, but it seemed to go off all right.

In the Dartmouth lecture-rooms which I was shown with pride, I had something of the same feelings as in that first super-kitchen I had visited, that the ends of education might be swamped by excessive attention to the means. The stalls were so comfortable, their swivel arm-flaps so nicely calculated to support the note-book, the air conditioning so perfect and the lighting so well-planned that I had a wry fear lest the waters of knowledge might perversely refuse to flow in such a well-dug channel, and that wisdom, which is a living thing not easily captured, might get sterilized out of the pre-digested, spoon-fed diet which appeared to be all that those well-dressed, well-exercised, and well-vetted students were expected to stomach. I think Ramon must have been a very unconventional professor. I know that he made his students swallow the whole of Proust unaided, and if they survived this dose and then showed enthusiasm, he would begin really to talk to them about French literature.

On this first visit to the Guthries the snow still lay upon the ground. Drifts were thick in the pine-woods and the steep valleys, and the roads going south had only lately become passable to cars. The students and the professors and their wives had only lately abandoned their winter sports and I was shown the ski-jump and the toboggan-run, and walked up to some of the log camping-huts on the heights. Next time I

AMERICA 209

came, it was summer, lush and green, with fireflies at dusk as thick as midges. From the Guthries' car I saw some of the handsomest of American country, well-wooded, well-watered and mountainous. I found a great charm in the tall clumps of trees standing in the greensward near the road and casting leafy shadows on the gracious white clap-board housefronts, set amid their own flowers but without fences or railing. The Americans are enormously house-proud and village-proud, and they achieve an effect of space and graciousness which our muddled English countryside cannot touch; as for the provinces of France, whoever heard of a Frenchman cultivating flowers for the benefit of the neighbours, or living anywhere but behind a locked gate, set for preference in a high stone wall ?

Those trees! How luxuriantly they overshadowed the dapper little shuttered houses. In New England where I painted most of my child portraits, the country was marvellously bowery and well cared for, but the sparsely-populated mountains of Vermont were grander. From the great window of the farmhouse barn which Red Lewis and Dorothy Thompson had made into their living-room, you looked right down an immense rocky valley of spectacular dimensions, on whose nearby slopes your eye might catch the red flank and pale antlers of a roving deer.

Painting Dorothy Thompson and her small son was the nicest job I had whilst in America. I did not resent the fact that she and Red seemed to have a great deal of money because they had earned it all by the sweat of their own brains.

We had a vast number of friends in common, and I soon began to enjoy myself. The luxurious informality of an American country home is delightful in any case, and when the host and hostess and all their visitors are literary folk instead of business people, the result is twice as happy.

Added to this was Red's disarming and unspoilt provincialism and Dorothy's warm-hearted candour. Neither of them had an ounce of side—and Twin Farms, South Pomfret, appeared to be packed to all its roofs with honest human sentiment. As the beetle-browed, passionate old cook said, "Never did I see a gentleman so devoted as Mr. Lewis is to you, mam." "Dear me, Mrs. Blake," replied Dorothy crisply, "you should get about more!"

The Twin Farms were quite separate. The first house contained Red shut up on the left with *Ann Vickers* and Dorothy shut up on the right with her articles for the *Saturday Evening Post*. Beyond this was Mrs. Blake's kitchen which led into the great barn, where all the social life of the establishment was centred. This was filled with grand old bits of furniture that had mostly been brought back from strange places in Middle Europe and looked perfectly at home against the oak beams and the big stone fireplace. The second farmhouse was run as a separate domestic unit for the accommodation of visitors and children. Here dwelt the son and heir, a brilliant baby of about three, and a small niece. Here also were swing-seats on a big porch, four bathrooms and an inviting little drawing-room where I was to paint my picture. The happy visitor could remain all day in this establishment if he felt unsocial.

How delectable are the fruits of success! How enviable is the lot of those who are well paid for doing what they like to do, who can buy privacy and peace for their work, and can afford to pursue the pleasures of conviviality and of parenthood amid lovely scenery, well-fitted with gadgets and motor-cars! The admiring visitor sees nothing of the grinding hard work that has gone into the making of it all; the headaches and the self-discipline and the perpetual, relentless effort through all kinds of personal storms that a literary and journalistic career entails.

Nor is that all. There has to be a Dorothy flying between the two farms in her little car to remind the gardener where he should set the roots this year, and which kind of beans had proved unsatisfactory ; to tell the nurse that since the little girl has gained two unwanted pounds she should have her cream reduced; to reconcile antagonisms between nursery and kitchen, and to tell Mrs. Blake that lunch must be kept back, and five extra arranged for. To be Dorothy, is to be three women in one with the vitality and organising power of six. To be Dorothy, in fact, is to deserve success.

How she loved her life! "This has been such an awful year for every one," she said (it was then 1932). "I'm simply ashamed to be having such a good time. Really, I am having the most marvellous luck and I do enjoy it."

I like people to admit it when they are happy! They so seldom do.

She and I used to walk through the leafy lanes and talk about life in general. I found her much more honestly feminine than I had expected. "You must accept what comes to you," she said, "let it all sweep right over your head. Don't fight it." The idea that you might be cold, and wise, and careful, and thus immune from hurt, did not appeal at all to her warm and generous soul.

But there were times when the careerist arose within her, and then she would set her house in order, bid farewell to all home ties, and sail forth with a contract in her pocket to report on the political plague-spots of Europe. She said that when she got home again, the establishment was always at sixes and sevens, and it all had to be put together again.

When I was there it was running beautifully. Red was on the water wagon for the sake of *Ann Vickers*, but fortunately this did not mean that there was no wine. As it was during prohibition, people who wanted wine had to make it themselves.

The Guthries, for instance, used to make a very tolerable wine from dried cherries in a big crock in the kitchen, but the Sinclair Lewises had it done on a large scale in the cellar by a visiting expert who first sold the appropriate grape-juice, and then came and fermented it, and finally bottled it as "claret" or "sauterne" or even as "champagne." Some of it was reasonably good.

The long table was always set before the great window and you had the view with your meals. Remote as we were, there would often be visitors who had motored for three or four hours for the sake of a two-hour visit. This nice American habit of motoring long distances for pleasure stood me in good stead, for it inspired Ramon to fetch me in his car from Waterbury to Dartmouth, and subsequently to deliver me to Twin Farms, and after I had finished my picture of Dorothy and the boy, Carl transported me in his Lincoln to Irita's beautiful farmhouse in the Berkshires, and thence to my next job. Thus was my life made very easy and thus did I see some of the loveliest country in the pleasantest fashion.

By the time I was well under way with my next batch of portraits, I was beginning to get dreadfully homesick for Julie. There is nothing to be done about homesickness. It is like being in love and simply has to be endured. I was staying in a grand house and had just been put through my paces regarding my attainments and qualifications by a business man who contemplated giving me another job. He had my little pictures hung on the wall and the children held forcibly below them for comparison! He was obviously pleased with the idea that in Paris, owing to the depression, there was now plenty of near-art and fine-art to be had for a song. He argued about the price.

I felt that I did not want the job. I felt that if only I could get my suitcase out of the house, I would run away in the night and never come back. But when I came down the stairs next morning, the leather-framed calendar which stood on the desk in the hall where my hostess conducted her charitable activities had been changed from Sunday to Monday, and the motto read:

"The Power that Others Have to Annoy me, I Give Them!" Very salutary.

I got the job, and another one in New Jersey to paint a posthumous picture of a notable gentleman for a hospital. All this was because I had done a little picture of Oliver Hueffer after his death, for Muriel, from a photograph and from my own memory, and she had liked it and written about me to the family of the deceased philanthropist. They asked to see my work, which was at Carl van Doren's in New York, and he very kindly received them and sold me to them quite successfully. The result was that I had a pair of large portraits to do, one from a photograph (always a horrible job) of a man who had died many years ago at the age of about forty-five, and the other of his wife, now seventy, who was very unwilling to pose. She wanted me to paint her also from a photograph, and submitted an ancient "artistic" blur of no documentary value. I was distracted. The job was very well paid, and I would have undertaken anything, from murals in the Hudson Tunnel to tinting post-cards, if it would have helped to buy security for Julie at home. But I could neither paint the lady from the blurred photo, nor match her age, from the life, with the picture of her dead husband. I said that I *must* paint a contemporary picture from life, and that I would come and stay near her in the country for the purpose, and would make do with seven sittings. She agreed, but in this instance the seven sittings were not enough, and they were all I got. I was not pleased with the result and I had a bad conscience about taking the cheque.

I really had a bad conscience about taking all the cheques. The whole thing appeared to me as a fearful racket. I started every portrait with the firm conviction that I should never succeed in getting a likeness, and I knew full well that the likeness was usually the only thing that I was being paid for, and was the only thing that I could not control. The really important elements in picture-making—composition, texture, and so on, were my private concern, and I was experimenting frantically, particularly with backgrounds, on people who believed me to be a "qualified practitioner" who could be relied on to produce a definite result.

All these experiments and all these experiences with sitters and clients were fast turning me into a qualified practitioner, however. The six months that I spent in America were absolutely invaluable as a forcing house for what latent skill I had, and for developing a stubborn resistance to difficult conditions. I have done much better work since, and I have worked with more confidence.

The other gift that I received from the U.S.A. was the delightful gift of a good time. After the grim period at the Villa Paul, the gaiety and friendliness of America fell like rain on thirsty ground. When I first tried to sleep in Katie's flat, alone amongst the flashing neon signs and roaring noises of West Eleventh Street and Seventh Avenue, I had all the classical sensations about being alone in the harshness and strangeness of the great city. But kind friends showed me how to ride the hubbub. I was taken to eat convivially at Mario's and at lesser and greater speakeasies; I was shown where to buy food, how to use the subways, where to get stamps, and how to make gin. I was taught to give up all thought of wine and to drink whisky—which I had hitherto despised. I soon learnt how to produce a meal for six people and hold a conversation with them at the same time, and I do hand it to the American

girls for their skill at informal entertaining. The food may
be a little stereotyped, since it all comes from the same delicat-
essen (I was extremely shocked when I asked for half a pound
of bacon rashers to find that I could not choose the cut, since
it was all done up in cellophane, and I thought the ready-sliced
loaf and ready-ground coffee were definitely retrograde), but
these party meals, eaten on the knee and served by an unruffled
young woman in evening dress, are a triumph. They show
what gadgets and ice-boxes can mean, when they are in clever
hands. They bring the kitchen into the parlour and release
entertaining from all the bother of wondering whether the
servants will revolt. Their possession could have saved me
years of time and strength, which might have been used for
painting. I can remember Jean Wright, just back from Hollywood, drifting glamorously round Carl's big room, handing
out twelve plates of delectable food with an accompaniment
of hot buttered rolls, strawberry tarts, coffee, and drinks,
to a hastily-summoned party. Paul Muni was there, pretending
to be "just a ham actor," but doing the most extraordinary
things with his handsome mask of a face in illustrating something a taxi-driver had said to him. He ceased, in fact, to be
Paul Muni and became the taxi-driver. So when his wife said,
"Isn't my Paul grand? Wouldn't you like to make a picture
of his face?" I said, "But he hasn't *got* a face. It's just an
indiarubber bag of tricks!"

Next day two people rang me up to ask if it was true that I
had told Paul Muni that he had not got a face!

What I had been trying to say, however, was not as silly as
it sounded. I know that for my kind of painting the fleeting
expression and the dramatic moment are quite wrong. What
I would always wish to get is something representing *all* the
moments—something timeless and tranquil. Thus the best
sitters are often those who offer up their faces naked and un-

conscious, as it were. In a well-ordered universe, such faces would be served up to me daily, in whatever quantity I might desire! That is my idea of Heaven.

In London I once painted the actor Hugh Miller. He had just made a great success in Paul Muni's original part in *Counsellor at Law*, and he was a grand subject physically. But I found myself disconcerted by his instant comprehension of the particular aspect of his face I was after, and his complete control over its expression. I was used to sitters who talked and changed and left me to piece together a composite impression. In the case of the actor, there seemed nothing left for me to do that the camera could not have done better.

The pleasures of New York were doubled for me after the return of Katie Seabrook from Mexico. She had not been in the flat for five minutes before she had established herself at the telephone and called up all her cronies. She gave a fine big cocktail-party for me—also in Carl's conveniently large room, which that good-natured man of letters was always ready to lend us—and she took me for a delightful week-end at Clare Spenser's place in Connecticut. Here was another little old farmhouse, complete with aged retainer, stuffy but adorable parlour, small bedrooms for the children, and an immense kitchen, and a stone's throw away there stood the great barn which had been converted to wholly hospitable ends. It was as tall as a cathedral and up one end ran the tapering flanks of a gigantic stone fireplace. The hearth was of a size for a dozen people to sit on its edge and grill their steaks at the glowing logs. Food, plates, knives and forks would be dumped before them, and after the meal, the guests would invade the farmhouse kitchen and dispose of the washing-up.

Opposite this fireplace was a gallery, underneath which were a series of little wooden cubicles, each with a deep-sprung bed and an electric plug for the breakfast coffee. These

were for female guests. The men were accommodated in a
bunk-lined dormitory at the other end of the barn, complete
with shower-bath. The women had a tub!

This place was crammed at week-ends, but no staff was
required to cope with it. Everyone waited on themselves and
talked, and talked, and talked. At night it would be round the
fire, and at noon on the sun-bathing terrace. Pleasant, very
pleasant.

Indeed the American genius for organising their out-
door and domestic lives, whether with money or without, is
quite wonderful. When I stayed with friends who had been
absolutely ruined by the depression, there was still a great deal
of physical pleasantness in their lives, although their mental
distress was growing. The Ruin was spreading. Folk who lost
their jobs knew that they would not find another—that shabby
clothes and broken-down cars could not be replaced. They
discussed the wisdom of breaking their leases—flitting from
inexorable landlords and apartments they could no longer
afford, and allowing their furniture to be seized. One young
couple I knew had found a solution by reversing rôles. The
wife still had a job with an advertising firm, but the husband
could find nothing whatever. They had a nice little flat and
the young man ran it entirely. He did every scrap of the housework and marketing and he did it beautifully. The wife was
waited on when she came back from work like any British
breadwinner, and the husband was too sensible and too realistic
to allow any notions of false pride to spoil this arrangement.
But then he was an American. Later, he got a fine job with a
publishing firm.

Another young man whose business had crashed and who
owned a charming week-end place in New Jersey had retired
there for economy and his wife took a job in a Newark store.
She was on her feet all day and deadly tired and earned only

what it cost her to have the housework done at home. So she chucked the job and took over all her own work, the rough as well as the smooth; scrubbing and washing, even to the sheets, as well as cooking and the rest of it. But being an American, she had an electric washer and cooker, a boiler and a frigidaire and a vacuum cleaner, and being a person of taste, the charm of her home lay in the effective disposition of simple objects on large bare floors so that it always looked beautiful, like a woman whose bones are so good that it does not matter what she wears.

It was in this household that I stayed when I was painting the old lady and her dead husband. The people I met there were poor, and young, and clever, and were all struggling along in their several country cottages with half-jobs or no-jobs, in moribund cars, and showing a resilience and courage that was like a tonic. It was nice to be again amongst people who were acquainted with insecurity, who knew what it was like to sing for one's supper, and with whom one did not have to pretend to be important or successful. It was nice to be with people who knew how to conjure beauty and grace out of poverty, and how to keep each other's spirits up. And they were so efficient and so good-looking and some of them were really gifted. I dare say they are all very successful by now.

My time in the United States was nearly up. The proposed three months had stretched to six; Julie was with the Marcoussis in Normandy and I was shaken by homesickness for her. The *rentrée des classes* was imminent and for that I must return.

One more tiny portrait—done in a scramble just before the boat sailed—of a small red-headed boy who lived at the seaside. Two more commissions offered—but I could not wait. I planned to come back six months later, and repeat this surprisingly successful visit. I had made enough money to pay off all my debts, and to live with Julie in the rue Boissonnade, where both studios were now unlet, for half a year. And surely a little work would turn up for me in Paris.

A farewell party at Carl's. Some careful purchases in the shops—a red dress for me, a little fitted dressing-case for Julie with her name on it, and a lovely winter coat with a real mink collar at a summer price. That'll knock 'em in Europe, I thought. Frocks for Julie.

It was rough on the *Paris*, and I was again a prey to the desolation that always besets me at sea. I was desperately tired. I had only one thought in my head, that Julie was waiting for me at the other end.

At the Gare St. Lazare, Alice Marcoussis rushed up to me with a child whose hand in my hand and whose body in my arms were bigger than they had been six months before. Disconcertingly bigger. "Voici votre trésor," said Alice, "and now forgive me, because I have got to be at the Hôtel Continental at eight o'clock."

There was no one else at the station. Julie and I hugged each other all the way home in the taxi, and I told her about her presents.

In the empty studio the *femme de ménage* had left some purchases of food. Four eggs, two rolls, a packet of sliced ham and some butter in a bag. The fire had not been lit.

CHAPTER TEN

England Again

AFTER THE STUDIO was cleared of debt, it took just six months to convince me that life in Paris was no longer possible. I became convinced for the simplest of reasons; I had no more money.

In six months I had only two small portrait commissions. I had the greatest difficulty in finding a tenant, at a much reduced rent, for the smaller studio, and my chances of returning to America in the spring became fainter and fainter. Finally the New York Bank Moratorium put the stopper on all my hopes. I could not get confirmation of the few commissions that I had been offered verbally before I sailed home, and the very friends who had jubilated at my previous success and foretold its repetition, now wrote and said "For goodness' sake don't come over this year. You will not make even your expenses." So there was nothing for it but to turn my attention to England, and see if we should be allowed to creep back there.

This realisation hit me like a sudden blow one lovely afternoon in early spring as I was standing on the Pont Marie. I was looking towards the Ile Saint Louis, where I was on my way to see the paintings Louis Marcoussis had been doing there. He had been lent an improvised studio by Madame Helena Rubinstein in a beautiful old house which she was about to pull down. The river had never looked lovelier nor the house-fronts of the quai de Béthune more warmly golden in the late afternoon sunshine. "Avez-vous remarqué," an old French painter once said to me, "que la lumière de Londres est rose, mais celle de Paris est dorée?" I had remarked it, and I was in no mood for London's pink sun, nor for the slack, slow and heavy tempo of London streets and London conversation. London offered no stimulus capable of dissipating your worries, but left you severely alone to build up all sorts of poisonous little phobias and obsessions. Paris on the other hand was an immediate tonic in times of trouble; her hard head and delectable bosom were always at your disposal, for comfort and advice. She could also show you such physical beauty that to leave her seemed impossible. Especially on the island!

That is where the Bradleys lived and where Jenny (now Julie's godmother) had given me the best of my French social education. That is where Julie was at this moment having tea with Madeleine Marcoussis and where, long ago, the *Transatlantic Review* had had its little office. Rich foreigners had bought some of the old houses on the quai and filled them with exotic decorations, but these appeared merely as extraneous ornaments on the prow of a tightly-packed ark which, anchored in the Seine, held an insular and even a provincial life peculiarly its own.

When I looked at it from the bridge on that sunny afternoon, it seemed to contain all France for me. In my private imagination, Montmartre usually shared this distinction because it housed the Marcoussis, and in spite of the fact that they were really Polish, to me they represented a considerable slice of French life. Julie and I used to climb what seemed just a busy village street on Sunday mornings to visit them in their tall studio with the great view from the top of the rue Caulaincourt. This studio contained the most charming of treasures —Aubusson tapestries, an ancient spinet, African masks and fetishes, Alice's ivory bracelets laid out in a long row, old faience tiles hung up, and a comic collection of glass bottles—all arranged against the simple domestic background of two hard-working painters. There were also Louis' cubist compositions and Alice Halicka's satirical-romantic decorations, and in particular there was their delightful daughter in person, who was Julie's best friend. Madeleine was as dark as Julie was fair and as quick as Julie was deliberate and they twittered together with a charming mutual devotion. There would be a proper French Sunday lunch with *hors d'œuvres* and a find salad and a bottle of red wine and fast and friendly talk, chiefly of painters and painting, and also of such common topics as how to dress and feed one's self without spending money. There was nothing about those Sunday lunches to make one homesick for the roast beef and Yorkshire pudding and the subsequent somno-lence of the English Sabbath. On the contrary.

On the day when I saw that we would have to leave Paris, the Marcoussis happened to be all on the Ile Saint Louis, along with those other friends and beauties and joys that I realised I was going to lose. For if Paris offers a good antidote to emotional troubles, she is adamant where money is concerned. She allows no blurred edges or wishful thinking on this stark subject. In London, you can kid yourself that things will come right in the end, that luck is just round the corner and the day of reckoning very far away. Paris permits of no such self-deception.

So I knew that we must go back to where my few pounds were still worth twenty shillings and where there was, perhaps, a market for portraits that no longer existed in Paris for a foreign woman painter.

With difficulty I found a tenant for my studio. He was a rich, neurotic and undisciplined American whose wife had just been trying to commit suicide. I hated leaving them amongst my things, but they paid me three months rent in advance. With deep misgiving I installed Julie—now twelve years old—

in a *pension de famille* to finish her school year at the *Ecole Alsacienne*, whilst I went prospecting across the Channel. The day I left, I took her to the Bon Marché to buy some necessary socks and vests and petticoats, and we wandered in a state of utter desolation amid the ugly displays of cheap underwear. That night, I sailed in the third-class women's cabin from Dunkerque to Folkestone. At midnight, listening to the creaking timbers of the vessel, I remembered that it was my fortieth birthday.

. . . .

In London, I found, as usual, that I had some marvellous friends. I found comfort, kindness, uncritical friendship and loyalty—all those English virtues that I had forgotten about in my enthusiasm for France. I was reminded of what an old French lady had once said to me concerning the vicissitudes of her life—"It was always my English friends who helped me when I got into a hole."

Muriel Hueffer had me to stay in Chelsea, and Aylmer and Phyllis Vallance in Hampstead. Dolly Osler offered me the use of her Cotswold farmhouse for the summer holidays, and I was charitably given two portrait commissions. At the beginning of the summer holidays I sent for Julie who came over with a man from Cooks. She had not been happy at the *pension*, but England was even more strange to her because she spoke nothing but French. We spent a lonely summer in the Cotswolds, and in September came back to London to try our fortunes.

I had some more luck. A London-Paris friend let me have her large Kensington studio at a nominal rent, and Julie was received at reduced fees at a co-educational day-school where she was allowed to do her lessons in French until she had picked up enough English. Margaret Cole—that same brilliant and forthright Margaret Postgate who, since her marriage to G. D. H. Cole, had become a considerable personality in the

Labour movement—introduced me to Mr. D. N. Pritt, K.C., and also to Lady Cripps, wife of Sir Stafford, who had their portraits painted.

This got me into circulation, but it did not make me feel at home. I was appeased, however, by the relatively slack and confident atmosphere of London after the anxieties of Paris. No one bothered about the sterling exchange rate; no one had to worry about getting a *carte de travail*; problems of nationality did not cloud the air, for the refugees had not yet begun to come. In Kensington, the prams were pushed as they had always been pushed by dawdling women, peering into unattractive, well-filled shops, and as one lay awake in the early morning hours, the clatter of the milk-bottles produced a comforting and sedative effect. It seemed that the English people expected no disaster, and had no conception of the strain under which the shifting populations of Europe were living. Insularity appeared to have its compensations.

Amongst my friends of the Labour movement I found myself in a world where my ignorance of politics was sadly shown up, but where, also, I was carried further away from the things that most interested me, such as conditions in France and in America, the international circulation of the Arts, and the prospects of building a world where currencies should remain stable and we should all be allowed to travel and to work where we liked. I heard much less about international socialism than formerly, and gathered that the situation had worsened to the point where setting one's own house in order was all that could be hoped for. This seemed much less interesting.

I was born without the slightest desire to instruct or to reform society. To preach or convert or persuade opinion is a thing for which I have no gift or inclination. But I came to London at a turn in my life when I wanted to know what I was and where I belonged. The personal life of the emotion no longer sufficed and I wanted something wider—some citizenship amongst people whose notions of the right way to live corresponded to some extent with my own; some comradeship of interests and beliefs.

I never found it. I dare say I have never known how to communicate with people in the English idiom. The knocking about that I have done has turned a shy person into a pretty good mixer, but maybe it is only in the sense that a New York taxi-driver is a good mixer—he can talk to anyone. But that is not the English way. In the interests of general conversation, you toss off a remark. In Paris or in New York the ball is quickly thrown back. In London, it crashes to the ground where it lies looking like a suet pudding under the cold and silent eyes of the company. Agony !

This makes it very difficult to know who are your potential friends. And another thing; however well you may get on with someone at a party, getting on with people is not considered important, in England, between people who are no longer young. By the time they are forty, Londoners are well established in their homes and careers and they do not seek to enlarge their acquaintance except for definitely social or business reasons. A proficiency at golf or bridge would do the trick in no time. But the enjoyment of mere conversation is not a factor in the English scheme of life. If it were, you would not on social occasions see all the women left high and dry at one end of the room, whilst the men forgather at the other, not to converse, but just to feel that they stand solidly together.

It is a perpetual surprise to me that people will associate with each other freely from habit, but very little from choice. I cannot think that they enjoy their lives as much as I reckon to enjoy mine.

Well, the enjoyment of life would appear to be a thing of the past. The story of our lives—Julie's and mine—since we came to England is a *diminuendo-rallentando* of enjoyment, leading into the present blackness that has engulfed us all, darkening the foreground of a picture that is already remote, of that rosy period of false peace between the two wars.

When first I came to England, an earnest and learned revolutionary of my acquaintance said to me that he thought that happiness was the last thing to take into consideration in estimating the value of life. I was quite shocked. If effort and sacrifice are worth making it was surely in order that more people shall have more happiness, and in the long view, freedom and education serve to increase this. Or one might even call it pleasure. Whether it is the enjoyment of a complicated but illuminating idea, or the simple bliss of relaxing in the sun, pleasure is enormously important. It is what we feel when our faculties are being properly exercised, and we all try to manœuvre ourselves into the position where we believe that we will feel it most keenly.

Unless one is a gangster at heart, one must believe in something. I have always found it quite easy to believe—roundly and simply—in good and bad, and I won't be argued out of it. I am not trained in argument and must stake my conviction of these things on my own consciousness of them; but I know a perfectly good case could be made out, not intuitively, but logically, which would prove that health is better than sickness, kindness than cruelty, freedom than slavery, and reason than unreason. It also seems easy to accept that justice is a desirable principle that can be defined and logically upheld.

Of course, I can see also that "good" things can have "bad" by-products and vice versa and that you can quickly get into a fine confusion between ends and means.

The difficulty is to avoid the perils of fanaticism as well as the paralysis that sometimes comes of seeing both sides at once. The loftiest wisdom ought surely to be able to see every side of everything simultaneously, but this kind of vision would seem to have no place in the world to-day. It belongs to a state of health and equilibrium, and society has become mortally sick. Drugs and surgical operations are the order of the day and the quack doctor is coming into his own.

The effective person is the one who says that "only one thing matters," but I have never felt that he was right. I have always thought that everything matters all the time and it is hard for me to realise that there may be times when it is not appropriate to think of everything, but only of one immediate necessity. I used to talk to many people who believed in the necessity for social revolution and were willing to resort to force. I was—and am—easily convinced that capitalism won't work any more. The "starving in the midst of plenty" is sufficient proof of that. At the same time, when a Communist writer declared to me with a flaming conviction that I could only envy, that to *sacrifice a whole generation* would not be too great a price to pay to stop man's labour being exploited for profit, then I was ready to cry mercy. Could even the sacrifice of a generation so change the quality of man's existence? Could even a perfect economic system, supposing that it could be insured by such a sacrifice, do more than make it more possible for him to lead a good life? Does not the good life begin after legislation and social planning have done their work, just as the sick man's life begins again after he leaves the hospital which has cured his disease, but cannot ensure his subsequent happiness? Does not the social reformer make the same mistake as the doctor in imagining that his function—either in providing economic and political freedom, or in establishing health—covers the whole of life?

"We must decide what we are going to do with the people's leisure." I thought these words were very sinister; I thought the social planner was planning to exceed his functions.

I wanted to know how a socialised society proposed to use the artists who, so far, had usually been hired by the leisured class that socialism was setting out to liquidate. I had a foolish hope that my own kind of rather straightforward painting might appeal to people of simple tastes and I thought how happy most painters would be if they could sell all their work at a low price, instead of a small proportion of it at the high one maintained by the dealer's interests. If there were any popular demand for pictures, how different, how enviable and how socially self-respecting would the life of the painter become. How agreeable it would be, too, to paint portraits of people who were free from the perpetual and uneasy vanity of the leisured. But alas! the proletariat does not care a hoot about painting and the capitalist is still the only customer; a customer who generally wants a suave and happy rendering of his next-of-kin without too much character in evidence. The trouble with me is that the character always creeps in more heavily and more insistently than I had intended. Then they say, "Of course I've often seen him look exactly like that, but it is not the expression I should have chosen," or, "Isn't it rather sad?" or, "I don't *really* look like that, do I?" or, "Of course, you have brought out all my wife's side of the family," as though I had done it on purpose!

It is often on just those occasions when I am most satisfied with a likeness that I fail to please and on those when I fall into a watered-down generalisation that I am acclaimed. On the whole, there is no limit to the amount of flattering that sitters desire. My own opinion is that most people have not got the least idea what they look like. Also that the problems of picture-making have got nothing to do with the problems of facial expression and it is just too bad that a painter can only sell his work if he is able to cope with the latter. Small wonder that "pure" painters despise the murky trade of the portraitist.

The story of the years which led us from Kensington to Hampstead and from Hampstead to the lovely cottage where we now sit waiting for the German invasion, is neither important nor interesting. It seemed important at the time, to persuade oneself that one was a craftsman as worthy of his hire as, say, a cobbler or a carpenter. It seemed important, also, that one should make up one's political mind and understand where the real cleavage was going to occur in the approaching earthquake, for the nineteen-thirties carried these problems in each minute of their anxious months and years. Events were forcing everyone to examine the roots of their security and the charter of their citizenship, and the preoccupations of the nineteen-twenties—love, æsthetics, individualism, and the personal life—got out of focus as they came within the range of the approaching storm. Now that the storm is here, it does not seem to matter much whether one used to be called a "flabby liberal" or a "dirty red." It does not matter whether one was a diligent wage-earner with an insurance policy and a hire-purchased home, or a thriftless artist who did as he liked and lived on luck and charity, for now we are all swimming for our lives in the same stormy waters. But in the nineteen-thirties our feet still walked on solid ground of a sort. We busied ourselves with building card-houses, which we attempted to insure.

My own efforts at sober wage-earning were never very

happy. Aylmer Vallance, then editor of the *News Chronicle*, gave me the job of writing up the art exhibitions of London, and no one could have worked harder and to less good effect than I did at my weekly article. I went to dozens of shows every Wednesday and was floored by the impossibility of saying anything significant about them. I could only succeed in voicing an opinion if I gave rein to my first impressions without ulterior considerations, and for this reason I found it best to keep clear both of painters and dealers. I thus became still more isolated. I was too heavily conscientious to make a good journalist and too ignorant of contemporary English painting—which appeared to me to be mostly a rather dull kind of impressionism—to make a good critic. I drew my salary with a deep sense of guilt, and except for the financial anxiety which it caused, I was rather relieved when eighteen months later Aylmer's successor gave me the sack.

Julie and I lived for several years in a nice quiet, light studio in Belsize Park. I had finally got rid of my Paris studio, but luckily had managed to salvage a good deal of the furniture. I held two exhibitions in the provinces and exhibited in various London shows. I sought diligently for the portrait commissions which, when I got them, paid so much better than anything else I could have done, but which sometimes left me for weeks or even months without knowing when my next job was coming.

I developed a technique for doing portrait sketches in two or three days and got a good many orders. But this way of working led me further from the small, tight and formal painting on panel which was my natural bent. The English love anything that looks as though it had been tossed off quickly and easily. They love to be told that something just "came" in an accidental and effortless fashion and do not like to think that painters, the importance of whose work they do not really believe in, may have to sweat and groan like anybody else.

Unfortunately sketchiness has never been one of my qualities. Nevertheless the quick portraits sold well and encouraged the delusion that I should some day achieve financial security by my brush.

I also painted several "conversation pieces," of whole families, with little figures of Hogarthian dimensions sitting about in their own homes. These I enjoyed more, in spite of the tremendous difficulties involved. They had to be painted in other people's houses and Julie got quite used to being sent to stay with friends until I came home again.

I never succeeded in getting the commission that I really would have liked, for a large group of people treated as purely formal decoration. I wanted further to develop the idea I had had for the "Nègre de Toulouse" because I was by now much better at portraiture but was getting less and less interested in "natural" poses and realistic light and shade. But I could not get my group, plus the appropriate decorations, without the co-operation of some club, or team, or lodge, or firm. It would have been jam to me to have had a lot of nice fleshy faces to portray, surrounded by their insignia of office, symbols or what not, all woven into a formal pattern. I was not frightened by the unfashionable word "decorative" and I was dismayed by the tedious realism of the "groups" that were painted to order by Royal Academicians and such. I happened once to be giving an exhibition in a university town and was shown a picture that had lately been commissioned of a college faculty. It depicted a group of professors in their common-room, on whom through a tall window there fell a cold and wintry light. They were arranged around a table, those on the near side being turned round sideways, so as to show their faces. One was handing a paper to another. This was to make it seem more natural. All the figures were the same size and in dark suits, but instead of using their similarities in effective repetition, desperate efforts had been made to break them up and make them look different. Only they didn't look different. They would have looked much more different if the painter had played up the sameness of their attire and concentrated on their facial characteristics. And the actual portraiture could have been much more intimate if the realistic lighting from the window had been abandoned. I knew all about the difficulties of posing people in groups because I had been struggling with my "conversation pieces," but what seemed to be just possible with five or six people of different sizes and sexes, became impossible with a dozen grown men in conventional dress. How I longed to arrange their faces in rows or in circles and dress them up in their gowns and fal-lals and perhaps stick in a bit of gold and even scrolly tickets to say who they were!

I should like to have painted the Emperor of Abyssinia in ceremonial robes, surrounded by all his family in their fantastic gew-gaws! Failing that, I would have liked to go to India and do decorative portraits for maharajahs. What a futile hope!

I never was happy in London. Since I was not allowed to paint ornamental flesh in the way that I wanted, I began to dream of painting flowers, just to please myself, in some idyllic cottage in the country. I wanted a garden. London might be dark and unsympathetic, but the English country held all the secrets of peace and safety and kindliness. When Julie had finished her education, perhaps. . . .

Meanwhile bits of Paris or New York would turn up. I had a party for Dorothy Thompson who wanted to meet G. D. H. Cole and Aylmer Vallance, and another one for Edith Sitwell and Pavlick. Once Alice Halicka turned up for the première of a Covent Garden ballet for which she had done the décor. She lay dead tired on my sofa and fulminated bitterly against all the producers, dealers and rich society patrons on whom her career depended. Once she sent Madeleine to spend the summer with us, and twice I sent Julie on a visit to her in Paris.

But the ties with our beloved France were growing more and more tenuous, although I had one lovely summer in the south with Ruth Harris who had come over from New York and taken a studio on the hill at Cagnes where she bade me join her. I stopped in Paris on the way for just three hours, to dine with Jenny Bradley. It was late on a summer afternoon and the houses of the quai de Béthune were once more gilded by level beams of sunshine. The people in the streets were even more alive, more eager, gay and shamelessly interested in their lives than I had remembered. The Ile Saint Louis was lovelier than ever and I wept a little under the trees at the corner. That made me feel better.

Next day brought me to Cagnes, that charming old muddle of houses which crowns a steep conical hill between Antibes and Nice, whose windows and terraces open upon vast views of sea and mountain and whose thick walls and steep stone stairways provide a background that demands only to be left untouched.

I found Ruth in a little square-walled garden, overhanging a cemetery that lay deep in the valley below. There were four orange trees under whose interlacing boughs was set an oval table with a yellow cloth. A goldfish pond was fringed with pot-plants and a pink bath-house in the corner contained a shower, a basin, a lizard and two spiders. The water from the tap was tepid from the sun-warmed pipes, and the air, too, was tepid even at midnight when we went across the garden in our nightgowns to the bath-house. The studio had once been a large stable but now it had a hard floor, a skylight and two shuttered windows. It belonged to Sandy and Tusnelda, who with their own hands had made a beautiful concrete cowl to the chimney and had painted a wavy blue line round the archway leading into the little pink alcove where I slept. On the kitchen table where we had our meals when it was too hot out of doors, there stood a large platter of grapes, eggs, onions, aubergines, peppers and courgettes, tomatoes and figs. Ruth was writing a book and I set up my easel for six weeks of blissful, uninterrupted work. Sometimes we would down tools and prepare a meal for Sandy and Tusnelda, who lived on the top story of the highest house in the town, or for Robert and Herma Briffault who lived next door in a house which from the outside showed nothing but a low, prison-like wall with a heavy door and a small barred window, but where once inside, you found yourself on the top story of an old house that clung to the side of the cliff and ended in round arches on a narrow, shady garden, way below the level of the village street but high above the road winding up from the sea. Robert and Herma in Paris had been hard-up, hard-working and worried, but now, owing to the success of Robert's book, *Europa*, Herma was having a chance to exercise those domestic gifts which were her especial glory. There was never such a cook, such a born home-maker, such a trainer-up of docile little maid-servants as Herma Briffault. Her métier was "ghosting" books for people who could not write their own stories and I have known her turn someone else's incoherent material into limpid and persuasive prose at the rate of five, six, or even seven thousand words a day. But housekeeping was her great hobby and the fact that Robert was an inveterate rolling stone was a real grief to her. Eleven moves in twelve years she told me she had had. And each time, she had transformed a mediocre habitation into a home of charm and trained up some local child to be a neat-handed, expert, and fanatically devoted little cook. But Robert always pulled up his stakes and the maid-servant wept and the Siamese cats got upset and Herma had to start all over again, leaving the fresh decorations and the well-stocked garden to be enjoyed by someone else. She and I used to spend many hours telling each other of the different homes we had had. The one in Mexico had been her favourite, and although not a sentimental girl her voice would become haunted and tender as she described the great piles of fruit in the darkened dining-room, the blazing light outside, the thick walls and shady courtyards and the simple ways and beautiful manners of the Mexican servants. I am sure that I bored her with descriptions of Bedham and its heart-comforting security and sweetness. I also told about giving up the cottage at Guermantes and the dear little attics with the flowery wall-paper in the Rue Vaugirard and losing the big studio in the Rue Notre-Dame-des-Champs. That had been one of the moves that I had minded most because it was more packed with good memories than any other place and its physical aspect had always delighted me. I had minded losing the studios in the Rue Boissonnade, of course, but they had become a worry and liability long before I gave them up. I lost them, as it were by inches, but I told Herma how, when I finally came over from London to pack them up and clear out, all the other tenants—the French painter downstairs, the Dutch one opposite with the red beard and the old Australian impressionist on the top floor—had all gathered round with offers of sympathy and affection and even of hospitality. I had had no idea I had so many friends in the house and had been very touched.

The Briffault's culinary standards being so high, we were naturally on our mettle when we had them in to dinner, and the procedure, at Cagnes, was to leave nothing to chance. You went in the morning to Madame Nickolai, who kept the village shop and you humbly begged her advice. You said you expected "du monde très chic" at your house to-night and she would advise a certain dish, according to what her husband could fetch that day from the Nice market. She would write down the recipe, which was generally something to be simmered for long hours on the charcoal burner and added to at intervals, and she would prepare the *bouquet garni* herself. Five of the herbs would come from her own garden and four more from Nice. One clove, she would say, "et je veux dire *un seul*. Deux seraient trop," one red pepper, two yellow and a green, etc., etc.

The result would always be marvellous and would necessitate a visit to the shop next day, to describe how it had been appreciated.

Poor Madame Nickolai! She was a notable cook, but she was killing her husband. He could not resist her dishes and she could not resist making them. Already he weighed twenty stone and already his son had to go to market in his stead. M. Nickolai just sat, vast and jovial and cracking ribald jokes with all the visitors to the shop. But the doctor was beginning to look very grave. . . .

The standard of cooking at Cagnes was altogether marvellous or so it seemed after London. We had a neighbour called Dorothy Whatley who was also a noteworthy cook and served lovely meals in a lantern-lit garden. But the greatest feature of Cagnes was Tusnelda, because she and Sandy had such an extraordinarily good time on almost no money at all. He was an American painter and she was a lean, strong, red-headed Danish girl with the most useful pair of hands and the wittiest tongue and the warmest heart I ever met. Of course she was just the person to have mended up a fellow who had had over a dozen operations as a result of the last war. She was an inexhaustible fountain of strong and natural life.

They lived in one of the oldest houses in Cagnes. Its upper story had been thrown into one room, and from its *terrasse* one looked over the roof-tops to the distant mountains and the sea, or down upon the dark or yellow heads and pinkish frocks of the children playing in the cobbled street. I stayed there once with Katharine Chorley, an English friend from an orthodox home of sweeping lawns and numerous young offspring. She was a learned person who was writing a large treatise, but the sweeping lawns offered little shelter for a lady who wanted to concentrate on research and prose style ; nor could her commodious Georgian home provide her with privacy or immunity from the telephone, the servants, the clamours of the obstreperous young. So I took her to Tusnelda's to finish her book. I was rather apprehensive as to how the conservative manners of my well-bred and well-tailored friend would go down amongst the easy-going idlers of that somewhat decadent village. I need not have worried. Tusnelda, looking more raffish than usual but behaving with her usual easy efficiency, provided the perfect conditions for the best spate of work that Katharine ever produced. People whose lives are dedicated to the upkeep of a bourgeois home may well envy the blissful simplicity of a life where there are no servants and consequently no fuss. Of course there was no time-table. The coffee was made by whoever got up first and after the briefest hour of household activity (no carpets, no smuts and no fires in that climate), I would set up my easel and Katharine would carry her typewriter on to the *terrasse*. At one-thirty someone would say, "what about lunch," and one of us would go down to Mme. Nickolai for a long loaf, some butter, black olives, garlic, sausage and a slice of ripe *fromage de brie*. A litre of vin rouge turned this into a feast and the lunch would prolong itself as a convivial occasion, fitting reward for a good morning's work. In the evening, we would proceed to a bistro for a 6 fr. *plat du jour* and a bit of conversation with the neighbours.

When Tusnelda gave a party, she would ask a dozen people and tell each one, firmly, what she expected them to bring. The poorest were asked for bread and the richest for meat. Wine, salad, cheese and fruit were all in the schedule and the cooking was done after the company arrived. They were very happy parties and Katharine was delighted. Poverty here was by no means the grim and bitter business that it was in England. I had to point out, however, that though the climate of Cagnes was worth £100 a year to anyone, it was quite impossible to earn your living there, unless you were a writer or a painter with contracts elsewhere. All the old problems of nationality, foreign exchange and the *Carte de travail* were again in the foreground. For a foreigner, the south of France could be nothing but a holiday ground, a reward for labours performed elsewhere. It was no use to decide that the South was your spiritual home; it was as though an adored person was not eligible to become your spouse and that you must be satisfied with intermittent concubinage!

But these trips made me less and less satisfied with London —and turned my thoughts more towards the simpler ways of living that England still offered. It is true that our misty isle could not match the climate of the south. But its green countryside had a sweet consoling quality and its old cottages still suggested a life of peace, security and ease of mind. And an English cottage garden, ah! that was something one could feel homesick for and even patriotic about. After all, a rainfall had its points. It meant that you could keep yourself embowered in greenery all summer long. And then the flowers. What perfect sitters they made! They could be woven into the patterns that I loved, and the trembling perfection of their petals held a life scarcely less vital than the flesh and bones of my usual human subjects. I began to promise myself that somehow, when Julie's education was finished, I would get into a cottage with a steep roof under a big tree, with roses round the door and poppies amongst the cabbages.

Julie's education, however, took an unexpected turn. All efforts to transform her into a conventional English school-girl having failed, she began agitating to be allowed to leave school at fifteen to study stage design. I thought she ought to matriculate first, but realised that the gaps in her English education were so formidable that it was going to be an uphill task. The go-as-you-please establishment which had received her so kindly when she left the Ecole Alsacienne, had apparently quite forgotten to teach her any arithmetic concerning English money, or any wide survey of English history. Her general knowledge was surprising but patchy, and her reading, for her age, had been prodigious. Indeed, that was what worried me most. There was scarcely a moment, when she was out of school, when her nose was not buried in some printed matter that had nothing to do with her school work. If it wasn't a historical novel it was usually quite a respectable French classic; but that did not help towards matriculation. She did not want to do exams and she did not want to play games. She wanted to leave school and go to the recently opened London Theatre Studio.

I let her. I was glad that she should learn to do some-thing with her hands, and her drawing of characters in cos-tume had always been good. She had the faculty of catching dramatic movements with a nervous line and her colour sense was satisfaactory. She had always adored the theatre and our chief hobby for years had been the making of cardboard scenery for her little toy stage. In Paris, she and Madeleine had even given a performance, with figures $1\frac{1}{2}$ inches high, of a grand satiric melodrama written for the occasion in rhymed alexandrines by Robert Briffault.

The three young women called Motley, who together had become a successful firm of stage designers, had charge of the décor section of Michel St. Denis' London Theatre Studio, which set out to train actors, producers and stage-managers, costume and scene designers. This admirable venture was one of the first casualties of the war, but during its brief life-time it was a hive of eager, gifted and brilliantly led young life. Julie, at school in England, had been a bad mixer. She was shy, shut-in and awkward. I saw that this French producer's forcing house of dramatic talent was likely both to appeal strongly to her imagination and put her on her mettle to rise to its demands. She was received with doubts and demurs on account of her youth, but was allowed to "play around" in the Islington workshops before starting her two years' course.

It all worked out very well. She was stimulated and inspired, tormented and overworked and thrown into contact with students of every nationality, under the influence of a mind that she admired. She was accepted as a contemporary by students older than herself and settled down with a happy feeling that she was in her element at last.

"Settled down" is hardly the word, however, for anything connected with the workshops and theatre of Providence Place. Islington High Street was infested with exotic young women in paint smeared slacks, straggling locks, lurid make-up and dye-stained hands, and with acting students whose heavy circular rehearsal skirts swept the dusty pavements with the authoritative air of Edwardian matrons and accorded strangely with the jersey-clad bodies and towsled young heads that emerged above.

St. Denis was a blond Napoleon with a cold and prominent blue eye of great intelligence, and he spared nobody. He was really a great producer and he had the great producer's capacity to extract the last ounce of effort, dramatic talent and imagination from the material at his disposal. It was the same with the décor students. He was merciless to a design that missed the subtleties of the play's atmosphere and sent people home in tears and in despair; but as Julie said in her still faulty English, "He makes you do what you are not capable to do."

Julie was taught the history of the theatre and the history of costume. She was taught the cutting and fitting of garments of all periods, how to make patterns, build up padding, make shoes, hats, properties, wigs and ornaments. She learnt how to do things with wire, rope, canvas, plaster and papier-maché. She learnt dying and block printing, spraying, golding, pasting, stiffening, softening and all the fascinating tricks of one of the most fascinating trades in the world. She learnt scale-drawing and model making and how to do carpenter's diagrams. She also learnt about the switchboard and her talk was all of tabs, flats, cut-outs and sight lines, or of floats, projections and the Baby Spot. She was also taught to stretch and prime canvas, mix colours to match her sketch and to reproduce it accurately on a surface many times larger than herself.

Every summer the school gave a short season in its own theatre, consisting of half a dozen items which were acted, stage-managed and mounted by the students. Those who were leaving were given varied parts to test their versatility, and were usually snapped up by talent-scouts from other theatres. The standard of acting was quite extraordinarily high.

Julie arrived finally in the "special group" from whom designers were selected to do the plays of the annual show. She got her play. It had five scenes and twenty costumes, with 1½ minutes for changes. She became engulfed in the colossal effort.

For four weeks before the shows, the big room presided over by the cutting-and-fitting mistress resembled nothing so much as a sweat-shop. The floor was knee-deep in debris and amongst it rushed the acting students, between rehearsals, to have their costumes fitted. Boys and girls in various stages of undress, taking no notice of anything except the job in hand, stood patiently about whilst the designers stuck pins into them, squeezed them in, padded them out and gave orders about their hair-styles, the neck-lines of their underwear, the height of their heels and their make-up.

They co-operated wonderfully, and if some of them already showed signs of becoming temperamental they were also learning to be pretty kind to each other's egotisms and vanities.

There was one girl designer who had sixty costumes in her play. That was more than it was humanly possible to cope with in the time allotted. She had got married the year before, and when the summer shows approached she was extremely pregnant, but it made no difference. She worked day and night. They all did. Sometimes they went home by the last train at 1 a.m. and came back with the milk, sometimes they just fell asleep on the studio floor and went on working when they woke up, and sometimes they worked all night and went home for breakfast, returning at noon. They wilted, staggered, sweated and slaved with a kind of inspired devotion that was marvellous. They were happy. If you speak to one of them now, about their last term at the London Theatre Studio, they are almost ready to cry with nostalgia.

I happened to be present at a "dress parade." I knew that the forty-odd costumes had been pinned and tacked and somehow thrown together in a desperate rush before the trembling and exhausted designer took her seat beside Saint Denis at the appointed hour. Behind her were "Motley" and the producer, all very leisurely and very critical. The curtain went up and showed the first costume in a blaze of light. "Yes," said Saint Denis, "that is all very well, but I want to see *there* (pointing to the stage) what I see *here* (pointing to the girl's design). The line should be *so*. More fullness below. More slope to the shoulder. She has square shoulders? I cannot help that. *They must slope*. Now lift your arms. Turn to the back. Bend. You are comfortable? You can make your movements? Do me a little dance. You are not constricted? Good. But the hem-line is drooping on the right."

What an education!

Julie had only twenty costumes in her play and was able to show a very decent amount of finish. Her scenery, also, swivelled round and folded and unfolded to make the five scenes quite successfully, and she had managed to preserve the necessary atmosphere in spite of the material difficulties. So I was pleased with her and grateful to the studio and delighted that she should have chosen a métier that appeared to absorb every waking thought and give scope to every scrap of talent and intelligence she might possess.

But when it came to finding a job, however menial, behind the scenes in a real theatre, there seemed to be masses of eager young people willing to do anything, for any pay, or none, for the sake of being within smelling distance of a size-pot. As for designing, former students with good professional experience all told sad tales of futile job hunting and hopes perpetually deferred. "Yes," said the director of an important and progressive provincial theatre to one of them, "your designs are very good. I will write your name and address on this card and put it with the names of the other young designers in whose work I am interested." He then opened a drawer entirely filled with similar cards and placed hers at the back.

This, however, was in June, 1939. The world has turned upside down since then and all those gifted youngsters are being used to man guns and milk cows and make shells. They are learning how to deal with incendiary bombs, how to stop hæmorrhage and how to carry an unconscious person from a burning building. Saint Denis was called up in the French army—where is he now? The Theatre Studio is abandoned, empty, and forgotten—the long skirts are folded away in the property baskets and the streets of Islington are no longer beautified by the presence of the strange children who wore them.

It was during the last term at Islington that Ford lay dying at Honfleur and sent for Julie, and I took her across the channel for the final visit. It was his heart, and it was clear that he could not get well, and we could only be glad that he had first been able to come home to his beloved France. For some time past he had been Doctor of Comparative Literature at Olivet College, Michigan, and Julie had not seen him since visiting him at Christmas in Paris, eighteen months earlier.

Janice was with him at the end and did everything that it is possible for one human soul to do for another, to comfort his last days.

Julie was profoundly moved by her father's death, which, added to the urgent expectation of a European war and the final ending of her activities at the London Theatre Studio, seemed to mark the conclusion of the period in which we had been living. Everything was finished, wound up, put away.

I had no portrait commissions in sight and was forced to face the fact that my probable earnings were insufficient to maintain us both in the London studio and that when war came, there would be no more portraits and—perhaps—no more London.

It was the moment for the country cottage, the safe spot, the place where one did not have to struggle, or fight, or worry about success. Julie's jobs, if and when she got them, would be temporary and intermittent. So would mine. A single room in London would suffice as a base from which to operate for these. We would seek this in the autumn, after establishing ourselves in the cottage of our desire.

That the cottage dream was ever realised is entirely due to the patience and energy of a good friend of ours who motored us round and round the home counties in a lengthy search. This friend was a soft-voiced, highly-cultivated woman who lived in furnished rooms in London and was herself leaning towards the idea of a country cottage for week-ends. We considered sharing. We soon found that there was nothing north, south or west of London that would suit our purses. That country was filled to saturation point with Londoners who were preparing bunk-holes for themselves in case of war. Essex was the only possible hunting-ground and Essex was directly on the route to London for German air raiders. For that reason it remained comparatively cheap.

I told myself that I would never be driven away by air raids. They would not be directed against the open country; they would pass over our heads and we would get used to the noise.

We hunted for many days and were offered many cottages to buy, but few to rent. At last we found Green End.

It lies in an insignificant little lane in an insignificant little hamlet about five miles from the Blackwater estuary. The village stands on rising ground overlooking the flat lands towards the sea. Behind, lies undulating farm country, open and unspoiled and decked with tall clumps of elm trees. There is a great deal of sky at Purleigh and a great zest of ozone in the air. There are no villas, no business men's Olde Worlde retreats, no spectacular picturesqueness to attract the moneyed week-ender.

I had received instructions from the owners of Green End as to the whereabouts of the key. I obtained this from an aged crone who emerged from a veritable bower of roses and indicated "our" cottage hard by and hidden behind a clump of willows. The lane brought us to a rickety gate, and the gate to a weed-choked path leading to a cottage which I saw at once was meant to be our home. Its high-pitched, mansarded roof of ancient tiles was broken by a charming dormer window. Its walls were of apricot-washed brick and its front door was framed by a red rose and a white, which sprang half-way up the roof and sprayed downwards in huge bouquets. There was a little plot of grass at the side in which were set some fruit trees, and beyond a patch of raspberries I saw currants, gooseberries, a row of scarlet runners and some peas. In front of the cottage was the remains of a small formal garden surrounding a lilac bush and overgrown by sturdy clumps of marguerites and golden rod and blue campanulas. At the side, lupins and more campanulas reared their blue spikes through a sea of grass and shirley poppies, and behind stood two tall elm trees. Roses were bursting everywhere into bloom and when we went indoors the cottage turned out to have lovely oak beams, a beautiful fireplace and water from the main laid on.

The last item decided it. We came back the next week-end and interviewed the owners, two nice London school teachers who were week-ending under their own thatched roof across the field.

They gave me Green End at a modest rent and promised our friend the adjoining cottage when it should fall vacant in the autumn. This cottage had a locked door which communicated with our own back premises, and we saw that we should only have to unlock this door to organise a communal system of meals.

We whitewashed the old walls and ceilings, stripped and re-papered the upstairs rooms, put up shelves and painted the doors and windows. We had never had so many rooms before.

When the furniture van arrived at Belsize Park to remove us, I felt very little of the usual remorse at breaking up an old home, for the new one (at one-third the rent) was so much sweeter. It marked the end of the struggle to wrest a livelihood from unwilling London; a real burning of the boats.

Phyllis motored us down to Green End on the night of July 25th. Our furniture was somewhere on the road. We spoke of the small foothold we would somehow achieve in London in the future. Next winter perhaps, we would find an attic and both come to town for jobs. Some day I would paint a lot of new and quite different pictures to please myself and would have a marvellous exhibition. Julie would get attached to a permanent theatre and we would have a lovely flat in town; but always there would be Green End in the background for the permanent things, for beauty, peace, silence and the tranquil spirit.

As Phyllis's great fast car sped over the dark and gleaming roads, all these things were clear and hopeful on the surface of my mind. But underneath I knew well enough that it was a forlorn hopefulness. The royal blue of the sky was pierced by searchlights, fifteen, twenty at a time, whose long batons of light wrote inscriptions on the clouds that were not difficult to read. They spelt war—no future—no safety. "The sacrifice of a whole generation."

Perhaps that was why Green End seemed so lovely. It looked so permanent, so inviting to life and growth and health, so packed with the beauties that money cannot buy and that are therefore not worth man's while to destroy. The lighted lamps shone warmly out through all the windows and illuminated wide paths in the tall-standing marguerites which bloomed thickly around. The blue searchlights playing on their cloud-targets looked cold and unimportant by comparison, an exercise in geometry for which, just now, we had no time.

Phyllis's first-born, Cordy, was with us on that night. She was Julie's "best friend" and Phyllis was the nearest thing to a sister that I had ever had. They warmed our home and they warmed our hearts and we made a meal at midnight and went to bed convinced that life was just beginning, after all.

Next day, our visitors departed and our furniture arrived and Julie and I embarked on the long job of creating a home out of chaos.

To-day, Green End is shaped to every domestic pleasure one could wish. The tent-like slope of my bedroom ceiling is pierced by the jutting tunnel of the dormer window, filled with sunshine at the crack of dawn. Outside there sway the long mauve tassels of the buddleia tree. Above my bed, supporting a frilly muslin canopy, there hangs that bunch of shining glass baubles that Pavlick once contrived for the Rue Boissonnade. The narrow old chest from Bedham just fits under the slant of the roof and on the faint pinkish bricks of the chimney I have hung my picture of the turquoise waters of the Mediterranean seen through the grey olive trees at Portofino. In the parlour stands the little old chest of drawers that Ford once bought for Julie and the writing desk I found at Castelnaudary. On the white walls, between the dark beams,

there hang the metal-encased mirrors with the ornate tops
and branched candle-brackets that came from the Paris flea-
market. The little *rustique* dresser that was bought for the
Rue de Vaugirard has had to have holes cut for its feet in the
concrete floor, that its head may fit under the low ceiling.
In Julie's room there stands the large mahogany chest of
drawers, inspiring her, I dare say, with the same illusion of
confidence and self-importance that I used to derive from it.
All these things appear to have come at last to their real home
—not one of them looks amiss—not one but helps create the
fond illusion that whatever may happen, life will still go on.

Life certainly goes on in the garden. I have dug,
planted, thinned, weeded, pricked-out and hardened-off, so
that to-day both tall and dwarf peas are bearing, and
lettuces, carrots, French beans, scarlet runners, beets, onions
and radishes are flourishing in tidy rows and the sweet corn
looks like racing the first frosts with its bearded cobs. I have
planted garlic and many herbs. Globe artichokes, too. And
the flower garden has had delphiniums and tulips and pink
perennial poppies, sweet peas and peonies, holyhocks and sun-
flowers, added to the original exuberance of its daisies and
campanulas and roses. I have made red-currant jelly and
black-currant jam. I have bottled gooseberries and intrigued
to get sugar for the plum crop. The apples I shall store again
in straw in the old tin bath-tub.

It has been the most exquisite spring. It is now the most
exquisite summer. I am reconciled to England at last.

We have become members of a community. We dig
when others dig, plant when others plant, and make jam
according to the recipes of our Mrs. Wyatt. Our Mrs.
Wyatt is another reason why I am reconciled to England.
She is as civilised in her way as her French counterpart, and
that is saying a good deal. She gives us two hours of her

valuable time each morning, during which we contrive to re-inforce our feminine *morale* for the day. She has a war-crippled husband and two charming children and she is good-looking and intelligent and a tower of strength.

She was greatly sympathetic when Julie got a job. It was to go to Bangor, in Wales, and do the sets for a newly-founded repertory company. She was hired, on the strength of her designs, for £3 a week by people she had never seen and was very frightened of going so far from home and of having to put the precepts of the Theatre Studio into practice without help or advice: "I wish I had listened more to Annette," she said. "Do I prime over old paint or not? How much dry colour should I order? I hope the stage carpenter will be all right with me."

The tears of her departure were soon followed by happy and excited letters, but alas! one set was all she did for the Bangor Repertory Company. She collapsed with an incapacit-ating sickness and had to be packed off back to London. She arrived at Phyllis's more dead than alive and there proceeded to turn yellow with jaundice.

Mrs. Wyatt said all the right things. "Poor Miss Julie, kind Mrs. Vallance. What a shame, but perhaps it's all for the best. It will be nice for you to have her back again, seeing it's war time."

For of course it was war time, although through the winter and the early spring we had been allowed to live our normal lives. Dig for Victory, they told us, and dig we did. But then the warm weather came and the invasion of the low countries and the incredible disaster of France.

If we could have had our Act of Union with France, what a cause that would have made! And what a chance to forget some of the bitterness we felt against a government that sold democracy in Spain and Czechoslovakia.

We are fighting for our lives, that is understood. But it might have been for so much more.

Ford used to say that ideas were more powerful, in the end, than arms. He also said that of all wars, those fought for religion were the bitterest. I don't know. Last time I was in France, the Facist posters were saying, "Pas de Guerre Ideologique!" That was clever, and it evidently succeeded. The Facists got their way, resistance was called off, and the words "Liberté, Egalité, Fraternité" have been effaced.

But what about those other words—"Of the people, by the people, for the people—the lawful judgment of his peers —thy neighbour as thyself—man's inalienable right to life, freedom, and the pursuit of happiness?" Millions of people have been willing to die for words like these, and millions still are willing. Do they mean anything? Can they embody a Plan?

Hitler's plan is plain to see, dark and illogical as it is. It has contempt for common humanity at its roots, and enslavement as its aim. The Communists had a plan that was logical enough, but they would seem to have lost it by using bad means to their good ends. Has Democracy got a plan? With head, legs, and belly? Is its shape emerging at last? Will it defend the Rights of Man, and set our economic house in order? Can it be born in England?

Until this is clearer, it is hard to guess where the final cleavage will occur. Who knows what new convulsions will leave us standing—where? On which side of what new chasm?

Meanwhile, we contine to fight for our existence. And we are getting nicer all the time, so that even a poor stuck-up painter can feel sisterly towards football-fans and people who eat prunes and tapioca. Surely that is an improvement!

I want to live through it. I want to see what happens. I want (vain hope!) not to be too frightened. . . .

It is now some weeks since the soldiers came to Purleigh. They have dug trenches at all the salient points and piled barricades beside the roads. Two of them keep watch, day and night, from the church tower, and streams of lorries full of young men and guns go crashing through to the coast.

The other day, a knock at the door revealed two officers, too tall for the beams of our low parlour ceiling. They were excessively courteous and informed us that " in the event of an emergency" (it seems that you never say, "If the Germans come"), they would wish to commandeer our cottage as an army first aid post. It was solid, they said, and well off the road and they could easily lay twelve men on stretchers on the parlour floor. We might go or stay as we liked. If we stayed, we should have to live upstairs. If we had good nerves we might be useful. . . .

Good nerves. . . . How could we tell?

And now the air raids have begun. We put cotton-wool in our ears, and hope to stay asleep when the sirens howl. If not, we sit downstairs in Julie's room. It is in the middle of the cottage and the big brick chimney-stack passes through it. If there are any bombs the cottage shakes and the windows rattle. The anti-aircraft goes wuff-wuff and the German planes fill the sky with a pulsating hum, like a swarm of evil bees.

In the morning Mrs. Wyatt arrives haggard and sleepy, having spent the night with her children in a neighbour's dug-out.

Sometimes we go and fry eggs for the soldiers at the canteen and sometimes we attend first-aid classes at the vicarage and learn to tie up wounds and fractures. We have bought a stirrup pump and been told how to deal with incendiary bombs and had our gas masks overhauled.

Meanwhile the sun shines and the sweet-peas are out and the poppies surpass all expectations. The French beans are ready to be salted down for the winter and I am putting in savoy cabbages as I take up the peas.

We will not go yet. Not yet, though we are now in a "protected area" and our friends, who are not allowed to visit us from outside it, are urging us to evacuate. When an "emergency" arises, we know that the roads will be closed to us. We shall have to stay put and take what comes.

Mostly I feel that one can face dangers at home that one could not face elsewhere. Mostly I feel that this is my last ditch. Why, I've had a bench made to sit on in the sun beside the front door in case some day I may become a grandmother. Clearly, one should try to protect one's home and stand by one's food supply. Food! It may soon become the most important thing in life.

Do we go or stay? To-morrow when I have finished this book, I must decide these things.

JULY, 1940.

THE END

Also of interest

LAUGHING TORSO

by Nina Hamnett
New Introduction by Edward Booth-Clibborn

Nina Hamnett (1890-1956), talented artist and determined pleasure seeker, was the legendary queen of Bohemian life in Paris and London. Her irrepressible autobiography, first published in 1932 and out of print since then, takes us from her birth in 1890 to early middle age. She leaves home, suffering from 'virginal hysteria and boredom', takes a studio in Chelsea and scrapes a living from her painting. She works for the magician Aleister Crowley; has Carrington and Mark Gertler to tea; makes batik for Roger Fry at the Omega Workshops. In 1913 she goes to Paris where she drinks in the Rotonde with Modigliani, dances naked in Van Dongen's studio, spends Christmas with Stella Bowen and Ford Madox Ford, wears bright yellow stockings and falls in and out of love. Hers is a marvellously entertaining picture of high and low life.